SAFE
TO LEARN

Rebecca Harris

Embedding
Trauma-informed
Student Wellbeing
Practices

amba
press

This book is dedicated to educators everywhere,
but particularly to those I have worked with at
Carlton Primary School. Many lives have been
changed as a result of the learning that happens
in that school, including mine.

Published in 2023 by Amba Press, Melbourne, Australia
www.ambapress.com.au

Internal design: Amba Press
Editor: Jacinta Dietrich
Proofreader: Rica Dearman

ISBN: 9781922607928 (pbk)
ISBN: 9781922607935 (ebk)

A catalogue record for this book is available from the National Library of Australia.

CONTENTS

INTRODUCTION

Welcome to *Safe to Learn*. This book is the culmination of my many years of work in education, with students, families, teachers and support staff – all the elements of a primary school. My work has made very clear to me that the story we tell of educational equity in Australia is a fallacy. As with all elements of our society, the more you have, the easier life is – education is no exception. I have worked with families who are well-off, well-supported and well-educated, and I have worked with students born in refugee camps, growing up in Australia, living surrounded by community violence. I see that while parental love, care and attunement are most definitely important, the structures around children can also have a profound influence on all aspects of their life, including education.

I wholeheartedly believe that those of us in schools have the capacity to have a huge influence on the students we work *with* and *for*. I believe we have the opportunity to mitigate adverse impacts that affect students, whether that is impacts from home, health, discrimination or societal structures. It is with this belief that I have written *Safe to Learn*.

Trauma, adversity and education

The impacts of trauma can be significant, and for those who experience trauma when young, the impacts can be cognitive, behavioural, social and physical. Trauma very often happens in the home, with just over 40 per cent of young Australians reporting having experienced abuse as a child (Haslam et al., 2023). Of those young people, half met the criteria for at least one mental disorder (Haslam et al., 2023). The rates of abuse, neglect and family violence tell us that it is unlikely any classroom in Australia is trauma-free.

Along with experiences of abuse, children are exposed to parental mental ill health, poverty, community violence, racism and other kinds of adversity that can cause chronic stress which has the same impact as trauma on a developing brain. I'm guessing you can see the reason trauma and adversity knowledge is important for educators.

Knowing about the prevalence and impact of trauma and adversity, we can't simply focus on educating the students in our schools with a one-size-fits-all approach. We see the impacts of trauma every day in classrooms – these impacts might be labelled as a behavioural issue, bad parenting, school refusal, lack of engagement or perhaps given a diagnosis. Frequently, students are suspended or expelled, as schools either don't know what else to do, or simply don't want to deal with complex and challenging students.

When adults in schools have a deeper understanding of their students' lives, a whole world opens up – there is capacity for compassion, care, and both intervention and prevention. What power schools have to positively influence a student living with adversity!

Purpose of this book

My hope is that readers of this book will develop a deep understanding of the ways that trauma and adversity impact a child, what that looks like at school and how we can support these students. Some of the information might feel big or overwhelming, but the aim is to give readers more strategies and interventions to support students, and also support those educators who are doing this vital work.

In reading this book you will explore optimal brain development and learn what happens when this development is interrupted. You will also learn about the nervous system and the ways that it does such a great job in being a protector – too good sometimes. You will explore more about how you operate and how this may be similar or different to your students' inner working. You will examine how all behaviour is communication, that students want to fit in with their peers and the barriers they may face in trying to act the same. You will read case studies, demonstrating the theory through stories, and you might recognise some behaviours in students you have known. You might reflect on students from your past and wonder what else was going on for them. But I hope you will feel empowered.

My educational experience

I was lucky enough to have had a public education in inner-city Melbourne. My classmates came from all over the world and I learned early that kids come to school from all different backgrounds. I was not an exceptionally academic student, but I learned a lot. I still remember being about ten years old and hearing from a kid in my class about the journey he made on a boat from Vietnam with some family members to come to live in safety in Australia. This had a profound impact on me and so did the various stories I heard over the years. We all brought our history to school as well as our experiences at home. Sometimes we shared with each other and many times stories were kept to ourselves. I remember the resilience in those I went to school with.

I continued my education in a primary school decades later, working only a couple of kilometres from where I went to school, once again hearing stories of seeking safety in Australia, from a different part of the world. Again, I was able to see the resilience and to recognise when there were untold stories. Through my adult's eyes, I could understand the ways that the educators in these students' lives could influence, for better or worse. Realising the ways that knowledge and understanding can help us to better serve our students, I became passionate about trauma-informed approaches in education.

Notes on a few things

I have included plenty of stories in *Safe to Learn* as case studies to better engage with the theories. While these stories are all based on real people, elements have been changed or stories have been merged to protect the privacy of those real people. I have opted to use gender-inclusive pronouns for this reason, too, and because I believe attempting to neutralise our natural biases regarding gender is always a good thing.

I want to acknowledge that there is no way I got everything right. This book has limitations. I am still learning, too, and I am working within the education system, which I know can harm even as it helps. My opinion will make itself known in numerous parts of the book, and it is likely that you will not always agree with me. I am sharing what I know and understand, and some of these things have changed as I have been writing, and might change again!

I have attempted to bring lots of practical suggestions to the book. Consider them a kind of pick-and-mix, noting what might resonate for you in your practice. Embedding student and educator wellbeing should be part of what we do every day, so the strategies and interventions I suggest often lend themselves to fitting in with your existing routine or practice. There are lots of ideas or options and it would be impossible to do them all, so it is best to choose whatever you think would work best for you and your students. I am a firm believer in moving toward the ideal, so any small change is great and should be celebrated.

Structure

I wrote this book with the assumption that educators are time-poor and don't always start at the beginning. You might be the kind of reader who skips around, or who just wants to get to the 'useful bit' (though I personally think it is all useful). The beginning of the book is pretty science-y. Here, I explore trauma and adversity, some brain science basics and nervous system basics. You might be interested in this or you might not. If you choose to trust me on the science and skip to the more practical chapters, they are Chapters 7 onwards. Here is a little rundown of what you will find in each chapter.

- **Trauma and adversity.** In Chapter 1 I outline what trauma and adversity is and how it can come from experiences at home, in the community or through societal structural inequity. You'll learn about how communities can be traumatised by natural disasters, war, colonisation and violence. You'll read about how trauma can be passed down through generations and how vicarious trauma works. You will also learn about the links between trauma, and physical and mental health conditions.

- **The brain.** In Chapter 2 we look at different parts of the brain and what they are responsible for, how the brain develops and how trauma impacts brain development. We explore memory and trauma's impacts on it. You will also find out about the brain's brilliant capacity to heal and change, through the process of neuroplasticity.

- **The nervous system.** Chapter 3 is all about our wonderful nervous systems. The way our brain responds to threat is examined, as is what happens when the threat is ongoing. You will learn about Polyvagal Theory and the way the nervous system responds in a hierarchical fashion. You will read about the links between sensing threat and the resulting behaviour, and you will see how children might feel under threat even when they are not.

- **Attachment, a blueprint for relationships.** In Chapter 4 we look at attachment theory. You will learn about the ways that our earliest relational experiences can impact all our subsequent relationships. We'll explore the difference between secure and insecure attachment, and what it might mean for our students. You will also read about the power of relationships to heal and mitigate the effects of trauma.

- **Trauma, the body and self-narrative.** Chapter 5 covers the sensing systems and the ways that trauma can impact its development. We then go on to look at the all-important sense of self and its development, and what happens when development is not ideal. We also look at shame and the impacts of shame on a developing sense of self, including the ways shame has been used in education.

- **Trauma, adversity, behaviour and learning.** In Chapter 6 we will look at the way trauma and adversity play out at school. We explore how all behaviour is communication and what a student might be trying to tell you. We look at learning, regulation and individual capacity, and how these can all be impacted. We also investigate developmental impacts on cognition, memory, focus and concentration, and what this can mean for our students.

- **Safety, resilience and sense of self.** Chapter 7 is where we look at the importance of safety for our students, and our role in this as educators. We discuss the positive impacts of feeling safe and look at resilience – what the evidence tells us and also the potential problems. This chapter is also where we delve a bit deeper into ways that we can support our students in building a positive self-narrative.

- **Relationships.** Reading about relationships in Chapter 8, we discuss the impacts of early attachment experiences and what this looks like at school. You'll read about student peer relationships and social experiences. Most importantly, you will be able to identify the powerful role that positive relationships play in recovering from trauma and building a sense of self that is steady and strong.

- **Classroom strategies for supporting student behaviour.** Chapter 9 is full of practical strategies that educators can use to support students to feel safe and connected at school. We focus on things that support a whole class, including what teachers can do each day as they interact with students. We discuss the importance of predictability and routine in a classroom, and how we can embed interventions that are great for all.

- **Behavioural strategies for individual students.** In Chapter 10 we turn to interventions that are designed for individual students. We know that some of our students need more supports and you will read about how important it is to employ differentiation strategies when it comes to behaviour as well as learning. This chapter will also look at structural inequity and the role of educators to address this as best we can.

- **Embedding a whole-school approach.** Chapter 11 is where we get to dream that we are working with a whole school ready to employ trauma-informed practice and embedded wellbeing strategies. We look at the things that can be embedded into the daily life of a school to support all students and help in mitigating the impacts of trauma and adversity.

- **How we teach wellbeing.** In Chapter 12 we continue to look at a whole-school approach and explore what it means to teach wellbeing. We look at empathy and how we can promote it in our students, as well as the research around having a whole-school program and we do a bit of a tour through some of the social-emotional learning programs that exist.

- **Embedding educator wellbeing.** In Chapter 13 we explore how to support educators. This chapter is where we get to shift the focus to ourselves. We look at how the strategies we use to support our students can also support us. We explore the joy of vicarious resilience and how we can be influenced by the resilience in our students, as well as other evidence-based, and accessible, strategies to boost educator mental health.

An invitation

Education is more than a vocation; it is a calling. If it is your calling, I hope that this book can support you in your ability to hold your own in the profession, and support you to notice and refine the positive impact that you most certainly have on your students.

I invite you to explore the references that seem interesting to you, or do a deep dive into any theories or ideas that resonate. I encourage you to listen to as many voices as you can, including your own. I am just one person with a passion, an opinion and a capacity to research.

1

TRAUMA AND ADVERSITY

When children have harmful experiences, their whole self is impacted, with Kain and Terrell (2018) stating '…early trauma takes a staggering toll on our physical, psychological, emotional, and social health' (p. 1). There are many kinds of trauma and many ways to talk about it, evident in the various words we use to describe these experiences. In this book I use the word *trauma*, but I also frequently use the word *adversity* and we can also use *chronic stress*, and *traumatic stress*. Including adversity in this list is a recognition of the way that structural issues can impact child development. Living with the structural inequity that leads to many of these adversities can be traumatic, creating compounding inequities. For those of us working with children and young people, understanding these impacts is vital. Thus, this chapter explores the various aspects and types of trauma and chronic stress as well as adversity, poverty, racism, homophobia and transphobia, exposure to community trauma and living in structures that harm.

What is trauma?

Trauma is all about the perception of an experience. The way a stressor (the cause of stress) affects someone is personal. When an individual experiences something so overwhelming that they feel unable to cope, this is a traumatic experience. What is traumatic to one person, may not be to another. What is traumatic at one point in a person's life, may not be traumatic at a different time. What one sibling experiences as traumatic, might not have the same impact on another sibling. As Atkinson (2012) states, 'Simply put, traumatic events are beyond a person's control. It is not the event that determines whether something is traumatic to someone, but the individual's experience of the event' (p. 11).

Trauma might be most commonly thought of as a one-off event such as an assault, a natural disaster, an accident, the loss of a loved one or a serious injury. In more recent times we have come to understand that trauma can be caused by ongoing stressors such as displacement, war, physical and psychological assault, repetitive damaging experiences or chronically stressful living situations. The work of researchers like Daniel Siegel, Bessel van der Kolk, Pat Ogden, Ruth Lanius, Judy Atkinson, Bruce Perry and many more, have expanded our understanding of the impact of chronic stress on children's social, emotional, cognitive and even physical development. More recently, studies around attachment, discussed in Chapter 4, and other influences have led to greater understanding of what can happen when children lack positive attachments or are exposed to other forms of early adversity. Here, we look at some categories of trauma, including what diagnoses we might see and how we might be impacted personally.

Childhood trauma

At the core of any trauma is a sense of complete overwhelm. It can play out in many ways beyond this core, but this trauma response is at the heart. *Developmental trauma* refers to the timing and type of the trauma, which leads to a significant impact in a child's development (discussed further in Chapter 2). Developmental trauma, also called *complex trauma*, generally occurs in the early years, continues for a long period of time and is usually abuse or neglect perpetrated by a parent or adult in a parental role (Kezelman & Stavropolous, 2019; Rosenfield et al., 2018; Sar, 2011; van der Kolk, 2005). As van der Kolk (2005) identifies, 'most trauma begins at home; the vast majority of people (about 80%) responsible for child maltreatment are children's own parents' (p. 402).

However, developmental trauma can also stem from other causes, such as regular hospitalisation or illness, separation from caregivers or exposure to violence outside the home. The impacts of trauma or adversity are cumulative, so a single traumatic event can be recovered from in a way that repeated exposure to family violence, for example, cannot. A series of events that are unconnected but all cause high levels of stress can combine to cause a significant impact, too. When these events occur in our early years, the impact, as Kain and Terrell (2018) identify, is intricately woven into our development:

> *Because developmental trauma occurs prior to, and during, the times of our most rapid development, its effects impact every area of our developing selves and imprint us in sometimes unique ways. (p. 40)*

Developmental trauma leads to both physical and psychological symptoms and responses, all of which can be exacerbated by stress. Common symptoms include anxiety, low self-esteem, aggression, violence, neediness, lack of resilience, impulsivity, dissociation, inability to maintain friendships, negativity, academic issues, depression and apathy, obsession with food, difficulty learning, lack of empathy and incessant chatter (Kain & Terrell, 2018). These differing symptoms can impact diagnosis, support and treatment, as complex and multifaceted trauma leaves our siloed systems of health, education and child protection unable to respond appropriately.

The trauma of structural inequity

To understand the trauma that stems from structural inequity, it is important to understand the difference between equality and equity. At a very basic level, *equality* gives the same to everyone regardless of need, while *equity* gives based on need. Teaching the standard curriculum to a class of same-aged children is an example of equality; differentiation is an example of equity. It is always going to be harder for those who live with layers of structural inequity than it is for those who struggle with a single barrier or those who face no barriers.

The range of non-medical factors that are known to influence our general health and wellbeing, the 'social determinants of health', highlight the fact that inequity in society directly influences the lives of individuals. Zubrick et al. (2014) identify that 'These factors extend to income, employment, occupation, poverty, housing, education, access to community resources, and demographic factors such as gender, age and ethnicity' (p. 94) and add further that 'Social inequity results in the unequal distribution of, and access to, resources required for the development and SEWB [social-emotional wellbeing] of adults and children' (p. 98). Looking at these statements, it is obvious that a person's community, resources and support systems have a dramatic influence on their likelihood of experiencing chronic stress and the degree of impact of traumatic events. For example, coping with a difficult universal experience, such as loss of a loved one, will be different depending on these social determinants. Could you take time to really grieve without the pressures of work? Could you find comfort in a parent, partner or close friend? Was there a complex relationship with the loved one? Have you already lost multiple people close to you?

It is the repetition of stress that makes it chronic or traumatic, and it does not need to be the same stressor repeated, but can be multiple stressors, cumulatively leading to chronic stress with a trauma response. So while single risk factors or one-off negative life events might have a minimal effect independently, when combined they can have a strong interactive effect. Similarly, exposure to multiple risk factors over time can have a cumulative effect.

Community trauma can occur from structural inequity, even when a family functions well. We often compound structural inequities with 'solutions', for example, public housing estates. Families might be showering children in love and care and attention but are unable to protect them from exposure to community violence and the impact of living alongside those engaging in it. To be constantly afraid of the next-door neighbour will have an impact not unlike being constantly afraid of someone inside your own home. We can see the ways that children living with societal structural inequity might experience the impacts of this as traumatic, or chronically stressful, even regardless of the protective factors in their life.

Poverty

For those living in poverty, stress is hard to avoid. Here in Australia, we have built a society that offers some universal access – to education and health – and yet, money will still gain you benefits that are not available to everyone. Living with a lack of means or access to necessary elements of life, such as health and dental care, fresh food and adequate housing, is very common and contributes to a stressful life. The Australian Council of Social Service (ACOSS) with UNSW Sydney identified in 2020 that 13.6 per cent of Australians were living in poverty, including more than one in six children, and more than one in eight adults (Davidson et al., 2020a; 2020b). When thinking about poverty, it is clear that the associated stresses can be a significant factor in determining trauma experiences.

Kain and Terrell (2018) identify that:

> *It is not poverty per se that is the problem; it is all that typically accompanies poverty: lack of safety, exposure to violence, neglect, diminished access to health care, and learning difficulties. Those same factors can also be present in the absence of poverty. (p. 105)*

The point is that all these struggles are frequently interlinked and exacerbated by poverty. Not only are they likely to lead to traumatic stress experiences, they also frequently do damage to educational and social experiences, too. As Kira (2001) states, 'Poverty translates into the arrest of intellectual development and into educational deprivation even for those who have no apparent organic limitations to learning' (p. 81). Similarly, for children born into poverty, evidence suggests they are more at risk of insecure attachment than those born into middle-class families (Craig, 2016). Considering the impact of stress on all the ingredients that create secure attachment, this makes sense.

The myth of equity in education is not borne out in experience, as anyone who works at a public school with many low-income families will know. It is vital that we do not reduce expectations for children who we know live with adversities, but rather that we make the accommodations required to offer them the same opportunities as those children arriving at school with privilege. Research by Patalay et al. (2020) indicates that children in lower socioeconomic status schools were more likely to have behavioural symptoms, however, schools with more positive school climates were more likely to see fewer students with mental health struggles. This research makes it clear that schools have a very privileged role in children's lives, with influence that can go some way to mitigating the impacts of adversity, making way for success and self-determination.

Discrimination

Coping with discrimination based on race, religion, sexuality, gender, sex, disability, education or any other reason can be a significant stressor in a child's life. Repeated studies have highlighted that perceived discrimination has a negative impact on an individual's wellbeing and discrimination can seriously impact a child's mental health, their sense of self and their educational outcomes (Anna Freud national centre for children and families, 2023).

The term *minority stress* (Cyrus, 2017) describes repeated exposure to stress based on societal discrimination. A meta-analysis by Schmitt et al. (2014) showed that the impact of discrimination is more significant for people in 'disadvantaged' populations, highlighting that those with less social capital are likely to experience higher levels of discrimination. Similarly, the more pervasive the discrimination, the more negative the consequences are for the individuals experiencing it. For most members of a minority group, it is likely they will experience inequity and minority stress within societal structures such as education and work.

This kind of stress may not be obvious to educators. For example, a teacher might not be aware they have an LGBTIQA+ student in their class, so may not be attuned to the impact of casual homophobic comments. For this reason it is vital that educators make an effort to view everything through a lens of equity and model this to students. While this may not be an easy task, it is vital if we are to make schools equitable places for everyone.

Cyrus (2017) notes that discrimination is cumulative for those who belong to multiple minority groups since, as previously noted, multiple stressors can contribute to adverse, and potentially traumatic, responses. Consideration of intersectionality is important for educators, as the risk factors are significant and need to be acknowledged and responded to.

Bullying

Bullying is a very specific, individualised form of discrimination. As with other forms of discrimination, victims of bullying are often targeted for a perceived sense of difference from the dominant group. It is important to note that bullying is repetitive and targeted. When dealing with aggression and unkindness at school, we most often deal with students who have been insensitive or unkind in a moment. Bullying, however, is continuous and much more serious.

As with other stressors, being the victim of bullying can induce a trauma response, with Cozolino (2014) stating '...being bullied can cause psychological and physical problems that can last a lifetime' (p. 115). Unfortunately, the crossover between those who have been bullied and those who bully is high. Children (and adults) who are already victims of abuse or bullying, or who have been exposed to violence or suffer in other ways, are particularly susceptible to bullying – both being a bully and being bullied (Craig, 2008; Cozolino, 2014). Similarly, Children who experience abuse from a caregiver often don't disclose what is happening, experiencing a sense of shame and self-blame (Hershkowitz et al., 2005; Lemaigre et al., 2017), and this same dynamic can play out in a bullying scenario, making it really important that educators can identify symptoms of student distress. Bullying between students can also happen outside of school and online, making it difficult for teachers and staff to recognise the subtle effects at school, when fear has already been established and little needs to occur to bring it to the surface.

Racism

Zubrick et al. (2014) define systemic racism as 'the inherent ways in which policies, practices and processes of institutions – such as education providers, government agencies or the police – operate, leading to systematic, entrenched inequality between racial groups' (p. 98). There are many examples of this, including lack of representation in the school curriculum, in books, in advertisements, in TV shows, in politics. This is possibly not noticeable to a member of the dominant culture, but not seeing yourself represented is a constant experience of othering. As Dudgeon et al. (2014) explore:

> *Subtle racism can be just as damaging as blatant racism for people who are the targets of racism – and conceivably it could be more damaging in that it is harder for such people to attribute negative outcomes to racism, and harder to avoid attributing such outcomes to qualities about themselves. (p. 16)*

The broad and relentless impacts of racism are a recipe for a trauma response. Zubrick et al. (2014) show:

> *There are six main pathways through which racism can lead to ill health: reduced access to the societal resources required for health (e.g. employment, education, housing, health care) and increased exposure to health risks (e.g. unnecessary contact with the criminal justice system); negative self-esteem and self-worth leading to mental ill health; stress and negative emotion reactions which lead to mental ill health as well as affecting the immune, endocrine and cardiovascular systems; disengaging from healthy activities (e.g. exercise, adequate sleep, taking medications); maladaptive responses to racism such as smoking, alcohol and other drug use; and injury through racially motivated assault, resulting in further negative physical and mental health outcomes. (p. 98)*

A school's responsiveness to racism requires a willingness to engage in difficult topics, and for acknowledgement of their contribution to oppression – as individuals, as educators and as people who work in an inherently racist structure. Knowing that an adequate response must include all domains of life that are affected, it is important that we make ourselves aware of opportunities for referral. There are many high-quality services that are specific to groups who have experienced trauma and racism – such as First Nations peoples and refugees – that cover physical and mental health, child and family services, and recreation. This is particularly the case for those of us who work in cities. There are also some excellent online learning opportunities that work to contribute to our individual knowledge base and ability to respond to our students.

Homophobia and transphobia

Members of the LGBTIQA+ community are at higher risk of mental health issues, self-harm and suicide than their heterosexual and cisgendered peers. Data from the LGBTIQ+ Health Australia's 2021 Snapshot of Mental Health and Suicide Prevention Statistics for LGBTIQ+ People found that 58.2 per cent of LGBTIQ+ fourteen- to twenty-one-year-olds had seriously considered attempting suicide. The report states that 'These health outcomes are directly related to experiences of stigma, prejudice, discrimination and abuse on the basis of being LGBTIQ+' (2021, p. 1). Similarly, the rates of high or very high psychological distress for transgender and gender-diverse people in this age group was 90.2 per cent.

The role of schools in supporting the LGBTIQA+ community is significant. School-age students enter the developmental stage where they are exploring their identity, and in many cases, identifying and expressing their gender and sexuality. A 2021 Australian study identified distressingly high experiences of homophobia and transphobia by both teachers and students, but also extremely positive effects of teachers who were supportive, both actively and passively (Ullman, 2021). The impact of early experiences in families and the home, and more broadly in society, the media and the law, can produce life-long negative impacts for LGBTIQA+ individuals (Bergeron et al., 2015; Paterson et al., 2019), but the impacts of repeated positive experiences can inoculate against the frighteningly high rates of psychological distress, suicide and self-harm.

Intergenerational trauma

Intergenerational trauma is trauma carried on through generations, where the first generation of survivors experiences the trauma, but the next generation inherits the effects, despite not experiencing the trauma. When this continues in future generations it is referred to as transgenerational trauma. This trauma can then become part of the fabric of a family or a community (Aboriginal and Torres Strait Islander Healing Foundation, 2013). Intergenerational trauma is relevant to a range of experiences. For a refugee, trauma may stem from tremendous loss, including home and loved ones, along with the challenges of finding a new community such as isolation, racism, lack of housing and job security. For others, trauma may stem from living in families who have survived war, deprivation or great losses (Atkinson, 2002; 2012; Yehuda, 2007; 2018). Similarly, since colonisation, First Nations peoples have experienced a loss of community, culture, loved ones, homes and belief systems (Atkinson, 2002; 2012). Other high-stress living situations such as poverty, violence, untreated mental ill health or addiction can also move through generations.

Likewise, being raised by traumatised adults can be traumatic. The experience of the parent who lives with traumatic stress can go on to cause traumatic stress for the child. Children experience their parents' survival strategies, which can be emotionally inconsistent, frightening and result in faltering attachment. In fact, even a parent who experienced childhood trauma but is an attuned, responsive parent to their own children can still pass on trauma as 'such parents might sporadically but repeatedly alarm the infant via (often involuntary or unconscious) exhibition of frightened or dissociative behaviour' (Hesse et al., 2003, p. 59).

The issue of whether or not the trauma has been processed is a vital one, as it is the processing of trauma that stops the passing of trauma to future generations:

> *The best predictor of a child's security of attachment is not what happened to his parents as children, but rather how his parents made sense of those childhood experiences... If, for example, your parent had a rough childhood and was unable to make sense of what happened, he or she would be likely to pass on that harshness to you – and you, in turn, would be at risk for passing it along to your children. Yet parents who had a tough time in childhood but*

did make sense of those experiences were found to have children who were securely attached to them. They had stopped handing down the family legacy of nonsecure attachment. (Siegel, 2010, p. 1)

This important research shows that adults who still suffer from symptoms of their trauma will likely pass on this trauma response to their children. The impact could look like trouble with interpersonal relationships; difficulty with attachment to their children; executive function; or coping strategies – all things that can harm a child just as direct trauma or adversity would.

However, for caregivers who have had the opportunity to dedicate time and energy to working through what happened to them, the impact on their parenting (and other relationship formation) will be mitigated. It must be noted that in many cases, such as for First Nations peoples, the luxury of 'processing trauma' is not available as the source of the trauma continues. Similarly, access to the resources required to process trauma are scarce, and not equitably available, with large financial and geographical barriers.

Collective or social trauma

Collective or social trauma describes the impact of a traumatic experience or experiences shared by a group or community, and can include the trauma of colonisation, war and natural disasters (Atkinson, 2012).

Colonisation

Of course, this is incredibly relevant in Australia, with the trauma of colonisation having an ongoing and relentless impact on First Nations peoples. Judy Atkinson (2012) describes why some frameworks for trauma do not adequately encapsulate the extremity of collective trauma as she refers to the complexity of a trauma that has multiple stressors, which are deliberate, interpersonal and systemic:

> *...Such experiences have been generational, and cumulative over time and space, and are compounded by poverty, poor housing, ill health, poor education – employment opportunities, and marginalisation through racism and prejudice. Today there is much more understanding how these adverse social situations are both cause and effect in generational trauma. (p. 11)*

Atkinson makes the point that it is impossible to unravel the cause and effect when it comes to the transgenerational impact born of collective trauma. While the original cause may be clear, such as colonisation, war or extended natural disasters, the symptoms of the collective trauma itself go on to create additional trauma – being both cause and effect of the trauma for subsequent generations, in some instances becoming 'cultural norms' (Atkinson, 2002, p. 81). This can be the experience for many students, and can be dramatically impactful when it comes to behaviours or symptoms. In her book *Trauma Trails*, Atkinson describes the way collective trauma plays out for many young First Nations people, identifying the tendency for past traumas to be played out by future generations. She explores how this trauma can look like traditionally Western psychiatric conditions, but that it is often not helpful, and sometimes harmful, to frame it this way.

As Parker and Milroy (2014) explore, collective trauma can be present as physical as well as psychological:

> *This phenomenon of 'malignant grief' is the result of persistent stress experienced in Aboriginal communities. Malignant grief is a process of irresolvable, collective and cumulative grief that affects Aboriginal individuals and communities (Milroy, 2005). The grief causes individuals and communities to lose function and become progressively worse; ultimately it leads to death. This grief has invasive properties, spreading throughout the body, and many of Australia's Aboriginal people die of this grief. The issue of malignant grief should also be viewed in the context of repeated generational trauma that affects some Aboriginal and Torres Strait Islander communities. (p. 30)*

Migration, war and conflict

Bentley et al. (2012) talk about the impacts of post-migration stress adding to the impacts of pre-migration traumatic experiences. People who left countries where conflict was ongoing fared particularly poorly, indicating that the collective trauma had been brought with them, and was ongoing and unresolved. This can leave individuals still feeling the trauma, knowing that though they are safe there are many others who aren't, which may include family members.

In addition to previous and ongoing trauma, many migrants face new stressors, too, such as social isolation, poverty and racism (Salinas &

Salinas, 2021). Physical symptoms are frequently experienced, such as stomach aches or headaches. It is very common to have these somatic representations of psychological distress (Bentley et al., 2012). The physical sensations are very real, and in fact constant stress can lead to a range of physical ailments (Centers for Disease Control and Prevention, 2022; van der Kolk, 2007; van der Kolk, 2014) most often associated with inflammation.

In our multicultural country, it is important to understand the trauma of forced, and unforced, migration. We can see clearly the ways that the experience of forced migration contributes to trauma symptoms, knowing that adversities such as poverty and racism also contribute to the loss and grief of migration. This is also the case for children born in Australia to migrant parents due to the impacts of generational trauma.

Climate change and natural disasters

Ongoing impacts of climate change mean that we are likely to see more natural disasters. Natural disasters, like bushfires, droughts and flooding here in Australia, can cause collective trauma when a community has suffered the shared loss of friends, family, community members, pets, homes and community facilities. The emotional recovery can be delayed, as practical matters such as housing can take an extremely long time to be attended to, leaving people feeling unsafe and dislocated for prolonged periods. The carers within the community are also affected, meaning appropriate community support needs to come from beyond the community itself. However, those coming from outside the community do not have the same knowledge and connection to the people or place. In instances such as these, the educators who would normally provide community care for students, are themselves victims of the collective trauma, placing them in incredibly vulnerable positions.

In situations of community trauma we rely on structural support, namely the systems that support the carers. When educators are both victims of the collective trauma, and those people providing support to the students and families, it is important that advocacy to the relevant department of education happens. We saw examples of this during the COVID-19 pandemic, and the lockdowns.

Support for educators in these instances might look different from school to school, or even from person to person, and the role of leadership in identifying and accessing support for staff is paramount – while also not forgetting to care for themselves, of course. Chapter 12 on educator wellbeing will have some guidance on how we can work to prevent burnout, but the more educators are able to share how they are travelling, the more able they will be to offer support to others in situations of collective trauma.

Secondary or vicarious trauma

The terms *secondary trauma* and *vicarious trauma* are used interchangeably and describe the traumatic stress response of a person who is exposed to someone else's trauma. It is called *secondary* as it describes being once removed from the original traumatic experience. The experience of hearing of or being connected to the trauma of another becomes a new trauma. This can happen to anyone, including family members, friends, community members and professional care providers. Reuben (2015) states:

> *When a therapist for a patient with PTSD hears a story of violence, empathetic imagining can inadvertently trigger a physiological reaction similar to what the victim may have experienced: a racing heart, shaking hands, nausea, and other elements of the fight-or-flight response. (para. 11)*

As with first-hand trauma, the effect can be strong enough to alter one's perception of the world, which could mean feeling less safe, having less confidence in others, or a loss in core beliefs. As with burnout, which we will discuss in Chapter 13, it can creep up, with gradual changes that make it hard to identify what is occurring. While burnout, which can be described as 'psychological strain' (McCann & Pearlman, 1990, p. 133), may be more of an issue for education staff, it can certainly be the case that working with particular populations, or indeed particular individuals, can make us vulnerable to vicarious trauma. I remember hearing such distressing stories from one family that I was left with images in my head of things I had not seen, and with no one to talk to about it because I did not want to pass it on. Trauma can be contagious.

It is important for us to be aware of vicarious trauma, for ourselves and for our colleagues, particularly those in wellbeing, counselling or support roles. The symptoms of vicarious trauma match the symptoms of traumatic stress, including anxiety, depression, loss of motivation, hyper-vigilance, sleep disturbances, intrusive thoughts, grief and numbness (McCann & Pearlman, 1990; Rueben, 2015). It is vital to recognise the symptoms and seek help if vicarious trauma is experienced as, untreated, it can become worse. Some strategies that can be employed to avoid vicarious trauma include passing information on to another, or even writing down responses, or ongoing counselling or professional supervision.

Krupka (2018) explores the ideas around secondary trauma. She questions who trauma 'belongs' to, since the words *secondary* and *vicarious* imply that it belongs to the individual. But why should our traumatised clients or students own trauma, when instead, we could consider their experience a collective responsibility. Krupka states, '...why shouldn't we be traumatised by the brutalisation of others, either known or unknown to us? Why should our witness pain be pathologized in this way?' (p. 8). I introduce this idea to call us educators into the world of these students. Their trauma is our trauma because we are members of the same society where the trauma was born. For me, this idea speaks to our sense of belonging and collective responsibility around care for all members of our society. While we need to take care of ourselves, we can also question our role as activists who work to prevent these traumas occurring in the first place.

Sanctuary trauma

Sanctuary trauma refers to when someone who has experienced trauma and seeks help or support 'encounter[s] a reception that is not as supportive as anticipated or needed' (Wolpow et al., 2016, p. 2). School is often a place that students or caregivers reach out to for support and we are privy to all sorts of information about families, either directly or indirectly. Wolpow et al. (2016) states:

> *The likelihood that children and their families will experience school-based sanctuary trauma is directly correlated to how well staff are informed. That is, if staff understands trauma's impact on relationships, behavior, and learning, and they have the support they need to act with compassion, children and their families are more likely to get the help they need. On the other hand, if staff is poorly informed and unsupported, the likelihood is that traumatic experiences will be exacerbated. (p. 13)*

This idea of sanctuary trauma highlights the incredible impact that schools can have. As we have explored in this chapter, traumatic stress is often born of experiences that are repetitive, cumulative and also systemic. School has the capacity to interrupt these experiences or build on them, and this can impact the whole family. Of course, our work is with students and yet our students exist in the context of family and community. It should be clear that when a school provides positive experiences for all family members, and has a high standing in the community, its reach can be broad and powerful.

There is a significant body of research that shows that when schools engage well with families, students do better academically, have better attendance, develop better social skills and stay in school longer (Australian Childhood Foundation, 2018; Brunzell & Norrish, 2021; Durlak et al., 2011; Hampden-Thompson & Galindo, 2017; The Victorian Foundation for Survivors of Torture Inc., 2015). This makes sense and provides more reason for schools to do this well. As with trauma-informed practice generally, the outcomes are positive and cover social-emotional outcomes, academic outcomes and life outcomes.

Similarly, we need to ensure that all staff members are provided with the right support and training to ensure schools are safe places. Often training and professional development happens for teachers, and sometimes classroom support staff, but often does not include administrative staff even though they are frequently dealing with families across a range of potentially traumatic experiences, such as financial issues, absences, illnesses or housing issues. We must not forget the impact of our front of house staff. School should be a safe place, for children and for families, and if we can manage this, we are going a long way to supporting all people who walk through our front doors.

Trauma diagnoses

The *Diagnostic and Statistical Manual* (*DSM*) is the final word on psychological and psychiatric disorders in many countries, including the United States and Australia. If listed in the *DSM*, it can be a diagnosis. If it can be a diagnosis, it can be supported by the medical system, including private health insurance, the National Disability Insurance Scheme (NDIS) and Medicare (in Australia). It is written by the American Psychological Association with input from practitioners and researchers. As the impacts of complex or developmental trauma are significant and life-altering, there was, and is, a push from some clinicians and researchers for developmental trauma to be added as an official diagnosis (D'Andrea et al., 2012; Sar, 2011; van der Kolk, 2005).

Unofficial diagnoses

The studies that identify the impacts of childhood trauma are still relatively new, and there exists an argument that there should be capacity to allocate a diagnosis describing the impact, thus providing the subsequent access to services (Kezelman & Stavropoulos, 2019; van der Kolk, 2005). However, in spite of there being no *DSM* diagnosis, the impacts of childhood trauma are widely described as complex post-traumatic stress disorder (CPTSD). CPTSD has been identified as a subcategory of the existing PTSD diagnosis, covering some shared symptoms along with other characteristics such as: damaged sense of self; self-harm, struggles with regulation; and dissociation (Kezelman & Stavropoulos, 2019; van der Kolk, 2005). As of January 2022, CPTSD exists in the World Health Organization's (WHO) *International Classification of Diseases* (*ICD-11*), which is a huge step in having the impacts of childhood trauma recognised, and while, as Kezelman and Stavropoulos (2019) point out, '...diagnosis is only one of several lenses through which to view complex trauma' (p. 25), recognition in the *ICD* 'makes recognition and more appropriate treatment of Complex PTSD more likely' (p. 25).

Alternative diagnoses

There are crossovers in the symptoms of trauma that we see in children and the behaviours or traits we see in attention-deficit hyperactivity disorder (ADHD), autism spectrum disorder (ASD) and other similar diagnoses. As Kain and Terrell (2018) identify, behaviours that we might associate with dysregulation can result in one of these diagnoses: 'Some of the common diagnoses given to children and adults with dysregulation are attention-deficit hyperactivity disorder, oppositional defiant disorder, spectrum disorders, anxiety disorders, and aggressive behaviours' (p. 187). Sometimes it may be the case that our students are diagnosed with one of these conditions, as their trauma responses meet the criteria for a diagnosis (Siegfried et al., 2016; Stavropoulos et al., 2018), or they may have combined symptoms of trauma as well as another condition.

The links between developmental or complex trauma and a range of adult psychiatric diagnoses are also significant. Without the capacity to give a diagnosis that reflects the trauma experience and the symptoms, the symptoms are seen as falling under various mental health diagnoses, commonly dissociative disorders and borderline personality disorder

(Kezelman & Stavropoulos, 2019; Sar, 2011). A range of diagnoses are given to adult survivors of complex trauma, but the CPTSD classification provides a link between experience and symptoms, identifying that symptoms of trauma are born of strategies an individual uses to cope with their experiences.

Adverse Childhood Experiences study

The Adverse Childhood Experiences (ACEs; Centers for Disease Control and Prevention, 2022) study is a longitudinal study that began in 1995–1997 in the US. Participants were taken from within a private health fund, and more than 17,000 adults were asked a series of questions about their childhood experiences and their health and health behaviours (Centers for Disease Control and Prevention, 2022). The childhood adversity questions were simple: ten descriptions of adversity, with a score for each one experienced before eighteen years of age. The ACEs fell into three categories: abuse, neglect and household challenges. The health and wellbeing survey looked at health history and behaviours (such as smoking). The research found statistically significant causal connections.

In the initial ACEs study, it was found that ACEs were, as paediatrician and now Surgeon General of California, Dr Nadine Burke Harris (2018) states, 'astonishingly common' (p. 38). Sixty-seven per cent of people had experienced one or more ACEs and 12.6 per cent had experienced four or more. The study's initial participants were predominantly from privileged backgrounds, generally white, employed people living in Southern California, with 75 per cent degree educated – people who, at first glance, were not living with the stressors of adversities. Yet still, in spite of having privilege, most of the participants had experienced notable adversity.

Later ACEs studies reinforced the original findings, and a survey sample from 2011–2014 with more than 210,000 participants went further to look at who was most likely to have ACEs. This study by Merrick et al. (2018) found that, while ACEs existed across all backgrounds, 'Children from minority backgrounds – whether based on race, socio-economic standing, or sexual orientation – were at distinctly higher risk of ACEs and their devastating life-long effects than middle-class white children' (Jamieson, 2018, p. 1). Some of the statistics to come out of the ACEs study were remarkable, for example, an ACEs score of four represents a 460 per cent increase in the chance of experiencing depression than someone with a score of zero.

That score of four also represents the chance of a cancer diagnosis being doubled. For those with an ACEs score of six, they can expect a reduced lifespan by twenty years. Early adversity changes us on a biophysical level, it:

literally gets under our skin, changing people in ways that endure in their bodies for decades. It can tip a child's developmental trajectory and affects physiology. It can trigger chronic inflammation and hormonal challenges that can last a lifetime. It can alter the way DNA is read and how cells replicate. (Burke Harris, 2018, p. xvii)

A broad range of physical and mental health conditions are identified to have links to early adversity, as van der Kolk (2005) makes clear:

[The ACEs study] unequivocally confirmed earlier investigations that found a highly significant relationship between adverse childhood experiences and depression, suicide attempts, alcoholism, drug abuse, sexual promiscuity, domestic violence, cigarette smoking, obesity, physical inactivity, and sexually transmitted diseases. In addition, the more adverse childhood experiences reported, the more likely a person was to develop heart disease, cancer, stroke, diabetes, skeletal fractures, and liver disease. (p. 402)

Work conducted by Burke Harris in her medical practice using the ACEs questions identified that, if her child clients had four or more ACEs, they had a thirty-two-fold increase of learning or behaviour issues at school as compared to children with an ACEs score of zero (Kain & Terrell, 2018). Statistically, there are many students who have experienced ACEs. In fact in an Australian context, 'An estimated 72% of Australian children have been exposed to at least one ACEs, with this rate being higher in some vulnerable Australian populations', according to The National Workforce Centre for Child Mental Health (para. 4, 2020).

The ACEs study is widely quoted, and the resources and data continue to be used due to the significant link demonstrated between childhood adversity and later life health and wellbeing. As Kain and Terrell (2018) state:

The results were – and continue to be – staggering, transforming the way we view childhood trauma and its impact on adult health; it has led to a paradigm shift in the way physicians, psychologists, psychotherapists, schoolteachers, and social workers view and treat patients, clients and students. (p. 101)

The ACE Resource Network (n.d.) has taken the original ten ACEs and added a second ten that it refers to as 'beyond the 10'. In doing this, it names adversities such as cultural trauma; discrimination; non-household forms of violence; racism; and adult responsibilities as a child as also being adverse childhood experiences. This work is an important addition to the original ACEs work and is supported by the science of adversity.

It is fair to say that in our society there is a degree of blaming an individual for their life circumstances, as Burke Harris (2018) says:

The belief of some that the increased risks had everything to do with behaviour... The popular thinking goes that if you live in poverty or have a rough childhood, you inevitably cope by drinking and smoking and doing other risky things that damage your health. But if you're smart and strong, you rise above what you were born and raised with and leave the bad things behind. (p. 40)

But as we explored earlier, for those that have experienced trauma, it is an additional blow to then be perceived as simply lacking the will to change difficult circumstances. While behaviour is an influence on health, it accounts for only about 50 per cent of an increased chance of disease (Burke Harris, 2018). So, while behaviour is definitely a factor in health outcomes, an ACEs score plays a significant role *regardless of behaviour*. It is therefore important to acknowledge that luck of birth is a huge factor when it comes to social and health outcomes for any individual in our country.

Schools have a vital role when it comes to mitigating the impact of early adversity and the impact of social and structural inequities. The impact that educators can have can last a lifetime. As a massive bonus, the most powerful interventions that we can enact, as we will discuss later, benefit each and every student, regardless of their exposure to adversity. As stated, we know behaviour accounts for only about 50 per cent of risk for disease. That means we have the capacity to mitigate the impacts of early adversity and to increase protective factors for all children.

There is a simple ACEs calculator available online; it is very basic and does not account for the importance of type and timing differentials in impact of adverse experiences and does not include all types of adversity. Should you like to look at it for yourself, be mindful that our fate is not determined by what happens to us. For ourselves, as with our students, we need to also look at protective factors and personal strengths when considering a predisposition for any negative life impacts.

Conclusion

Trauma can take many forms. In this chapter we have looked at many different categories of trauma that all lead to physical and psychological impacts. This knowledge offers such great opportunity to positively impact the lives of our students. In the words of Dan Siegel:

> *A teacher's understanding of trauma's impact on the mind and the brain makes all the difference between a reaction driven by an educator's understandable yet preventable frustration versus a sensitive and informed response empowered by knowledge, empathy and compassion. (in Jennings, 2019, p. xv)*

In Chapters 2 and 3, we will continue building this important knowledge base as we look at the brain and the interplay between experience and development.

2

THE BRAIN

To understand how trauma affects the brain, we first need to understand what typical and ideal brain development looks like. In this chapter we look at brain development, the impact of type, and timing of trauma and adversity on brain development and function. Vital brain functions such as memory have a huge impact on our capacity to learn so it is useful to discover the ways that these functions develop. This is a fairly simple exploration of regions of the brain because brains are really complicated! While knowing about each part of the brain is not necessary, a gist of the development and function will serve educators well, allowing us to better understand that sometimes when we think we are observing a personality trait or a behaviour choice, we are actually observing a brain wired for survival.

The development of the brain

The brain develops sequentially, with development beginning in utero, requiring positive input to develop optimally. Development is impacted when this positive input is not received, or when negative input is received instead. The brain is part of the nervous system, constantly sending and receiving messages to and from the rest of the body. This communication occurs via neurons, which are nervous system cells, and there are rather a lot of them:

Each neuron has an average of ten thousand connections that directly link it to other neurons. Thus there are thought to be about one million billion of these connections, making it 'the most complex structure, natural or artificial, on earth.' (Siegel, 2020, p. 25)

Neurons send electrical impulses to other neurons, via contact points called synapses, which act to give an instruction. We're going start with a look at different parts of the brain and the way neurons develop, and then consider what happens when trauma impacts development.

Parts of the brain

The brain is divided up into different areas, some of which we will explore, with each area maturing at different times. All areas work together, so while it can be a bit misguided to define the role of a specific area, it is worthwhile noting the relationships between areas of the brain and brain function to help us understand the impacts of early experience.

The brain is often described as having three main regions, called the triune brain (Siegel, 2010a). While this is a little simplistic, it can be a helpful way to think about the evolutionary development of the brain: the brain stem first, then the limbic area and finally the cortex. The lower regions are the oldest and are responsible for homeostasis – keeping us alive; the central parts of the brain are newer and linked with emotional input, output and regulation; and the most recent development is the cortex, our thinking region, setting us apart from other species, capable of higher-order thinking.

As we investigate the parts of the brain, and the relevance of their specific sensitive periods of development, it makes sense to begin at the bottom, where we find the part of the brain that is oldest and also the first to develop.

Brain stem

The brain stem, often referred to as the reptilian brain (van der Kolk, 2014), is the oldest and first developed part of the brain. Development begins pre-birth, continuing up to around eight months old. This part of our brain is responsible for our most basic survival functions like heart rate, body temperature and blood pressure. Think about a newborn – entering the world with capacity for life-maintaining functions such as breathing, sleeping, eating, crying, responding to pain and discomfort, and ridding the body of toxins – this is the brain stem in action. The brain stem also plays an important role in passing information between the body and brain.

Cerebellum

The cerebellum sits at the base of the brain, behind the brain stem. It develops from birth to two years old and is responsible for our movement and interpreting physical sensory stimulation – it helps us to know where our body is in space and helps us balance. Some animals also have a cerebellum, and it is another evolutionarily old part of the brain. The cerebellum is small, but it plays a big role as the receiver of information from our sensory systems, the spinal cord and other parts of the brain responsible for sensation and movement. It has a large number of neurons in relation to its size, which is key to it being able to take in so much information. The cerebellum appears also to be able to transfer information across hemispheres, and thus may be responsible for a range of important 'informational and integrating processes' (Siegel, 2020, p. 37).

Limbic regions

The limbic system is often referred to as the mammalian brain and all mammals who care for young have one. It develops both pre- and post-birth, primarily between the ages of one and four, and develops according to experience alongside genetics.

The limbic regions are in the central part of the brain sitting above the brain stem. The limbic structures take in information from the upper brain and the brain stem region. The parts include the amygdala, hippocampus, thalamus and hypothalamus. The connection with the structures of the brain both above and below allow for coordination and integration of many of the brain's functions, including meaning making, understanding others' signals and generation of emotion (Siegel, 2010a; Siegel, 2020). It can be described as the emotional centre of our brain, helping us to interpret and regulate emotions (Siegel, 2020) and identifying what is dangerous or safe.

Diencephalon, thalamus and hypothalamus

Just above the brain stem we find the diencephalon, which contains the thalamus and the hypothalamus. This region develops pre-birth and plays a role that includes hormone regulation, relaying information up to the cortex and regulating the sleep cycle. It is important for taking in and sifting through information, identifying what is important for survival, continually sending information to the amygdala to check for threat and to the cortex for decision-making.

Siegel (2020) refers to the thalamus as a 'gateway for incoming sensory information' (p. 32). It collects and filters information about physical sensations using all five senses and helps to create a link between physical sensation and the awareness of the experience of the sensation. It brings together information from the brain stem, the limbic regions and the cortex contributing to the creation of autobiographical memories and self-narrative.

Amygdala

The amygdala is mature from birth. It is a cluster of neurons with a role akin to that of an alarm system (van der Kolk, 2014), warning us of potential danger before our thoughts even have a chance to catch up with our response. This perceived danger could be the sight of a snake, or it could be the observation of small facial muscles heading into a frown. The amygdala takes it all in, constantly vigilant to threat. Along with absorbing messages of potential danger, the amygdala also sends this important information out to the body, with warnings that cause emotional and physiological arousal and prompt immediate action. The amygdala also plays a role when it comes to memory, specifically the emotional memories that are less about events or recounting information, but more about an emotional response. The signals of danger that the amygdala sends out are recorded alongside the event that caused the signals. This can lead to fear being associated with a location, for example, where a frightening event took place. Thus, the amygdala also has a role to play with regard to the attachment system and our ability to find safety in relationships (Siegel, 2020).

Hippocampus

The hippocampus is responsible for the development and retrieval of explicit memories, including those that tell the story of who we are. It also plays a part in knowing where we are in space and time, and understanding routes and places, as well as linking the associated experiences with places (Moser et al., 2008). It also has a role in memory relating to recall and autobiographical facts (Siegel, 2020). It continues to develop after birth and, once fully matured, allows for those explicit memories to develop and be retrieved (Perry & Winfrey, 2021; Siegel, 2020).

Cerebrum

The cerebrum is the main part of the brain and the largest area, divided into the two hemispheres, left and right, connected by the corpus callosum running down the middle. There are four identified lobes in each of the hemispheres of the cerebrum: occipital, responsible for receiving and processing visual information; parietal, involved in spatial awareness, language and object differentiation; temporal, used in sound recognition and linking words with their meaning, memory making and retrieval; and frontal, contributing to memory, speech and language, and personality (Jawabri & Sharma, 2021). The frontal lobes also act as a kind of 'lookout' with an overview of all that is occurring, ready to engage higher-order thinking and reasoning (van der Kolk, 2014).

The cerebrum does not fully develop until well past legal adulthood, possibly around age twenty-five. Interestingly, it is widely accepted that a biologically female brain will reach maturity earlier than a biologically male brain.

Cortex

The cortex is the outer layer of the cerebrum, the 'grey matter' that has all the folds that we typically associate with the image of a brain. This is evolutionarily the youngest part of the brain. Sometimes referred to as the neocortex, it develops from two to six years old. The development of these frontal lobes, the prefrontal cortex, are what allows us to communicate with speech, as well as reason, rationalise and problem-solve. The prefrontal cortex stores explicit memories about people, places and experiences, and has an important function when it comes to working memory and focus (Siegel, 2020). It is also responsible for meta cognition. The prefrontal cortex houses mirror neurons, cells that respond to watching someone do something, the same way they respond to actually doing the same thing (which we will explore later in the book). The prefrontal cortex also prioritises and acts as a complex problem-solver and decision-maker, contributes to the managing of stress and emotion and has the capacity to calm the amygdala when the amygdala is eliciting a fear response. Important for all kinds of learning, the prefrontal cortex continues to develop into young adulthood, fully maturing at around twenty-five years old. This important part of the brain remains structurally and functionally vulnerable to environmental stress until the mid-twenties.

Corpus callosum

The corpus callosum is a connection of nerve fibres that runs between and connects the hemispheres of the brain. The two hemispheres of the brain are responsible for different, specific brain functions, combining to give us function in areas such as memory, speech and visual perception (Siegel,

2020). It begins development in utero and continues to develop over a person's lifespan. When working well, the corpus callosum links our right brain and left brain, allowing us to give words to feelings, to interpret social cues and to understand our own experience.

Trauma's impacts on brain development

As you can see, the brain develops and matures at very different rates. Thus, the timing of damage to the brain via injury or experience will have a significant impact on what functions are affected. The optimal development of the brain relies upon optimal input from the environment. When the environment is not optimal, things do not develop as they ideally would. Here, we look at some of the impacts of trauma and adversity on different parts and different functions of the brain.

Parts of the brain and trauma

As stated, timing has relevance when it comes to the impact on the brain of traumatic experience, as a still developing part of the brain responding to trauma is particularly vulnerable (Kain & Terrell, 2018; Perry & Szalavitz, 2017; Perry & Winfrey, 2021; Siegel, 2020; Teicher & Munkhbaatar, 2020). Teicher and Munkhbaatar (2020) reference this impact on brain development as 'adaptations', rather than viewing the changes as damage. This reframing acknowledges the powerful instinct the brain has for survival, as van der Kolk (1994) says, 'even under the most miserable conditions' (p. 55).

Sensitive periods come when there is a significant amount of neural growth. These sensitive periods are genetically programmed, reflected in the fact that babies and children tend to gain particular skills at roughly the same age (Cozolino, 2014). These sensitive periods can lead to dramatic impacts from trauma. For example, a child experiencing some sort of maltreatment from age seven will experience brain changes, or adaptations, particularly in those areas not yet fully developed, while an infant experiencing the same maltreatment from birth will have a different experience, as almost all areas of brain development are likely to be affected. As Perry and Winfrey (2021) explain, 'Put simply, if you experienced trauma at age 2, it will have more impact on your health than the same trauma taking place at age 17' (p. 108). The earlier adversity is experienced, the more significant the impact on brain development.

Evolution is responsible for creating a human brain that has become ever more sophisticated, and yet does not always serve us well. If we consider our evolution as the ways in which humans adapt to our surroundings for optimal species survival, then consider the benefits of a brain adapting to living in a harsh or harmful environment, we can see how early adversity impacting brain development is adaptation, increasing the chances of survival. Looking back over the areas of the brain, we consider the ways that brain function may be impacted by trauma during sensitive periods.

Brain stem

Damage to the brain stem is often life-threatening because without a functioning brain stem, we are not capable of maintaining homeostasis. Damage even in utero can end, or dramatically alter, the chances of survival.

Cerebellum

Damage to the cerebellum would likely impact balance and movement.

Limbic regions

When impacted by trauma, the limbic regions can contribute to misinterpretations of sensory input as being dangerous, due to emotional memory being tuned toward fear (van der Kolk, 2014).

Diencephalon, thalamus and hypothalamus

An ineffective or suboptimal diencephalon negatively impacts self-regulation, attention, arousal and impulsivity.

When impacted by trauma, the important processes of the thalamus become less synchronous, meaning that the link between a physical experience, and the awareness and understanding of that sensory experience, are not aligned, creating a disconnect between the physical experience and the awareness of the experience. As the memories are created about a physical experience, the disconnect continues, leaving the memories not as a narrative that can be understood or told, but as an untethered collection of memory fragments experienced as intense emotion. Consider a trigger response, which we might see as a child 'flipping out' for no apparent reason, but is actually a rush of emotion caused by something that is essentially unknowable for the conscious mind.

The hypothalamus plays an important role in responding to stress. However, this stress response system can become over or under responsive with early trauma, leading to being especially sensitive or unable to identify when situations should induce the experience of stress.

Amygdala

The amygdala is an important brain feature when it comes to sensing fear. It is active when we are having a threat response. It is our alarm system and identifies fear-based experiences as important. The amygdala processes information that arrives through the thalamus, before the rest of the information from the cerebral cortex lands, so the heightened state may arrive and stay, even after the rest of the information is present (van der Kolk, 2007). For people who have experienced a great deal of fear, such as a child living in a violent home, the alarm system gets overworked. It can respond to this by always remaining switched on, creating hyper-vigilance, a state that sees a great deal of energy focused on searching for threat rather than other areas of engagement. This can also be the case for a person who has experienced a traumatic event, such as a bushfire or an attack – a sense of fear becomes the norm, and the perception of threat where there is none can be common. Some fear systems will respond to overuse in the opposite way, effectively losing the capacity to sense fear, creating the ability to live with danger without the associated emotional and physiological response. When this happens, a person becomes hypo-vigilant, unfazed, switched off.

Teicher (2016) refers to studies that demonstrate that severe abuse tends to reduce the size of the amygdala, while neglect increases the size. When it comes to timing significance, pre-puberty impacts tend to lead to the hypoactive response, whereas post-puberty trauma including bullying, was more likely to lead to hyperactive amygdala activity (Teicher & Munkhbaatar, 2020).

Hippocampus

Studies have identified poorer development and smaller hippocampi in adults with experiences of childhood maltreatment. The impact of this can include reduced capacity when it comes to understanding emotional memories and putting them in context. Without this ability it becomes hard to learn from past experiences and increases the potential to repeat past experiences in spite of their negative impact. Similarly, neuroscience suggests that a suboptimal amygdala and hippocampus working together serve to embed fear-inducing experiences in our memory (LeDoux, 2015 as referenced in Kain & Terrell, 2018).

Other identified impacts are lack of capacity when it comes to short-term verbal and visual memory, attentional struggles, lack of inhibition and reduced mathematical ability (Teicher & Munkhbaatar, 2020). One study suggests that the impact of maltreatment on the hippocampus ceased around age eight, suggesting that the sensitive period for this part of the brain is before eight years old (Rao et al., 2010). Interestingly, this appears to only be the case for boys. There appears to be a biological sex difference when it comes to the hippocampal impact of early trauma, with differences noted in both when the most sensitive periods are and also the influence of the trauma. This appears to result in poor hippocampal development in biological males and poor capacity to cope with stress for biological females (Teicher et al., 2018). In both cases the timing of the trauma was more relevant than the type, duration or even the severity of the trauma (Teicher & Munkhbaatar, 2020).

Cerebrum

As the cerebrum is the main part of the brain, injury to the cerebrum has different impacts depending on the location of the injury. Also, since this area isn't fully formed until the mid-twenties, it is vulnerable to the impacts of trauma for a long time. The development of the cerebrum requires particular inputs and lack of damaging inputs. As Porges (2017) and Siegel (2020) identify, the brain develops relationally, so damaging relationships impact development. Teicher (2016) details the use of electroencephalograms pointing to links of early abuse with a-symmetry in the cerebrum, with abnormalities particularly noticed in the left hemisphere of the brain, with greater chance of temporal lobe epilepsy and reduced verbal IQ. In addition, the specific type of abuse impacts the brain differently, for example, verbal abuse is more likely to impact the language areas of the brain – the left hemisphere, frontal and temporal lobes – whereas witnessing violence impacts the visual areas located in the occipital lobe.

Cerebral cortex

The impact of trauma on this part of the brain can impact its size, with an overall reduction in grey matter being found in traumatised individuals (Teicher & Munkhbaatar, 2020). The all-important executive function area was found to have a significant period of development at around fourteen to sixteen years old, whereas other areas of the cortex were impacted at much younger ages (Anderson & Teicher, 2008). The areas within the cerebral cortex are vital and adaptations might see an individual struggle in areas of decision-making, inhibition, emotional regulation and impulse control (Teicher & Munkhbaatar, 2020). Some specific changes are associated with types of abuse, for example, the visual cortex reduced function is associated with sexual abuse, potentially resulting in impacts to visual memory, including facial recognition.

Corpus callosum

Damage to the corpus callosum can result in the important communication between hemispheres being diminished. Other impacts include emotional dysregulation and extremes of mood, and difficulties problem-solving (Teicher & Munkhbaatar, 2020). Similarly, reduced function in the corpus callosum can indicate early trauma and is a risk factor for later mental health disorders, specifically borderline personality disorder (Teicher, 2016). Again, the research identifies differences in biological sex when it comes to the way that this part of the brain is impacted. Neglect and sexual abuse have both been identified as specific forms of trauma that impact the corpus callosum. There is also an indication that emotional abuse from peers can impact this part of the brain, with eight to nine years old being a critical period (Teicher, 2016; Teicher & Munkhbaatar, 2020).

Memory

Early chronic stress impacts memory in a range of ways. Memory capacity is impacted not just by the experiences themselves, but also by the coping strategies used in moments of these experiences. Many structures of the brain are involved in memory making. The amygdala and right hemisphere get a workout with our unconscious memories, and the hippocampus is vital for those memories that are explicit. The corpus callosum is vital for the transfer of information between hemispheres, and it has been proposed that the communication between the two hemispheres is important for the consolidation of memories. All these areas are known to be impacted by early trauma and stress, with continued impacts when the trauma remains unresolved (that is, it has not been processed; Kain & Terrell, 2018; Siegel, 2020).

The amount of stress experienced is very relevant, with moderate amounts of stress being helpful, while large amounts of stress negatively impacting memory. The ways that large amounts of stress impact memory tends to relate to the coping strategies, or 'defensive accommodations', that are used. In addition to this, the stress hormone cortisol has the capacity to actually damage the hippocampus when released too frequently (Kain & Terrell, 2018). There are still studies investigating what role different parts of the brain play when it comes to memory making and memory retrieval. The use of functional magnetic resonance imaging is very helpful, but the research is still coming.

Explicit memory

There are many types of memory and all can be impacted by traumatic stress. Often when we talk about memory, we are referring to *explicit memory*, that is, when we consciously remember something. Explicit memory can be of facts or events. It requires the development of the hippocampus to store the memories and then recall them. Explicit memory requires a focal moment to become encoded and thus, available to us later. Long-term memories become consolidated so that they are able to be retrieved without using the hippocampus. Explicit memories can be divided into declarative, semantic or episodic:

- Declarative memory is memory that can be described using words.
- Semantic memory refers to the recall of facts and develops around one to two years old.
- Episodic memory is of oneself in a moment in time.

Another type of memory is autobiographical memory, which is the recalling of things, events and experiences about yourself. It develops from about age two and increases with age. It is a combination of semantic and episodic memory. We also have memory specifically related to what you were doing; the recall of mood; memory of the senses; and the memory of how the body felt.

Vital for learning is working memory. Working memory is the memory we use all the time. It lasts thirty seconds or so, if there is no repetition. It is the memory we use to hold on to a phone number until we dial it. The lateral prefrontal cortex is thought to be the most relevant brain structure for working memory, but likely includes other parts of the brain, too. Impaired working memory significantly impacts learning and might manifest as the inability to follow multiple instructions, struggling with concepts and the need for more repetition than peers.

Implicit memory

A significant type of memory, particularly relating to high stress experiences, is implicit memory. Implicit memory exists from birth and likely before. In the time before the hippocampus is well-developed, our brains are only able to encode this type of memory. Quite different to moments when we are aware we are remembering, implicit memory is unconscious. Kain and Terrell (2018) state, 'In this way our lives can become shaped by reactivations of implicit memories, which lack a sense that something is being recalled' (Kain & Terrell, 2018, p. 131). Implicit memory is behavioural, emotional, perceptual and somatic.

The amygdala plays a part in our implicit memory, as do structures specifically in the right hemisphere, which is dominant in our early years, and is considered to be the more unconscious side of the brain (Valent, 2006). The right brain can be thought to hold trauma 'coded in emotions, sensations, automatic behaviour and attitude patterns' (Valent, 2006, p. 4). Studies of trauma survivors tend to show unbalanced hemispheric activity, with more action in this right side (Kain & Terrell, 2018).

This unconscious form of memory has no sense of time or place and, when an implicit memory surfaces, it is without a sense that memory is being recalled. Implicit memories are more likely to be stored when events are particularly emotional and may return to us without our control. It might be a reaction to a smell, music or even a response we have to a person or place without knowing why.

Trauma and memory

Consider what we know about the brain's response to threat, especially in terms of the 'thinking' part of the brain going offline. With explicit memory, this leaves the brain less able to identify a focal point of the experience and less able to create an explicit memory for later conscious recall. However, trauma does not inhibit implicit memory (van de Kolk, 1994). Rather, traumatic experiences are likely to leave an individual with implicit memory of the event, even if there is no explicit memory.

Trauma, memory and relationships

Early attachment experiences become implicit memory, whether they are a sense of love and safety, or a sense of threat or confusion. These implicit memories can be triggered by other close relationships with adults, like teachers. For a child with caregivers who caused fear or confusion, those early experiences will leave their mark unconsciously, later popping up as emotions detached from a conscious memory, when confronted with another close adult.

At around one year old, these repeated relational experiences will powerfully influence the memory. Attachment studies show that, even at this young age, children can demonstrate differences in behaviour with different attachment figures. At this point, brain development is likely leading to a child being able to, it is thought, bring forward an image of an attachment figure to support self-soothing, using evocative memory. At around two years old, children can recall and share memories of recent events. They build on this with a capacity to understand the sequencing of events and prediction based on previous experience as well as also gaining some spatial understanding.

When a child is brought to feel a strong emotion repeatedly – love or fear – these emotions become readily accessible and can eventually look like personality traits. A person who could be described as aggressive or uncaring might actually be someone expressing the impacts of living with a constant degree of fear and hyper-vigilance. Similarly, implicit memories can be unconsciously expressed, shown through the body and face, even when a separate narrative is being told. This might look like someone expressing that they are feeling happy (the narrative) while looking quite unhappy (expression of an internal implicit response). People can accept and believe a false narrative even in the face of the experience of their implicit memories. Being exposed to this incongruence in another can be unsettling and plays a part in the relational difficulties that a person with early relational trauma may experience.

Trauma, memory and self

We are more likely to remember things that carry an emotional element. Might this be why we remember that one multiplication equation that we got wrong in public that we will now never forget (or is that just me)? Our brain has to find a way to identify what is important and what is not, so selecting those experiences that carry an emotional charge makes sense. Teaching through storytelling is an example of making use of these emotive reactions and what we know about memory. Even when a story is not ours, we still are likely to have an emotional response to information that is related to a human connection, rather than information on its own, thus increasing the chance of bedding down a related memory.

Trauma impacts the memory in many ways that can lead to struggles with relationships, learning and sense of self. As the Australian Childhood Foundation (2018) states:

> *Trauma dramatically affects children's memory capacity. It serves to degrade children's memories. Children's working memory is extensively reduced. They find it difficult to learn. They are not able to remember events and the sequence in which they occurred. They are unable to build a narrative about their lives which draws out meaning and understanding. In many ways, trauma reduces children's ability to remember who they are. (p. 1)*

This means that trauma experiences, especially those that carry a strong emotional element, can serve to impact not just a child's memory of their experiences, but also their sense of self. We will explore this further in later chapters.

Epigenetics and neuroplasticity

While a person's DNA is final, our genetics are not our fate (Teicher, 2016; Tronick & Gold 2020). Our genes are not all created equal. Some are more likely to 'switch on' and influence who we are, while others remain unexpressed, 'not actually altering the underlying DNA sequence itself but rather the *expression* of those genes' (Kain & Terrell, 2018, p. 41).

Though our DNA remains the same in every cell in our body, it is the activation of genes that determine what function each cell will have. Genes switch on and off at various times throughout our life, and more recently it is understood that genes can be modified by our experiences – a process called *epigenetics*. This process does not affect our genetic make-up, but rather takes what we have and causes some genes to switch on. It is worth noting that not all epigenetic changes are irreversible. It is also important to note that epigenetic changes can occur before birth. Things that can impact epigenetic changes include the inutero experience, nutrition, smoking and experiences of high stress or trauma (Centers for Disease Control and Prevention, 2020; Teicher, 2016; Zubrick et al., 2014).

Trauma's genetic influences

In relation to the impact of early childhood experiences, gene predisposition has been linked to a vulnerability when it comes to receiving less than ideal parenting experiences (Siegel, 2020), increasing the likelihood of adapting to these difficult circumstances. In addition, it can work the other way: the negative early experiences can cause epigenetic changes which can then be passed along to the next generation (Siegel, 2020). Challenges in early life, with parenting, attachment issues and other struggles can pass through generations in many ways – epigenetically is one significant way. Gene expression and predisposition can make it particularly challenging for some individuals to break these cycles.

The impact of early trauma or stress varies depending on the type and timing of the experience, genetics and existence of protective factors (Teicher & Munkhbaatar, 2020). The brain in early development, wired for survival, becomes a reflection of its environment, adapting to attune to family, community and culture (Perry, 2009). Put simply, a child growing up in a stressful environment will develop a heightened ability to recognise and respond to stressors. This adaptive response becomes maladaptive when the associated behaviours are inappropriate for the situation the child later finds themselves in. What was once helpful, becomes harmful. For example, if the brain has adapted to cope with abuse from adults, then goes on to experience a friendly and caring teacher at school, the brain does not have immediate access to an appropriate response. The new response must be learned and this is not easy.

Epigenetic influences can include early trauma. In fact, children whose parents experienced trauma such as war or abuse are more vulnerable to both the genetic impact as well as the environmental impact of what may potentially be the effect of their parent's manifestation of their trauma. A person who has a parent who experienced the Holocaust is more likely to develop disorders generally associated with traumatic events, even if they themselves have not experienced these events (Kain & Terrell, 2018). This impact can go on for generations, and we only need to observe the ongoing, damaging impacts of colonisation to see the compounding impacts of this form of generational trauma.

The Hunger Winter

A fascinating story of epigenetics and the adaptive brain is known as 'Dutch Hunger Winter' in the Netherlands' during World War Two. In 1944, Dutch railway workers went on strike in an effort to stop the movement of Nazi troops. As punishment, the Nazis cut off food supply to the Netherlands. Though the war ended the following year, more than 20,000 people had died as a result of the famine caused by these actions. This horrific situation provided a unique opportunity to study the children conceived during the famine. This study, conducted in 2013 by L H Lumey and colleagues at Columbia University, researched hundreds of thousands of Dutch people conceived both during the Hunger Winter, as well as before and after. The researchers took blood samples from those still living and examined the death records of those who had since died. They identified some interesting characteristics of the group conceived during the famine. This cohort tended to be heavier than average by adulthood; by middle age they had higher cholesterol, higher rates of obesity, and higher rates of diabetes and other metabolic illnesses (Tronick & Gold, 2020; Zimmer, 2018). This research theorises that a certain gene had altered its expression, in utero, as a result of food scarcity, preparing for birth into an environment where food may not be readily available. Though this was not the environment they found themselves in, the scene was set (Tronick & Gold, 2020; Zimmer, 2018).

Other studies have also identified that maternal trauma or stress during pregnancy can cause a trauma response in the child, since stress hormones are shared with the foetus. Research by Perry and colleagues, as reported in Kain and Terrell (2018), identify that this experience is 'associated with increased risk of miscarriage, shorter gestation, and lower birth weight' (p. 46). Along with these risks, infants are harder to soothe when upset, and tend to be fussier and more reactive. These children can demonstrate hyperactivity and general emotional struggles, and the impacts appear to be lifelong (Perry et al., 1995).

Rachel Yehuda is known for her studies on epigenetics, including studying survivors of the Holocaust and the generations following. She acknowledges that while the science is not yet definitive, she identifies that 'There is now converging evidence supporting the idea that offspring are affected by parental trauma exposures occurring before their birth, and possibly even prior to their conception' (Yehuda & Lehrner, 2018, p. 243).

COVID-19

Closer to home and the present, research is currently being undertaken looking at children conceived during the COVID-19 pandemic. In one example, researchers identified a link between mothers' prenatal pandemic-related stress and the resulting temperamental dysregulation of infants at three months old (Provenzi et al., 2021). We can expect many more examples of the epigenetic impact of this period of time.

The study of epigenetics has the capacity to help our society address some of the deep inequities that exist. As we learn more it becomes clearer that by protecting people from the impacts of early adversities such as poverty, racism and abuse, we are protecting future generations. It also helps educators be aware of some of the uncontrollable factors that exist in a child's life, including their DNA. When it comes to school, Cozolino (2014) suggests, 'The central epigenetic question for teachers is how we can shape the learning experience to optimize the impact on the structure and function of our students' brains' (p. 55).

Neuroplasticity

It was thought, until relatively recently, that brain plasticity was only relevant in childhood, that any injury to the brain was permanent and unchangeable, and that the adult brain remained static, aside from deterioration with aging (Fuchs & Flügge, 2014; Gage, 2004). Although early research was happening around the mid-1900s (and one study in the 1920s), the extent of both child and adult neuroplasticity was not widely accepted as fact until around 2007 (Doidge, 2015).

We now understand that the brain continues to adjust throughout life, altering as a result of experience (Doige, 2015; Kain & Terrell, 2018). During the early years of life, the brain produces an excess of synapses, which are later 'pruned' based on use. Repetitions strengthen these connections in the brain while lack of use leads to pruning. This ability to prune, consolidate and strengthen is what is referred to as *neuroplasticity*.

Kain and Terrell (2018) describe research that identifies that neuroplasticity can work as a counter to epigenetics. For example, rats bred with a tendency toward anxiety can have this tendency mitigated when paired with 'especially competent mother rats' (p. 44). They also describe research results that show that stimulating environments, with toys and play opportunities, can be a factor in encouraging positive gene expression in rats. As Seigel (2020) points out: nurture *is* nature, love and care alter biology.

The idea that different parts of the brain can step in and take over from parts that have been injured or damaged is also new. Doidge (2010) writes about studies as far back as the 1860s that investigated the idea that specific areas of the brain were responsible for specific human function – such as language or movement. Investigating the link between impairment and damage to specific brain parts supported this brain mapping. It was one hundred years later that somewhat more sophisticated testing was able to identify that the idea of 'one function one location' shifted to a realisation that areas of the brain could be responsible for many functions (Doidge, 2010).

Neuroplasticity in recovery

Some of the very factors that make trauma so damaging to the brain can also be used in recovery. For example, remembering something or picturing something can cause neuronal activity in the same way as when we actually encounter that object or experience (Doidge, 2015). While this means that remembering a distressing thing will bed down the impact of the distress, remembering a happy experience will trigger the same brain activity as when we experienced it the first time. There is quite a lot of research that demonstrates that mental practise – 'the cognitive rehearsal of a task in the absence of overt physical movements' (Bernardi et al., 2013, p. 1) – has a significant impact on actual motor performance, demonstrating that there is capacity for neuroplasticity to aid in strengthening neural connections with positive lasting impact.

In later chapters, you will find interventions that schools can use to support students who have experienced early adversity or trauma that are designed to positively impact the brain in a way that aims to be healing.

Neuroscience and education

Neuroscience has great capacity to continue to inform educators. Understanding children's brain development alerts us to challenges and opportunities in teaching. Knowing what may be happening for a student whose capacity for thinking and reasoning is diminished because it has been hijacked by their brain's threat response can give insight into the internal landscape of a student who either appears 'offline' or confusing or overly emotional. We will likely continue to learn more about the intersections of early experiences, neuroscience and education as current research continues.

Conclusion

The world of our brains is fascinating, and while we know a tremendous amount more than we did just one generation ago, the research still has a long way to go. Looking at brain development, the functions of the brain and the impact of early experiences, it is clear that neuroscience can inform education systems and educators. The ongoing research will no doubt bring more insight to inform better education. As it stands, neuroscience can support our understanding of our students, the ways they learn and importantly, the best ways for us to educationally support those students, for whom life's experiences are impeding their access to the education they deserve.

3

THE NERVOUS SYSTEM

Exposure to events that represent a real or perceived threat to safety elicit subcortical mammalian, or animal defences that are not mediated by the cortex; in fact, they actually disable cortical activity when engaged. These animal defence strategies are adaptive at the moment of immediate threat, but tend to become default behaviours and inflexible action sequences. (Ogden, Goldstein & Fisher, 2012, p. 11)

It is important to understand the way our brains respond when we are under threat. Having just looked at various anatomy and physiology of the brain, understanding what happens in the brain when we are threatened will allow us to better understand how we respond to threat. This understanding helps us to better know ourselves and our students, and what happens when differently calibrated nervous systems encounter each other.

The autonomic nervous system

Our bodies decide if a situation is safe or unsafe. The nervous system has the important job of collecting information about our environment and deciding what response our bodies should have. The peripheral nervous system includes our sense organs and sensory nerves. It constantly takes in information about the body and the environment and sends the information to our brain and spinal cord – the central nervous system – where the decisions about appropriate responses are made. These decisions about what the body should do are sent back via the peripheral nervous system to get the bodily responses happening (Porges, 2017).

The autonomic nervous system (ANS), part of the peripheral nervous system, controls the bodily systems responsible for homeostasis like heart rate, digestion and breathing. As the name suggests, we do not need to consciously decide to breathe or cough or vomit to stay alive – they occur involuntarily as the ANS does its job. Similarly, when responding to perceived threat, the ANS does its best to keep us safe, enacting what we might know as the fight, flight or freeze response.

The ANS has two branches – the sympathetic branch and the parasympathetic branch – both of which use information that travels via nerves to the brain. Put simply, the sympathetic branch is responsible for the mobilised body responses of fight or flight, and the parasympathetic branch's initiation in the face of threat leads to the immobilised freeze response. These systems also work when we are not experiencing a perceived threat. We rely on our parasympathetic nervous system to have a regulatory calm influence on our body, while we would have a lot of trouble cooling down (sweating) or waking up without a little kick from our sympathetic nervous system. As the science of the nervous system has developed, it is now widely accepted that the ANS is somewhat more sophisticated than fight, flight or freeze would suggest, and we will go on to explore Polyvagal Theory later in this chapter.

A brain that experiences threat has a very specific response. The areas of the brain mentioned above, along with hormones linking the brain to the rest of the body, combine in an attempt to protect from threat. Our ANS is responsible for the patterns of response designed to keep us safe from a perceived threat, regulating our internal organs into an appropriate survival response. It is important to note that it is *perceived* threat that sends the ANS into action – the threat does not need to be real or present (as anyone afraid of an innocent spider will tell you), it just needs to be felt as fear.

Sympathetic nervous system

The sympathetic branch can be thought of as the active mobilised response. This controls our bodies in ways that allow us to take action. Heart rate increases, digestion slows, airways widen and muscles strengthen – we are ready to fight or to run. Anyone who has encountered a snake may have had this very experience – I certainly remember being in flight before my conscious mind even realised I was escaping a very large snake. It was as though an image of the snake remained in my mind until I was ready to take it in, by which stage I was already many metres away and moving quickly.

The sympathetic branch develops predominantly up to age one (Siegel, 2020). The helpful elements of this activating branch, when not under threat, are ideally engaged lots during this first year, in a positive relationship with caregivers – playing, laughing, exploring.

Parasympathetic nervous system

Meanwhile, the parasympathetic branch of the ANS controls the freeze response when under threat, also sometimes called 'tonic immobility' (Wynkoop, 2017). This is a more basic, less sophisticated approach to survival, the survival message to predators being something along the lines of 'I'm dead, don't bother'. When we are not under threat, the parasympathetic response allows us to rest, to calm, to digest and to heal. The parasympathetic nervous system is ideally present when a threat has passed. Once the sympathetic nervous system has done its job of activating us to respond, the parasympathetic response should slow us down, calm the system, stop the release stress hormones and slowly return us to normal functioning. It is under very extreme situations of overwhelm that this system is relied on not for recovery, but for survival.

Anyone who has seen a cat or dog with a smaller creature in its mouth may also be familiar with a creature that appears dead, but upon release, can activate its flee response. Given the freeze response is more likely to occur in situations where we feel unable to fight or flee, it makes sense that this is a state that many infants and children experience when threatened. In fact, there is a strong correlation between sexual assault and immobilisation (Möller et al., 2017), and in the face of such terror it is very understandable as an adaptive response. The psychological response of dissociation, where a sense of time and space and self can be lost, can occur alongside this physiological parasympathetic response (Kain & Terrell, 2018; Möller et al., 2017).

The parasympathetic response develops between one and two years of age, stepping in to help that mobile youngster from wildly pursuing every exciting thing in their world (Siegel, 2020). It is this inhibitory response that comes when a parent exclaims 'No!' to stop an infant from doing something dangerous.

All these responses are very reasonable when encountering threat. However, when a brain is regularly so overwhelmed it feels it cannot cope, this response can become ingrained and the brain can become hypersensitive to a point where *all change feels like a threat* (Australian Childhood Foundation, 2018).

Polyvagal Theory

Polyvagal Theory provides us with a more recent approach to understanding the nervous system and centres around the vagus – the longest nerve in the human body – which plays a very important role in the parasympathetic nervous system. The understanding that goes along with the theory was first introduced by Stephen Porges in 1994, and is now widely accepted and used in therapy to understand more about nervous system responses, and to support recovery from trauma (Australian Childhood Foundation, 2011; Dana, 2018, 2021; Kain & Terrell, 2018; Tronick & Gold, 2020).

Polyvagal Theory is a theory of the evolution of the nervous system that centres on the two subbranches of the vagus nerve: the *dorsal* vagus and the *ventral* vagus, each with a different approach to the parasympathetic response to threat. While historically the ANS was seen as two opposite and antagonistic approaches to threat response – fight or flight (sympathetic) and freeze (parasympathetic), Polyvagal Theory posits that the freeze response is not the only way our parasympathetic branch protects us from danger. The theory identifies that the response to threat is hierarchical and evolutionary, with only mammals having the 'newer' ventral vagus. In Polyvagal Theory we see that the threat response system begins with the most sophisticated approach to avoiding threat and moves through the ANS options until reaching, if required, the most primitive response of feigning death, the freeze response (Dana, 2018; Kain & Terrell, 2020; Porges, 2017).

Here, we will delve a little deeper into the basics of Polyvagal Theory, as a useful basis for understanding behaviour and the motivation behind it, both for our students and for ourselves.

Dorsal vagus

The dorsal vagus, sometimes called the primitive vagus, exists in most vertebrate animals. This subbranch of the vagus nerve connects to and regulates organs below the diaphragm, and is slower than its ventral counterpart in its responses (Tronick & Gold, 2020). When in a safe situation, the job of the dorsal vagus is to support homeostasis. However, when engaged as a defence response, the role shifts to one of immobilisation, slowing heart rate and digestion, and in the case of some reptiles, temporarily stopping breathing (Porges, 2017). This response can be triggered by acute fear of death. If we are confined, such as being isolated or restrained, our nervous system reads cues and functionally wants to immobilise (Porges, 2017, p. 66).

Ventral vagus

The ventral vagus is alternatively known as the smart vagus due its myelinated state, myelination being a process of an insulating sheath being formed around nerves, allowing very fast and accurate messages to be sent (Tronick & Gold, 2020). This is the evolutionarily newer branch of the vagus and connects to and regulates the organs above the diaphragm. The role of the ventral vagus goes beyond the traditional view of the defensive response as being two opposing physiological responses of fight or flight versus freeze.

The ventral vagus links to the tiny muscles in the face, ear, throat, eyes and neck, which are used to connect with others. This social engagement is what we use in times of safety and connection, for example, a parent and baby delighting in each others' faces. This social engagement can also be used more deliberately as an initial approach that our clever brain can use in response to threat. Consider all the things we do when connecting with others, particularly when we are trying to help someone feel safe. We alter the prosody of our voice so we are speaking in a gentle tone; we smile with our whole face; we tune in to the voice of another; we focus on their face and make eye contact. All thanks to the ventral vagus. Polyvagal Theory recognises that this social engagement response, sometimes called the fawn response, or the feign response, acts as our starting point for connecting with others and thus feeling safe.

There is evidence of babies using the social engagement response in moments where they are unsure of the adult in front of them, perhaps trying to elicit a smile from a caregiver, as in the still-face experiment discussed later. As a threat response, social engagement is likely incredibly familiar to women who are in a state of low-level fear around men who may pose a threat. The ventral vagus response mimics true connection, a fear response that sends the message 'No need for any confrontation, I'm engaging!' When not in a state of fear, the ventral vagus supports us to engage with others, to attune and connect. Educators will likely be familiar with the impact of attuned connecting with students; the use of face, voice, eye contact, breath and posture can facilitate very positive learning outcomes. It is also important to note that teachers are responding with their parasympathetic nervous system, too, when they are feeling under threat from an unruly classroom (we will look at the benefits of befriending your own nervous system later).

The use of the fawn response is one that can become overused just like the other nervous system responses, possibly with less dramatic outcomes for those around the person than other responses. Someone with a fawn threat response will possibly be hypersensitive to anyone being displeased with them, and will be a typical people-pleaser.

The nervous system and regulation

As discussed earlier, our nervous system is our first line of defence against danger. When danger is regularly experienced, the nervous system has lots of work to do, so when it is activated repeatedly as a child, these responses become deeply ingrained in us – no longer a response, but a way of being. When our threat response is directing us to do something, but we think we should do something different, we are in a state of dysregulation. For example, consider a phobia response. Despite knowing you are not in danger, seeing a spider (or whatever you're phobic about) generates a physical fear response. Being able to override a powerful fear response is incredibly difficult. A child once described their experience of dysregulation to me as, 'I was telling myself to not get angry, but then I got angry and hit him'. Even with insight, and attempts to engage the thinking brain, our nervous system can get the better of us. Dysregulation is possibly the biggest behavioural challenge that children who have experienced early chronic stress face at school.

We would expect that when the sympathetic nervous system response is active, that the parasympathetic response is not active and vice versa.

However, it is believed now that in some cases both can be active at once or both can be inactive, causing 'the body to work against itself' (Kain & Terrell, 2018, p. 78). The nervous system might work in these ways as the result of accumulated stress, and this act of the body working against itself can lead to behavioural issues in children (El-Sheikh & Erath, 2011). This form of dysregulation must be incredibly challenging to experience, with no path toward physiological reprieve from the conflicting messages the brain is sending.

When in a threat response state, we are in no position to learn or even to take in the information around us. Our clever brains and bodies are working purely for survival, perhaps listening for those low-range sounds that relate to predators while scanning faces for anger, or perhaps numbing to a point of not being able to really hear or see anything. Sadly, there are children in our classrooms who spend a great deal of time in these states.

For those lucky enough to experience a great deal of safety, they become attuned and spend time settled in the ventral vagus with all systems operating calmly. The more time we spend in this state, the easier it becomes to return to this state, should we need to move into a hypo- or hyper-alert state. This is how it is supposed to work – a threat response sends us into our fight or flight response, with our parasympathetic response there to calm us when the threat has passed. The freeze response is reserved for only the most dire of situations, where there seems to be no escape. These states are hard work and we are not designed to be in them for long periods of time. The ventral parasympathetic 'vagal brake' is there to bring us back to baseline, and yet for many children and adults, baseline is anything but calm.

Regulation

The term *self-regulation* could be seen to be somewhat of a misnomer, as regulation almost always occurs in relation to another. For example, though it might sometimes be the case that just one highly dysregulated student can disrupt a whole class, our aim would be that a calm class will have a positive influence on one dysregulated student.

Caregivers provide infants with a framework for how to react to different stimuli. Internally, our reaction to being very excited can be similar to being afraid. Co-regulation with a caregiver, and the sense of safety that this brings, provides a model to differentiate these and other feelings. Without a solid model, children might struggle to differentiate between their different internal experiences and, as such, may react as though afraid when overstimulated, even if to a positive experience. A child who lives with a nervous system that is in overdrive will struggle with self-regulation, which in turn impacts their ability to learn and ability to engage with others. For example, think about interactions at school where a student responding in an unexpected way negatively impacted others and became a barrier to relationships.

When a child misses out on the key factors of a healthy attachment experience, they also miss out on the experience of a consistent and reliable adult, able to support their regulation when they are not able to. This model for regulation is vital: co-regulation is a biological imperative, and positive early co-regulation experiences provide a child with a model for self-regulation that can last a lifetime. Dysregulation is a whole of self-experience, existing in the body, the mind and the emotions. Students whose early experiences lead to struggles with regulation are missing out on skills that are protective in a range of ways, for resilience, for education, or possibly interaction with police or other authority figures.

When regulation is hard

Kain and Terrell (2018) refer to 'foundational dysregulation' (p. 76) or 'foundational lack of regulatory capacity' (p. 90), describing a pervasive experience of lack of safety, leading to constant states of dysregulation. Having a focus on supporting regulation in response to behaviours we believe are related to trauma or stress, means taking a 'bottom-up' approach. Remembering the bottom functions of the brain are the basic functions for homeostasis, a bottom-up approach begins there, engaging the basic functions such as breathing and heart rate, and working with the relevant nervous system responses guided by this lower part of the brain. Trying to talk ourselves, or another, into a state of regulation would be a 'top-down' approach, using the cortex – perhaps talking ourselves down when we realise that snake is actually a hose.

When students have never learned how to regulate themselves, the regulation skills to be taught must match their development, meaning that we need to consider the developmental *stage* of students, rather than what we might expect from the chronological *age*. This generally means we need to start from their basic functions, using the bottom-up approach discussed above, as the bottom-up approach is responsive to the developmental stage. As is the case with all differentiation, and indeed all development, the foundational learning must come first.

Going back to the beginning means starting with safety and co-regulation. Teachers and other school staff play a very important role when it comes to supporting students to experience a sense of safety. It takes time and consistency. When there is opportunity, teachers are able to provide opportunities for co-regulation, maintaining their own equilibrium with the class, attuning to students, offering predictability and adaptability, and connecting with students one-on-one where possible. These opportunities contribute to a sense of safety. A teacher's ability to self-regulate is a vital key when it comes to supporting the building of regulation skills in students.

Even when it is difficult, or impossible, for students to connect with educators for co-regulation, it will most likely be possible with time. We need to be prepared to be misinterpreted, tested and have frustrating interactions. Offering predictability can be frightening for a child who has not yet experienced this, however, it demonstrates an alternative way of being that, with enough repetitions, can be recognised as safety. For those students who have experienced feeling safe early in their development, they will be able to re-experience this feeling more easily, supporting their learning and relationships at school.

Students with significant behaviour and regulation struggles may be given a diagnosis, however, it can be difficult to identify from where the symptoms arise and there are varying views about the benefits of diagnosis. Gabor Mate (2021), in 'The Wisdom of Trauma', identifies the alignment between stress responses and symptoms of behaviour-based diagnoses, suggesting that diagnosis is actually a description of behaviours (Benazzo & Benazzo, 2021). What is important for educators to keep in mind is that we treat our students with care and compassion regardless of whether we know their background, their diagnosis (or lack of) and if there is inclusion funding allocated to them. We should always respond to the individual in front of us. The strategies we will discuss for building self-regulation skills are likely to be appropriate for any student in a dysregulated state, and the preventative strategies are good for all students, regardless of their life experiences.

Window of tolerance

The idea of a window of tolerance can be a useful way to look at how a person operates with regard to their nervous system. Coined by Dan Siegel 'to describe the optimal window within which we can respond to a stimulus without becoming overly aroused, and then be able to settle naturally' (Kain & Terrell, 2018, p. 121), a person might have a narrow window, leading to frequent states of hyper-arousal (sympathetic response) or hypo-arousal (dorsal parasympathetic), or a wide window, meaning they demonstrate resilience to emotional triggers and an ability to recover well from being dysregulated.

Each of us has nervous system responses, and ideally we can recover and return to a safe and social state in a timely manner. Everyone has a different range – some people tend to operate higher or lower and some live constantly just outside this window. We rely on the ventral parasympathetic response to aid our recovery from dysregulation, helping to calm and put us in a position of readiness to take in what is around us. When within our window, we are operating with optimal arousal, taking in what is around us, but not overly distracted, allowing us to listen and learn, concentrate and connect. Outside our window, we may be hyper-aroused, with our system switched on ready to respond to danger. In this state we might be quick to anger, to be jumpy, to want to leave where we are. We would be less able to tune in to voices and might struggle to take in information. Alternatively, we might find ourselves below our window, hypo-aroused, tuned out, possibly dissociated, not hearing or being aware of what is happening in our surroundings. Anything can cause this loss of regulation – it might be someone yelling, being late for a meeting, presenting to an audience, a near miss while riding a bike. The stimulus can be anything, the reaction and recovery are what impacts us.

Everyone will have a baseline that they return to when threatened. It can be helpful when working in any stressful job to know what your tendency is. Do you tend toward mobilisation or immobilisation, or are you a people-pleaser? When you are angry, do harsh words come out of your mouth or might they stay in your head? Do you withdraw from conflict or stand in it and fight back? Even if you feel you are right, do you appease others? Though we are all capable of all states, we all will have a leaning toward one or the other (Dana, 2018; 2021). Knowing which you do can be incredibly helpful. Letting your team at school know about your warning signs, and your nervous system responses, can also be helpful.

For those of us who go to hyper-arousal, we might appear tense, we might be scanning the space around us, we might find it difficult to tune in to others, we might seem angry or aggressive, we might talk quickly or seem hyped. However, when in hypo-arousal, we might appear passive or disinterested, unable to find words, without much facial expression, disconnected from those around us, we might feel numb, tired or uncaring. You have likely developed strategies to deal with these experiences.

Children also move out of their window of tolerance, but have had less time to learn how to mask their experience and generally have less awareness of what is going on. For some of our students, they might never be in their window of tolerance, and what *looks like* being in the safe vagal parasympathetic space might just be as close as they get. Reactivity can be a key here. When students appear calm, but have instant big reactions, it can be an indicator that what appears to be their window of tolerance might actually be a state of hyper-arousal and hyper-vigilance, even when appearing relaxed. The student who can describe what is happening in their body is able to find clues and give caring adults information about what is happening for them. As adults, when we can recognise hyper- or hypo-aroused responses, we can work to teach children about themselves and give them the skills to respond to their nervous systems.

I knew a student who had experienced a huge amount of early trauma. Their parent had shared their story with the school, which was a safe space for this student and their mother, where they were able to let their guard down. The student most definitely tended toward hypo-arousal, including regression and dissociation. This student had a soft toy for comfort and behaved more like a child five years younger. They would frequently fall deep asleep in class, possibly a form of dissociation when things were challenging, but possibly a release knowing there were plenty of adults taking care of them. While this student was not able to engage with the curriculum expected for their age, they were able to build their knowledge about feeling safe through regular experiences of expressed care and protection that would hopefully counteract some of the negative impacts of their unsafe experiences.

As mentioned, some students might never be within their window of tolerance. They might experience what Kain and Terrell (2018) refer to as a 'Faux Window'. When a very narrow window exists, someone might be able to create an approximation of the window. For example, always being in a state of arousal, yet the lower areas of arousal appear as though regulated. This would be gained with the accommodations we mentioned earlier. Perhaps regulation strategies such as video games, disordered eating or self-harm might create enough of a release to get close to the top of the window. The same could exist on the hypo-arousal side of the true window, with actions like taking stimulants, aggression or stealing providing enough of a high to get closer to the bottom of the window. It is important to note that for some of our students, life is only ever experienced in a state of dysregulation. They will come as close as they can using strategies, or defensive accommodations, that they have refined over years. For those who experience the co-activation of both hyper- and hypo-arousal, this is life lived in chaos. It is difficult to know what we can do to support students in this situation. In viewing the attempt at regulation as actual regulation, we reiterate a faulty system. However, we can take action by being vigilant and expanding our own knowledge, including of individual students, to help us have the most accurate understanding possible.

As with the situation that sees an individual have both sympathetic and parasympathetic activation either simultaneously or not at all, the system might take shortcuts in an attempt to find a state of optimal arousal. Ideally, once heightened and the threat has passed, a nervous system will engage the vagal brake – that is, the ventral parasympathetic response to calm us. This system is designed to calm, to down-regulate and return to a state of equilibrium and homeostasis. However, this system, also the social engagement system, does not always make itself readily available to those who have experienced developmental trauma, or who have not experienced a quality attachment relationship. In this instance, a clever nervous system, knowing that the sympathetic activation state of hyper-arousal is not sustainable, might access the dorsal parasympathetic physiology as an alternative brake. This option takes someone from their hyper state into a hypo one, rather than one of ventral vagus calm. This may indeed be the case for some of our students, going from angry, for example, to collapsed, with no way to visit that gentle state that allows for calming and connecting. This can take a huge toll on the system, as neither threat response – sympathetic or parasympathetic – are designed for long periods.

I worked with a student who had experienced a great deal of trauma in their young years, exposed to adults who offered neglect and abuse rather than love and safety. As you would expect, we witnessed frequent zipping around the nervous system states. Often the student would be violent, lashing out with words or kicks and punches toward students and adults. The actions, at times, appeared deliberate and considered, but underneath there was an incredibly frightened and out-of-control child. After a particularly extreme episode, hitting a teacher across the face, the student stopped, lay on the floor, accepted the offer of a big blanket, pulled the blanket up for complete coverage and fell asleep. Here is a clear example of a child without a working vagal break – the choices are hyper-aroused or hypo-aroused, with the nervous system doing its very best to manage.

For each of us, our window of tolerance varies based on our situation. When we are tired or stressed, it is smaller. When we are relaxed and with our safe people, we can tolerate more. For those who might have been pushed outside their window repeatedly, they may have a strong resistance to finding themselves at the challenging edges of their window.

Conclusion

In this chapter we have delved into the physiology of the human response to threat. Understanding these concepts can assist educators to better support themselves and their students. When we can reframe behaviour to look for unconscious patterns of threat response, we are in a better position to focus on tuning in to our students and working on creating safe and predictable classrooms. This will be a step toward centring student wellbeing and calming nervous systems on high alert.

ATTACHMENT, A BLUEPRINT FOR RELATIONSHIPS

Humans have an incredible ability to read faces. Without consciously understanding what we are taking in, we notice all the actions of the tiny muscles in the face. For some people, particularly children exposed to unpredictable adults, they will be highly attuned to the emotion displayed in faces. Porges (2017) refers to how we unconsciously read another human as safe or unsafe as *neuroception*, identifying that this is the action where we 'evaluate risk in the environment without awareness' (p. 68). It is important to note that not everyone has a completely accurate neuroceptive sense. Repeated exposure to unpredictability from others will lead to greater sensitivity in identifying others as threats, with associated threat behaviours being more common, too (Kain & Terrell, 2018). Our early relationships create a blueprint for future relationships, so it is helpful for educators to have an understanding about attachment and the link to sense of self and relationship models, because we see the echoes of attachment every day in our classrooms.

Attachment

Attachment is the word we give to the connection between an infant and their caregiver. It describes a relationship that is vital to the infant as it provides safety, both physical and emotional. Children who do not grow up with positive attachments to caregivers will experience a potentially lifelong impact on future relationships. We all have attachment experiences and it can be very useful to understand attachment for ourselves and for our students. Early attachment experiences that are repeated go on to become encoded in our implicit memory, creating a core understanding and expectation about connection and relationships. These early experiences also influence our capacity for emotional regulation, our sense of self and our comprehension of our self-story. As Siegel (2020) explains, 'these salient emotional relationships have a direct effect on the development of the domains of mental functioning that serve as our conceptual anchor points: memory, narrative, emotion, representations, and states of mind' (p. 168).

The biological imperative for a baby or infant to form an attachment to an adult is the only option for keeping safe. As a result of this imperative, attachment is also a system linked with a vigilance to danger, where separation from an attachment figure can result in fear. The power of attachment is such that for a child with no attachment figure, there is a disorder identified as 'reactive attachment disorder', a developmental disorder that signifies a range of issues. Cozolino (2014) states, 'Experiences of early disconnection and abandonment are at the heart of most human pain and can be the source of lifelong feelings of brokenness' (p. 60). Meanwhile, a child experiencing secure attachment benefits from the protective nature of this experience and is more likely to have resilience in a range of areas. Attachment experiences are also predictors for one's parenting style, and for child and adult mental health issues. We parent based on our own experience of being parented, and a parent's cohesive self-narrative is a significant factor when it comes to an individual's wellbeing (Siegel, 2010a).

Our early attachment experiences continue to shape us throughout life, particularly with relationships. There are plenty of relationship advice books for adults that focus specifically on attachment styles. It is important to note that while attachment experiences can lead one to have tendencies, there are also many other factors that influence development.

Connection-seeking in infants

Ed Tronik's *Still Face Experiment* (UMassBoston, 2009) demonstrates the sophistication of a baby's ability to read the face of their caregiver and is a good example of the use of the ventral vagal approach to threat.

The experiment involves a caregiver going from interacting as normal to having a flat affect – a face with no expression. What this experiment shows is that even infants experience the fear that comes with a potential threat, in this case the loss of safe engagement (Tronick & Gold, 2020). The experiment sees babies respond in a series of ways – they coo, search for eye contact, make cute noises, wave their arms, point – all the things they do to receive a positive response when their caregiver is attuned to them.

In the experiment it has been found that babies' stress levels rise, then there is a great reduction in stress when the caregiver connects again. However, the babies do not return to normal levels for hours, with the stress hormones remaining in their bodies. These babies are using what they have available to them to first identify threat and then to respond (Tronick & Gold, 2020). Were this threat to continue, for example, a situation of neglect, their response would likely escalate through the threat response options, hierarchically, ending with no crying, no response, but collapse (Perry & Szalavitz, 2017). Since infants are vulnerable to threats and lack the ability to respond effectively to threat, adults can act as both threat and protection. The parasympathetic response is the most powerful protector an infant has outside of a co-regulating adult.

Attachment theory

Attachment theory is a developmental theory that is a useful framework to explore an individual's internal design when it comes to relationships. The initial attachment relationship with caregivers creates a blueprint for later relationships – though these are not static.

Attachment theory has its origins in the research of John Bowlby and Mary Ainsworth, whose revolutionary research began to show the impacts of early caregiving. While their work has been built upon, the basics are still very much a part of psychology today. Prior to their work, understandings about what infants needed to grow and prosper were based on behavioural theory, which understood that a baby or infant would create an attachment to an adult that fed them. Bowlby generated a different theory that went deeper and included the importance of an emotional connection between adult and infant when it comes to healthy attachment. Bowlby brought relationships into the picture of an infant's survival needs. Not only are the requirements for survival physical, they are also psychological.

Bowlby's own experience in his early years, both as a child and as an attachment figure, influenced his research and interest in attachment. His research led him to the understanding that humans had a need for attachment, and not receiving adequate early attachment experiences could lead to behavioural issues. Bowlby worked on the idea that the mother, understood as primary caregiver, was responsible for creating a sense of safety for the infant that would then become essential to the child's healthy development (Bowlby, 1944; Hesse et al., 2003; Teyber & Teyber, 2017). Bowlby conducted a study in 1944 entitled 'Forty-Four Juvenile Thieves: Their Characters and Home-Life' where his subjects were identified as sharing some key characteristics including lack of empathy, wilful destruction and a disconnection from others. The study linked these characteristics with a maternal separation and identified that this separation and loss of a maternal relationship had a direct causal relationship with the character and behaviour of the boys (Bowlby, 1944; Kain & Terrell, 2018; Teyber & Teyber, 2017).

Mary Ainsworth, who had been doing her own work in the area, began working with Bowlby in 1950 and in their work together they tested and refined the key understandings of what we continue to know as attachment theory today (Bretherton, 1992).

Important elements and timing in attachment

Bowlby also identified the ages when critical attachment milestones were occurring and where attachment might be at risk (Bowlby, 1969). The stages are pre-attachment at birth to six weeks; attachment in the making from six weeks to eight months; clear-cut attachment from eight months to eighteen months; and formation of reciprocal attachment from eighteen months to two years (Bowlby, 1969). These stages all exist pre-verbally, and before explicit memories are formed, so this way of being is unconscious. We now identify four components of attachment required for healthy attachment between an infant and caregiver.

Safe haven

This is the identified space that exists between caregiver and infant where attachment needs are met, where the infant, unable to self-regulate, can return in times of stress to be soothed.

Secure base

The attachment figure acts as a secure base from where an infant can leave to explore, then return for safety. This exploration is vital to building independence as a child ages. Bowlby identified the link between the early attachment relationships and later relationships with partners and friends. The experience of a secure base can lead the individual to later have the confidence and capacity to rely on others in difficult times.

At school, adults act *in loco parentis*, and as such, may be fulfilling roles like the safe haven and secure base.

Proximity maintenance

The idea is that a child will learn to explore their world gradually, always able to return at a moment's notice to the caregiver. Consider a crawling infant or walking toddler exploring their new surroundings in a park, ready to call out for rescuing should a stressful event occur. Think about yard duty as a way that we mirror this at school.

Separation distress

Ideally, the well-attached child will be able to endure separation from the caregiver safe in the knowledge that they will be reunited. Without this sense, a child would experience distress at the prospect of losing contact, fearful of it being lost forever.

These elements are understood as being essential for a child to grow up with resilience and healthy relationships (Kain & Terrell, 2018).

Attachment styles

Mary Ainsworth began her own research in 1954, when she moved to Uganda to study the practice of sending a child away for a few days to support weaning, a process that was thought to help to 'forget the breast'. Ainsworth learnt the language and ended up producing a book in 1967 that explored the features of attachment that she identified as universal. Ainsworth also became well-known for her work with her assistant Barbara Wittig, developing 'The Strange Situation', a study that put children in a short state of separation stress to identify the differences in child participants' responses, which is still used today in attachment research.

In this study, a situation is created that allows observers to witness two separations and two reunions between mother (always in the initial study, while later studies acknowledged that the adult in attachment relationships can be any caregiver) and infant. As a result of this study, which included a year of observing mother and infant relationships as well as the separation, three distinct categories of attachment style were identified. Later work by Mary Main and Judith Soloman added an important fourth category. Given how attachment styles can follow a person from childhood through later relationships, knowing this information about attachment can be very helpful for all who work with children (or people!). The four attachment styles are:

Secure attachment

This is the ideal scenario, where a relationship includes an adult who is responsive, attuned, caring and nurturing, who produces a securely attached child. We would expect a securely attached child to cry on separation and to be happy upon reunion. A child with this experience may go on to be an adult who is comfortable being independent within their relationships, neither clingy nor aloof (Kain & Terrell, 2018; Perry et al., 2017; Teyber & Teyber, 2017). Kain and Terrell (2018) describe the impacts of secure attachment when they state:

> *When safety and security are consistently available to the infant, she develops what is categorized as secure attachment, which supports healthy relationships and sufficient confidence to explore the external world. We expect those with secure attachment to also have a foundational capacity for self-regulation and to meet the criteria for healthy resilience. (p. 169)*

Avoidant insecure attachment

Children who were identified as having the avoidant style of insecure attachment displayed a lack of interest in the mother, both at her leaving and her returning. They also displayed a lack of interest in their surroundings. While some children in this category would not make any attempt to move toward the mother during reunions, others made an attempt, but then stopped short. Notably, the children in this category were later – with research using heart-rate monitors – found to have internal responses to their mother leaving and returning, but these responses were not externalised (Kain & Terrell, 2018). The crux of this style is the belief that the caregiver is not a source of soothing (Cozolino, 2014). This attachment style has been associated with conduct problems (Siegel, 2020, p. 191), and adults maintaining this attachment style are referred to as *dismissive*.

Anxious-ambivalent insecure attachment

Children in this category demonstrated high levels of distress even with their mother in the room, as well as when she left and when she returned. Two subgroups were identified within this category – one group demonstrated negative feelings toward the mother for leaving, while the other expressed a 'helpless passivity' (Kain & Terrell, 2018, p. 17). Similarly, reunion sometimes resulted in resistance to the mother's attempts to comfort. This attachment style is associated with caregivers who are often intrusive, inconsistently involved with their children, or unsupportive of a child's independence (Cozolino, 2014; Teyber & Teyber, 2017). Siegel (2020) states that we might expect children with this attachment style to have a 'vulnerability for anxiety problems' (p. 191). The term for adults with this attachment style is *preoccupied.*

Disorganised attachment

The later research by Mary Main and Judith Solomon produced another leap in attachment theory, with their identification of a fourth category – insecure attachment, where children reflected characteristics of both the avoidant and the ambivalent categories.

Children with this attachment style did not cope well and were sometimes unsure what to do. Their responses at reunion were not consistent, sometimes moving toward, sometimes moving away, and they generally experienced caregivers who were frightened or frightening. The children's behaviour came across as confused, disorientated or apprehensive when their mother was present, possibly turning in circles or freezing (Cherry, 2020; Cozolino, 2014; Hesse et al., 2003; Kain & Terrell, 2018).

This fourth group has the highest risk factor for attachment and emotional struggles throughout life, including dissociating, and symptoms associated with personality disorders (Siegel, 2020, p. 191). There is also the increased risk of becoming a victim of bullying (Cozolino, 2014). In the classroom, Cozolino (2014) states '...these children may do everything possible to avoid attention, including behaviours such as keeping still and hiding in the back of the classroom. Alternately, they may exhibit odd and unpredictable behaviour driven by their anxiety and fear' (p. 61). Without a doubt it is these students who will struggle the most at school, and who teachers will also struggle with the most. Adults who maintain this attachment style are referred to as *fearful* or *unresolved*.

Attachment and our students

The rates of these categories in the general population can give us a snapshot of who we might find in a classroom. It is worth noting that the rates of secure attachment appear to be reducing (Kain & Terrell, 2018). While there are studies identifying numbers in various populations, the number of securely attached people seems to come in at around 60 per cent. As a multicultural society, knowing that culture plays a huge role in parenting practice, which is the primary contributing factor in attachment styles, it is important to note that there are variations based on influencing factors such as parental country of birth, ethnicity, culture and religion (Agishtein & Brumbaugh, 2013).

Along with these influences, there are other relevant factors when it comes to attachment. It is important for us to consider that for children who live with risk factors such as poverty, parental mental illhealth, substance abuse and family violence, these factors are likely to impact their attachment experience. Attachment is one way that risk factors in families can lead to certain behaviours in children. For example, although disorganised attachment is uncommon, for children with abusive parents it is a likely result and 'epigenetically, disorganized attachment can be passed on for generations' (Kain & Terrell, 2018, p. 50).

It is not necessary for us to understand the attachment styles of our students and, as always, these kinds of measures are not one size fits all, but rather can be a helpful lens with which to observe the interpersonal relationships we see and participate in at school. It can also be considered as a source of information that can help educators find compassion with challenging behaviours and, when considering our own early experiences, we can gain some insight regarding our own interpersonal responses. Educators should also remember their own influence, as Cozolino (2014) suggests, '... teachers have the ability to stimulate neuroplastic processes and reshape brains in a positive, more adaptive direction' (p. 62).

In referencing a longitudinal study that has been going for forty-five years – The Minnesota Longitudinal Study of Parents and Children – Siegel (2020) reflects on the study's demonstration that the impact of attachment follows a child to school and impacts how their peers and teachers perceive them. The study identifies that those with avoidant attachment styles are perceived by their peers as aggressive or mean, that children with ambivalent or avoidant histories are much more likely to be a victim of bullying, are less liked by peers and less socially competent. The securely attached children get along with others the best. The study observed teachers and identified that they were likely to be warm and respectful to the securely attached children, but, while still warm, controlled the situation more and had lower expectations for the anxiously/ambivalently attached students. For the avoidant students, teachers were less warm, also controlling and got angry at them the most frequently.

Unsurprisingly, the teachers mirrored the students' attachment style. Our interactions carry the ghost of our attachment style, particularly for children, and this creates situations where we induce expected behaviour from others. Cozolino (2014) identifies the importance of attachment relationships at school, noting that attachment styles are likely to come to the forefront during times of stress, and that positive relationships between teacher and student can mitigate this, providing a sense of security and safety.

Early experiences and later relationships

Our very identity is shaped by our relationships. (Siegel, 2020, p. 196)

Relating well with others involves constant interpretation of social cues and the reading of others. These skills are both learned and taught. Even simple social norms, such as turn taking in conversations, are learned. If this has never been modelled, it is not necessarily a natural thing to do. Early experiences with fear or unpredictability set us up to struggle to read others accurately. As discussed in the section on Polyvagal Theory and the nervous system, our threat detectors are finely tuned and, when overused, can become hyper-sensitive. The need to stay safe will be prioritised ahead of seeking connection (Dana, 2021). Research has identified that frequent exposure to very frightening people render someone less able to identify a range of emotions in other people, with a bias toward identifying even neutral faces as contempt or anger, rather than emotions like happiness or fear (Brackett, 2019; Pfaltz et al., 2019). This may be an adaptive learned behaviour when watching out for danger and does not support the building of positive relationships. 'Human connections create neuronal connections' (Siegel, 2020, p. 188) and those connections stay with us as a foundation for our understanding of how to connect.

Empathy is impacted by early adversity. At its heart, empathy is about connecting with others, something that we know can be perceived as dangerous for children who have experienced unsafe relationships. To know how others are feeling, we need some degree of connection to our own feelings, something that is often dampened in the course of experiencing damaging early relationships. A strategy such as not connecting with emotion, or not attuning to the emotions of others, is very adaptive in the face of interpersonal violence, but very unhelpful when trying to build positive relationships.

When caregivers do not provide safety, but instead are a vehicle for fear, every subsequent relationship is modelled on this early one. A child becomes wired to spot an unsafe person, so much so that they see it where it does not exist. How difficult it must be to move beyond a sense that the world is unsafe and the people within it are harmful. Schools are in a powerful position to provide our students with alternate models for interaction. Over the course of a day we have many opportunities to demonstrate positive ways of connecting. If we succeed in this approach, we have a chance of offering an alternative to the idea that people are unsafe.

Neural repair in relationships

When we consider those children for whom the impact on brain development was caused by relational trauma, it makes sense that the healing is also going to happen in relationships. Siegel (2020) identifies that a positive therapeutic relationship will facilitate regrowth of neurons, promoting neural integration. He highlights how this integration is so important, being vital for self-regulation, which is essential for learning, for positive relationships and the capacity to articulate the inner emotional landscape and needs. Parish-Plass (2020) reinforces this idea when she adds that the neural integration that occurs in healing relationships:

> *is likely to improve the function of the neural networks that were damaged by the maltreatment, perhaps improving the ability to decode facial expression of emotions in others and facilitating the ability of the client to develop emotional language through the therapy process. (p. 6)*

The relationships that educators have with students have immense power to be therapeutic. For those students who might display challenging behaviour or may appear to be always checking out, our predictable attuned and caring presence can make up for those early relationships that may have been mis-attuned, unpredictable and inflexible. Unfortunately, this is nowhere near a quick fix – early damage can happen quickly, but later repair takes a very long time.

For healing to take place, a sense of safety is vital. As we have explored, the brain in a fear state is not taking in information. When we create a sense of safety for a child, we enable healing, helping to facilitate neural connections being made and new neural connective tissue and synapses (Parish-Plass, 2020; Seigel, 2020). Badenoch (2017) states '…our embodied brains are far more capable of recovery/rewiring than we ever imagined; and a cradle of safe, warm, responsive relationships provides the support most in tune with our brain's inherent developmental and healing processes' (p. 1). When this occurs in the traumatised brain, it is likely that all relationships will improve and that negative or anxious feelings will decrease (Parish-Plass, 2020; Seigel, 2020). The kind of healing that happens in relationships may be something that you yourself have experienced. It is powerful stuff.

Conclusion

All humans are united in having an attachment experience. This experience can be positive or negative, or a mix of both. As educators, we find ourselves in attachment-style relationships with students, as we play the role of caregiver when students are at school. When we bring an understanding about attachment, we can neutrally observe what occurs in these relationships and we can have some control over creating positive relationships. Exploring attachment allows us a lens through which to see our students and ourselves to better understand the way we relate to each other. We should explore and consider attachment without judgement. We consider and take note, understanding that there are many factors that lead to the way that a caregiver parents.

Considering attachment styles might bring up questions and feelings about our own early experiences, and there is always plenty of work that can be done to better understand ourselves in the context of attachment. It is important to note that we can change our attachment style.

5

TRAUMA, THE BODY AND SELF-NARRATIVE

Now that we have looked at brain development, the nervous system, attachment and relationships, and the impacts of trauma and adversity on each, here, we consider what suboptimal early experiences and subsequent impacts look like in terms of development and sense of self.

Trauma, adversity and sensing systems

While we are very familiar with our five senses of taste, hearing, smell, touch and sight, collectively called *exteroception*, there are other ways that we sense things. Here, we look at interoception, the way we sense our internal state, and neuroception, that 'gut feeling', intuition or sense of safety of another person. We will also investigate proprioception and the vestibular sense and ways they can also be impacted.

Though some bodily symptoms of trauma might be easily recognised by educators, such as a propensity toward dysregulation and a struggle to return to a calm state, there are some other physical symptoms that are less obvious. For example, it is often the case that the face and voice of a child or adult who has experienced trauma might display a 'flat affect' – a reduction in expression of the upper area of the face or a lack of prosody of voice (Porges, 2017). Those same areas that Polyvagal Theory taught us are specific ways we 'read' other people, become unreadable in traumatised individuals. The work of an overactive nervous system can include easy activation as well as numbing, depending on whether it is the sympathetic or parasympathetic system that is the go-to. Some physical symptoms of freeze might not always stand out to us as trauma responses, for example, students who are often sleepy, seem to be constantly daydreaming, who cannot tell when they are hot or cold, or continue to have toileting accidents as they get older.

Interoception and neuroception

We show our emotion with our face, our body and our energetic output. You know what it feels like when someone says they are okay, but you know they are not – we have the capacity to be highly attuned to the internal states of others. Individuals come with a range of experiences and understandings about attunement, with some people highly attuned and maybe not quite realising it, and some shut off from that sense. In addition, people have varied capacity to understand the impact of their non-verbal signals on others. It is often a surprise to a student when we let them know that we have observed that something is not okay, even without them saying anything. When we do this for our students, we are teaching them about connecting in this way. The sense that someone recognises our internal state can be described as 'feeling felt' (Siegel, 2010a) and the process can be described as neuroception (Porges, 2009, 2010, 2017). What a powerful feeling it is! This is a vital ingredient for attachment relationships and for all close relationships. Demonstrating this to a student can offer them something that is of deep significance and, in some instances, might even be a new feeling for them.

We can put language to the ways that the cues from inside us – interoception – and outside us – exteroception – contribute to neuroception, offering our students understanding and a way to talk about sensing and feeling. We are constantly taking in the world, both inner and outer, and assessing risk. Information is firing between brain and body. Neuroception can easily perceive threat where there is none, leading to the enaction of threat-response behaviours that are not necessary. This all happens unconsciously, but when we have words to describe it, we are in a stronger position when it comes to regulation – as Siegel (2010a) says, 'name it to tame it.'

Interoception

Interoception describes the way we notice how our body is feeling. When we have a visceral response, that is interoception working. Interoception gives us clues about our environment and works to keep us in balance. The body and brain relay messages, working together to maintain homeostasis. If we are attuned to our body's interoceptive receptors, we get messages about being too hot, or too cold, or hungry, for example.

As we know, we have a physiological reaction to emotion, so the physical and emotional are intrinsically linked when it comes to interpreting and responding to our body. For example, that sense of a churning stomach that we are likely all familiar with might be brought on by social engagement fear, such as fear of conflict, or by physical fear, like a fear that the plane we are on might crash. Without that churning stomach we might never have a fear of flying, but we may also not recognise when we are facing someone who is getting angry. This gut feeling gives us information about our physical state and about our emotional state based on its relationship to our physical state.

Many children struggle to notice what is happening in their body. It is a skill that requires teaching. In an ideal situation a child learns this when they are small through caregivers' feedback, for example, 'do you need to go to the toilet?' for the squirming child, 'time to take your jumper off' for the sweaty child, 'is that yummy?' at dinnertime and 'does that feel better now?' after a big cry. All of this teaches a child about their own sensory experience. Children may miss out on this teaching, perhaps due to a parent not attuning or being busy with many children and other stressors, or perhaps due to a parent who acts as an external monitor responding to a child's perceived internal experiences without engaging them about it. At school these are the students who never take their jumpers off, who don't ask to go to the toilet until it is almost too late (or actually too late), who might regularly get hungry or thirsty because they did not eat lunch or ran around all lunchtime without having a drink. Without this access to their internal world, some of the more sophisticated understandings of nervous system responses are beyond comprehension, and thus regulation is out of reach.

My friend tells the story of her three-year-old. He gets very grumpy when he needs to go to the toilet, or when he is overheating, or when he is hungry or thirsty. As a baby, when being grisly, his parents attempted to mitigate his grizzles by checking these things, but it is different with a three-year-old, who is more independent and can manage these things himself. What this little person's parents realised was that although he is indeed capable of managing these things, he gets caught up in what he is doing and is not tuned in to his body. They developed a quick check-in that went 'food, drink, hot, toilet?' to facilitate the important tuning in to the body. As a result, they are teaching their child interoception and exteroception that will serve him well for the rest of his life.

For some children, all needs are anticipated by a caregiver and attended to in advance, meaning interoceptive states are not engaged and the child may have difficulty tuning in to their interoceptive state in the long term. At school we can be guilty of this and it happens to us as staff, too – we eat and use the bathroom at breaktime rather than listening to our bodies. I'm sure all teachers will relate to ignoring bodily alerts to wait for the bell.

Interoception is a relatively new area of study, with research looking at its link to specific parts of the brain, and to sense of self and cognition as well as impaired function and links to psychiatric disorders (Payne et al., 2015). Recently, a program based around the use of interoception activities has been used in schools in South Australia, with a resource that highlights links between interoceptive skills and learning and activities to build these skills (Department for Education, South Australia, 2019). Students with sensory processing struggles are likely to require skill building in the area of interoception.

Neuroception

Porges (2017) refers to the way that we unconsciously read another human as safe or unsafe as neuroception. It is important to note that not everyone has a completely accurate neuroceptive sense. Repeated exposure to unpredictability from others will be more likely to result in identifying people as threats, even if this is not the case, and their body will respond accordingly. Porges (2017) refers to this as *faulty neuroception*, whereas Deb Dana (2021) prefers the term *neuroceptive mismatch*. Both are ways to describe a system that either struggles to calm in a safe environment or doesn't adequately tune in to defence in an unsafe environment (Dana, 2021).

Consider the student who thinks everyone is against them, always perceiving everything another student or adult does as an act of aggression. These students constantly feel like the victim – they feel vulnerable and so they respond as though they are being threatened, often with violence or verbal abuse. What happens next is generally a version of exactly what they thought was happening in the first place! And so a kind of self-fulfilling prophecy is enacted. The vital thing for us to remember in this situation is that if we only attempt to address the behaviour, without addressing the root cause, we will not be doing the best job of supporting these students and helping them to recalibrate their neuroceptive sense (Kain & Terrell, 2018).

I worked with a student with incredible skill in neuroception, who struggled with expressive and receptive communication generally but was able to observe a thought flitter through my mind as we were engaged in conversation. On one occasion, without my knowledge or intent, my face gave something away and the student worriedly asked me what was wrong. Upon reflection, I had indeed had a thought that must have shown on my face. Perhaps in response to struggling with other forms of communication and understanding people, this student had developed a hyper-attuned ability. When we put our faces in front of students every day, we need to be aware that for some of them, they will be looking to us to know that they are safe, reading our faces, body language, tone of voice, all to work out if we will remain a safe and predictable adult for them.

Without adequate interoception and exteroception (the five senses), neuroceptive ability is compromised, leading to a lack of ability to read other people accurately, in which case one cannot connect well with others, unable to easily be in relation. The impact spills over into capacity to self-regulate, and a student who cannot self-regulate becomes unpredictable and potentially dangerous for other students (Kain & Terrell, 2018).

Proprioception and the vestibular system

You may be familiar with the vestibular system – responsible for balance and stability – and proprioception – how we sense where our body is in space using internal, musculoskeletal sensations. We also use sense perception for pain perception, temperature perception and vibration perception. All these systems are influenced by external factors and are different for each of us. Two people can have the exact same experience and respond very differently.

These systems, as with all bodily systems, are impacted by the physiology of trauma and stress. Not only are sensory systems altered by trauma, sensory integration is impacted (Malchiodi, 2021). Consider your own experiences of stress. Do you experience jumpiness at loud sounds, loss of appetite or increased appetite, heart palpitations, dizziness, ringing in the ears or a croaky voice? These can all be physiological symptoms of stress, acute or prolonged. There are a range of bodily responses triggered by our nervous system that impact our senses. For example, research suggests that the muscles in our middle ear change when we feel fear – they become more able to discern lower frequency sounds and less able to hear human voices (Kain & Terrell, 2018; Porges, 2017). This and other responses to digestion, vision or balance can be tracked back to the nervous system response. Considering the way our senses are impacted by stress, the context of our ability to sense our inner and outer world is impacted, too and, as always, context is relevant.

In addition, or sometimes related to stress and trauma, students can have processing struggles with any of the sensory systems. This can be in the form of being over- or under-sensitive to sensory input or having trouble sensing or discriminating the exact nature of the input (Occupational Therapy Helping Children, 2022). Vestibular system challenges might look like struggles with balance, ball skills, letter reversals, rhythm, fear of heights or falling, or standing too close to others. Interoceptive struggles can impact self-regulation, being a flexible thinker, problem-solving or social skills. When a child has issues with proprioception we might see sensory-seeking actions, kicking furniture, breaking things or messy work (Occupational Therapy Helping Children, 2017; 2019). We will look, in later chapters, at how we can work with these systems.

I once worked with a young student who was not keen on sitting on the floor. Lying on the floor and rolling around, however, was very appealing to this student. They would often crash into things and were pretty heavy-handed with toys and equipment. These behaviours were likely a way for the student to connect with the proprioceptive system, gaining comfort from experiencing the sense of the body in space.

Taking a sensory lens to the behaviour of our students sees us asking what sensory-seeking or sensory-avoiding behaviour might we be witnessing. As we tune in to the senses, we might even begin to recognise that some of the decisions we make ourselves are based on our own sensory experiences, and this can help us to better understand our students, too.

Sense of self and self-narrative

Our early experiences are lived somatically, meaning through the body. This is where our earliest memories live, without the narrative to accompany them. Early somatic senses are likely to carry the theme of safety, the most important thing to a child. These experiences become a strong sense, something that is *known physically*. Early experiences of lack of safety create physiological changes and a blueprint for the future. They generate a narrative that can be carried for life, but not always explained. When we teach children about how to sense their internal state (interoception), or how to experience repetitive safe experiences, we can support the shifting of the blueprint. Anything that has been established in those very early years, however, will require continual exposure to differing experiences to shift that somatic narrative.

When a child does not gain a solid sense of who they are, where they come from and how they fit in, it can mean that their sense of self is negatively impacted. We all need a cohesive self-narrative. When children are living with situations that do not make sense to them, there is no way to experience a cohesive self-narrative and their 'sense of self is threatened' (Tronick & Gold, 2020, p. 121). For a child to develop the confidence and ability to approach unknown or tricky situations, they must first have the experience of a safe relationship that has occasional bumps and then repairs. For example, when a caregiver might get cross but later apologise and reconnect, this experience demonstrates to a child that a brief interpersonal disruption can occur within safety. This allows a child to feel a steady sense of self, knowing that relationships do not need to be perfect, to be safe.

Until trauma has been processed, it is extremely difficult to maintain a cohesive narrative about the trauma, and indeed about oneself (Siegel, 2020). As explored in Chapter 1, a parent's trauma can be transferred to a child and this link between unprocessed trauma and a lack of coherence tells us that while the trauma of the parent has interfered with the production of a cohesive narrative, it is this lack of a cohesive narrative that contributes to the creation of generational trauma.

Another aspect of the influence of parental self-narrative on a child's sense of self can be found in the idea that for those parents with a cohesive story about their history, they have the capacity to see a situation from different perspectives (Williams, 2010). That injection of objectivity brings more clarity to a story. The skill of seeing things from various perspectives improves parenting, as the child's perspective is also considered. This skill also allows for better social and relational skills, as anticipating what might occur in any given situation with another person is more likely. So, a caregiver who has a cohesive self-story and is able to share this with a child, and participate in storytelling generally, is able to provide a child with this same capacity to see things from multiple perspectives. With varying contexts and through sharing their own experience, a caregiver is able to provide the child with some knowledge of different situations, thus preparing a child for later relational experiences (Williams et al., 2009). Ideally, the child's own experiences are shared and explored with a caregiver, providing opportunities to build a sense of self and to explore ideas about the self and relationships. Children who have had these positive family storytelling experiences are more likely to understand context in a situation and to understand that they need to respond differently in different situations or with different people. There is immense power in the sharing of narrative stories, particularly within families.

Memory and self-narrative

The impact on memory can also cause trauma to damage self-narrative. Implicit memory rules when it comes to trauma. It impacts us tremendously, but we don't necessarily know why. Since our very early memories are implicit, our working model regarding relating to others is based on these early experiences and unconscious responses, which lack an accompanying narrative. For our students who struggle to relate well to their peers, it is possible that they have a working model that does not provide a positive and productive way of being with others. That can be hard to undo.

When a child is re-experiencing something from a very early implicit memory, they may seem to be overreacting, or having a big emotional response to something seemingly innocent or safe. We need to remember that while the story that a child might be telling us is not accurate, this does not mean that the emotion they are experiencing is not happening or not valid. A useful phrase here is 'story follows state' (Dana, 2018, p. 35), meaning that while the body's state arises from the nervous system's reaction to stimulus, it does not apply meaning, resulting in our mind trying to understand by creating a narrative to match what we are feeling.

One student would often start the day with me, as the entry to class was a challenge. If this student arrived at school heightened, I would often hear a story about something that happened at home. One day the student was sitting in the wellbeing room with me, quite agitated and upset, telling me about what happened that morning. The story involved details about injuries sustained by this student, about blood running down their arms. Very dramatic and distressing. When I asked to see the injuries, the student willingly showed me... but there was nothing to see and no evidence of injuries. The distress was very real, the injury felt very real, but it was not physical. The story was created to follow the state of this student. Without the words to explain why there was so much distress and pain, a story came forth to explain everything.

This story demonstrates that the feelings can be real, painful and difficult, regardless of the story's accuracy. Our job here, along with establishing any accuracy, of course, is to listen to the feelings, attempt to create a sense of safety and emotional resonance, and find the motivation behind the story. It can be very difficult in a busy school day, particularly when the work needs to go in to identifying the accuracy of what you have been told, however, it is a powerful thing that we can do as a safe adult, to hear, see and respond to the state, not the story.

Another way to think about it is that a narrative must be created to express the implicit feelings, reactions and responses, so this narrative is a representation of the implicit memories. When we are quite sure what we are being told is not the true story, we can refocus on hearing the story for what it is – a way to talk about something that does not exist within any kind of cohesive, accessible narrative. Any educator who has been told that they are yelling when they are using a regular speaking voice will understand this idea; that the words we say, or the way a student feels, can mean they hear something that is not there. As Kain and Terrell (2018) explain, 'Our own story of our lives is correct as we experienced it from the inside. It is an accurate representation of our subjective experience, whether that lines up with what others might see from the outside or not' (p. 156).

Narrative creation as protection

The misremembering of events can operate as a protective measure, too. A child, or adult, can have a story about a fabulous childhood, or about a caring parent, or about normalised things such as holidays or parties – none of which may be factual. Again, this can be a shifting of the factual narrative into one that fits what society tells us must be true. Exposure to books and films and others' stories might contrast with our actual experience, so a new narrative is created to fit with a larger societal narrative.

The repetition and normalisation of early experiences of trauma can lead to the creation of various other narratives. This can include a narrative of being bad, or sometimes an illness narrative. When listened to, without being dismissed or queried, a child is able to express a traumatic experience, or a feeling they might not understand, or indeed a fantasy that helps them to cope. In doing this, they begin to process, with the hope that in a number of these small expressions, big things can be expressed with whatever capacity is available to the child. Over time, that capacity builds.

A student I knew was often getting into trouble. They were part of a big family and tended to be the one who was most likely to be doing something they shouldn't. One day their father was at the school and announced to the Principal that she should not worry about this child because they were 'the bad one'. Clearly the child was meeting expectations that were laid out for them.

It is common for children to internalise the hurtful aspects of their parents' treatment of them. In this way they protect the parent, and thus the connection with them, by blaming themselves (Teyber & Teyber, 2017). These ideas or judgements about the self, whether internalised or externalised, including by others in the family, allows the justification of all manner of mistreatment of the child, while the idealised idea of the parent is protected and societal expectations are conformed to.

Those in schools are likely to be familiar with the magic of an ice pack (the new Band-Aids!). An illness narrative is a way for a child to explain their 'experience of helplessness, powerlessness, lack of safety or dysregulation' (Kain & Terrell, 2018, p. 158). Given the link demonstrated in the ACEs study between early trauma and a child's development as well as later issues with illness and disease, it is one that makes sense (Centers for Disease Control and Prevention, 2023; van der Kolk, 2014). It is also a way to potentially receive attention and care. While it is in no way a school's responsibility to do any medical diagnosis, those 'frequent fliers' to sickbay might really be benefitting from some kind words and that Band-Aid or ice pack that they don't physically need.

Shame

Shame is still something being researched and we don't yet have a common narrative around it. We can use the word *shame* to refer to a feeling that is unhelpful to us, even toxic, whereas feelings such as guilt or remorse are indeed helpful and can be a guide to correct behaviours to better align with our values and our desire to engage with others in socially appropriate ways. Guilt tends to be relational – another has been wronged and the situation can be remedied with acknowledgement. A helpful distinction can be the difference between thinking 'I did something wrong' (guilt) or 'I am the wrong thing' (shame; Brown, 2012). Siegel (2020) describes the ways that shame can end up as root of our sense of who we are:

> *If shame has played a part in our repeated interactions with our caregivers, how we sense our self may have the inner felt quality of something being bad about the self, along with a cognitive belief that the self is defective. (p. 385)*

This linking of shame to a sense of self can be referred to as 'identity trauma' (Hooton, 2019; Kira, 2001), a powerful term reflecting the impact of deliberate shaming.

Guilt and shame as teaching tools

Guilt or remorse, or what we might also call *healthy shame*, is an important feature of a developing sense of self. Being part of a group means that it is important to put the group first sometimes – this is certainly the case for a classroom. However, anyone who has ever spent time with small children will know that this does not come naturally or easily to many – it is something we learn. One of the ways we learn this is to have a solid sense of self, a connection to our group and a healthy relationship to shame. The bad feeling from being selfish or hurtful helps to guide behaviour and the reward comes from helping the group that we feel a part of. For children who have never learned to have a good relationship with shame, they are not guided in the same way as those who have a pro-social relationship to shame.

Historically, shame has been used as a teaching tool. Unfortunately, like fear, while it may appear to work, often it does more harm than good. For shame to be helpful, it needs to be ended and repaired quickly, with a reminder that it is the behaviour that is not okay, rather than the individual. This is the kind of situation that may occur as a small child is learning what is acceptable and what is not. When we talk about separating the behaviour from the child, reducing shame is at the heart. As explored earlier, a sense of self is reinforced constantly as we seek out confirmation of what is believed. So, for the child who believes *they* are the wrong thing, feelings of shame will reinforce that belief. Experiencing shame followed quickly by reassurance that who we are is not the problem means that the shame does not stick, but instead may be useful. However, when experiences of shame are repeated and not repaired, the shame becomes toxic.

Shame in the body

The experience of shame can manifest as a sense of being bad, wrong or dumb; it can come with a hot face, a sick stomach or a rush of sweat. Alongside these responses, with no repair shame can mirror the freeze response, resulting in lack of connection to others, dissociation and an offline cortex. As Hooten (2019) states:

> *Chronic or toxic shame is a condition that repeats when there is a real or perceived threat of being shamed again. People are shamed by being belittled, ridiculed, excluded. This condition rules the lives of those so afflicted, even when there is no conscious awareness of this underlying state. The constant stress of chronic shame has effects on all organs of the body and can lead to chronic illness in later life as shown by the Adverse Childhood Experience (ACE) study. (p. 31)*

Consider a time you felt shame – it is likely you have a visceral response to the memory. Shame lives in our body and is expressed in our body. Chronic shame interrupts connection. Lack of eye contact often accompanies shame, especially in children who experience toxic or chronic shame, creating an added barrier to connecting. Depending on what a student's experience of shame has been, their response to feeling shame might be to withdraw, or to fight, or to try to please. Shame can sometimes serve as a substitute for regulation meaning, that when a child might feel that they are afraid of doing something wrong, such as becoming angry or violent, they use their sense of shame to temper that instinct, rather than a healthy way of self-regulating (Kain & Terrell, 2018).

Interpersonal shame

Shame is particularly common as a result of interpersonal trauma from someone in a trusted or caregiving role (Platt & Freyd, 2015). When a child attempts to attune, but is rejected, shame becomes associated with attempted connection (Siegel, 2020). This shame is most likely to show itself with the experience of perceived interpersonal threat. In a situation where a caregiver repeatedly shames a child, it will be hard for them to be an engaged student. Exposure to an adult authority figure may immediately bring forth the experience of shame. Everything becomes filtered through the shaming, with experiences reinforcing ideas about the self.

In cases where children have experienced frequent shaming, the shame state becomes very easily accessible – it may be triggered by a look, a tone of voice, even by the anticipation of being shamed. The more shame has been experienced, the more likely it is to be triggered in a neutral environment (Hooton, 2019). Likewise, epigenetics (transgenerational trauma) can bring with it a core sense of shame. These deeply held somatic templates for shame can be challenging to resolve (Kain & Terrell, 2018).

Shame that impacts identity can come from many places. It can be related to attachment experiences, to negative judgement for being different or 'other' (consider the impact of neurodivergence or sex, sexuality, or gender diversity, or not sharing the dominant culture), or to abuse experiences. When shame settles in the body, the individual assumes, often unconsciously, that it belongs there due to a fault with them. When shame is part of a person's identity, they live with the internalisation of that shame. Cozolino (2014) refers to 'core shame' (p. 92) as the experience of being inherently not worthy of love. This core shame can cause responses that include bullying, which becomes an antidote to a sense of powerlessness, or rigidity and anxiety and protective responses, particularly from authority figures. Core shame will 'impede creativity, exploration, and learning' (Cozolino, 2014, p. 93). The students living with this will be incredibly challenging to teach.

Conclusion

Early trauma has many impacts, including on the body and on the creation of a sense of self. At school we see these impacts played out daily. We see students who need to move, or who struggle to move, we see students who struggle to connect, with us or others. We see the constant reinforcement of self-narratives, with a confirmation bias ready to fortify our beliefs. The classic 'I am dumb' narrative can be reinforced with the noticing of every mistake made throughout a normal day, or the sense of being a difficult person can be strengthened with every awkward interaction or miscommunication.

While it is overwhelming to consider all these elements of trauma's impacts, we have the power in schools to be a protective factor, to change lives and even to save them. The following chapters are where we look at what we can do, as individuals, as groups, as classes and as whole schools, to improve outcomes for students who have experienced early adversity.

6

TRAUMA, ADVERSITY, BEHAVIOUR AND LEARNING

In this chapter we will consider what the impacts of trauma and adversity on our students might look like in our classrooms. We will look at behavioural impacts and learning impacts, and how these two responses play out in class.

The job of educators to identify barriers to learning includes looking for cognitive barriers, which includes trauma. However, many trauma symptoms mirror the learning and behaviour characteristics of other things such as autism, ADHD, oppositional defiance disorder (ODD), speech disorders, language disorders and other learning disorders (Alvarez et al., 2016; Siegfried et al., 2016; Stavropoulos et al., 2018). It can be the case that a diagnosis of one of these conditions is given while trauma is overlooked (D'Andrea et al., 2012). This is curious given the prevalence of trauma in comparison to the prevalence of some other conditions. It is vital that educators take a student's whole life into account when assessing for learning difficulties and other disabilities, which might be co-occurring with experiences of traumatic stress or might indeed be symptomatic of traumatic stress. When we understand the impacts of trauma, we can factor this into our investigations of students' learning barriers. When schools are trauma-informed, what happens is that 'teachers are empowered to respond actively to the impact of trauma on learning, and to design their classrooms with attention to wellbeing principles, the benefits for students are long lasting and far-reaching' (Brunzell & Norrish, 2021, p. 30).

Behaviour

I think it is fair to say that dealing with student behaviour is one of the most difficult and confronting elements of teaching, and one that is generally, and inexplicably, not given adequate time or attention in teaching degrees. When student behaviour is explored within teacher training, it is so often referred to as *behaviour management.* This is such a telling choice of phrase. Teachers teach, and ideally, they teach behaviour, too. All children can demonstrate behaviour that challenges the adults around them, however, it is very likely that the students who will be the most challenging in any class will be those who are dealing with the most struggles. I wholeheartedly agree with Brunzell and Norrish (2021) when they say, 'We believe strongly that when their unmet developmental needs are addressed, students have the best intentions to learn and can be supported to self-regulate and engage in the classroom' (p. 65). Our students want to be enjoying class and connecting with their classmates. This is how we are wired – for connection and belonging. It is not always possible, though. Just as self-regulating is a skill that is learned, social niceties and expected behaviours are also learned. Not all students are exposed to positive behavioural models and in these cases it needs to be us, at school, who model healthy behaviour. Further, even a student who does have their developmental needs met is still driven by internal urges that they learn to control with support and guidance. As Cozolino (2014) states:

> *Children are born with millions of years of animalistic instincts; they want to be the centre of attention, win all the prizes, and be adored for everything they do... On the other hand most parents want a child to be respectful, hardworking, and well behaved. Gradually shaping children's primitive self-centred instincts into healthy and realistic self-esteem without crushing their spirit is central to both parenting and teaching. (p. 92)*

Students who have experienced early-life adversity are likely to have a range of unmet needs. So it makes sense that they will bring these needs to school, without the understanding that these needs are present. Unconscious, unmet needs are likely to result in behaviours that are not compatible with the classroom. Looking at the motivation behind behaviour, we can anticipate that behaviour is enacted with the aim of getting something or getting away from something. For our students with traumatic stress, they may be seeking to reinforce a sense of self, attempting to get away from something causing a threat response or seeking proximity to a safe adult. They may also be seeking further sensory input or trying to avoid it. While these behaviours might be directed to an adult or peer at school, it is very likely that the underlying source of the feelings and behaviour are nothing to do with anyone at school.

Foundations of behaviour

It is often the case that early experiences do not lay the foundations that support self-regulation, and without self-regulation, learning at school is tricky (Blair & Raver, 2015). As laid out in the first part of this book, it will be those children exposed to early adversities who are more likely to have suboptimal brain development which impacts self-regulation skills. In addition, it is fair to say that for low-income families the preference is likely for children to begin school as soon as possible, meaning they may be some of the youngest students in a class and behind developmentally simply due to age. It can be incredibly helpful in the early years particularly, to remember that a child at age five and a child at age four should have different behavioural expectations.

Foundations of emotions

Parents act as a kind of emotional interpreter for children – they recognise the emotion by reading non-verbal signals and put words to the emotion they see, allowing the child to build their emotional vocabulary and contribute to building a more nuanced approach to emotion. As with everything, a child's cultural background, home language and the micro-culture of their family will influence how this does or does not occur – some modes of emotional manifestation are more naturally expressive, whereas some cultures may be more likely to mute emotion in verbal expression; some languages have many words related to emotion, while others have fewer words available.

Some students arrive at school with a comprehensive emotion vocabulary, and some struggle to name many emotions at all. So often in class I have heard children describe how they felt as 'normal', an expression of the idea that emotion is felt universally and that everyone shares a baseline. Having our emotions recognised is something that feels good to most of us and finding words to describe how we feel has the power of letting us know that our feelings are recognised and shared by others. When students don't have an understanding of, or ability to talk about, emotion it has an impact on behaviour. Moving through life with feelings without capacity to appropriately express them, either for lack of words, or from lack of trust in an appropriate response from others, leads to those feelings coming out as behaviour. Beginning a list of emotion words is a simple way to build vocabulary and also an interesting insight into perceptions of emotion.

Impact of environment on behaviour

A recent study has identified that unpredictable or inconsistent parents impact the development of a child's emotional brain circuitry, with a link to later life mental illness and use of substances (Baram, 2022). Another recent study identified links between neighbourhood disadvantage and child behaviour, finding that 'Youth growing up in disadvantaged neighborhoods are more likely than their advantaged peers to face negative behavioral and mental health outcomes' (Suarez et al., 2022, p. 1). This makes it very clear that rather than punish students for acting out learned behaviour, we need to explicitly teach what we expect.

Another longitudinal study looked at the behaviour and school readiness of children in Kindergarten, and again found that when households were chaotic or disorganised, children's executive function skills, essential for both learning and self-regulation, were negatively impacted (Vernon-Feagans et al., 2016), leading to less capacity for self-regulation. The study noted this impact was above and beyond the risks that come with poverty, and that parenting quality was the most important factor, scaffolding acceptance and responsiveness. The study identified that '...the disorganized chaotic household appears in this study to disrupt positive parenting, such that parents may not be able to scaffold children's early EF [executive functioning] and regulatory skills' (Vernon-Feagans et al., 2016, p. 15). These longitudinal findings point to the fact that the state of our students' households are important when it comes to their capacity for behavioural regulation in our classrooms.

Coping strategies

Children will use a range of adaptive strategies to cope with any early stress or trauma. As humans, we use a range of *accommodations* – a word first used by Freud, expanded upon by Piaget and developed more recently by Brandchaft – as a coping strategy for dealing with difficult things that might not make sense (Kain & Terrell, 2018). For example, society, including education, might tell a child that Mum and Dad are loving people, that we make cards for them because we love them and we express all the great things about them. For a child whose experience of a caregiver is of a frightening or absent person, they will need to make some psychological accommodations as a survival strategy, commonly referred to as *defensive accommodations*. A collection of commonly used accommodations are denial, regression or acting out, repression, dissociation, projection, compartmentalisation, reaction formation, sublimation, intellectualisation, rationalisation (Corey, 2021; Kain & Terrell, 2018). These accommodations are used by all of us and tend to operate unconsciously.

Here, we have responses to untenable situations that, when viewed from the outside, might be perceived as poor behaviour, personality or habit. As educators, we can question the simplicity of labelling a child as aggressive or vague. We have the power to look beyond the behaviour to question what is behind it. These defensive accommodations can be difficult to work with, for example, the conversation with the child who denies all wrongdoing in the face of evidence (denial); the child who takes out their anger at a caregiver or teachers or students (projection); a parent who insists their physical punishment is for a child's good (rationalisation); or a colleague who derides students for not showing them respect, yet speaks disrespectfully to others (compartmentalisation). Having a level of understanding about why these behaviours may be occurring is an opportunity to feel compassion, which can help to cope with these undesirable behaviours.

Unfortunately, the subconscious and embedded nature of these strategies means that it is not easy for children to understand why they are doing what they are doing without a great deal of professional intervention. However, in school there is space to remind them of some things like acknowledging the feeling, 'I can see that you are really angry', rather than focusing on the interaction, 'Why are you angry at Alia? She didn't do anything wrong, you need to apologise'. Though you may be pointing out the truth, pushing a student to acknowledge an unconscious drive simply will not work (you can give it a go with colleagues, though). In later chapters we will look further at the kinds of behaviours, or defensive accommodations, we frequently see in the classroom and how we can work with them.

Self-regulation and physiological responses

Self-regulation, including but not limited to attributes such as focusing and maintaining attention, regulating emotion and stress

When in a state that sits outside our window of tolerance, we need to find strategies that will get us back. We can't underestimate the impact of being dysregulated, after all, we are invoking a physiological response that is based around threat and survival. We might need to work ourselves, or support a student, to widen our window generally or in specific situations. For this to occur, we need to feel safe, otherwise our threat response will kick in. In addition to a sense of safety, we need to be able to recognise what is happening in our bodies and have some strategies in place to self-regulate.

Think about the nervous system responses and what that might look like in a classroom when a student is activated or elevated. The fight response can look like anger, aggression, swearing; the flight response can look like throwing work away or ripping it up, like leaving the class or school without permission, like hiding; the freeze response can look like daydreaming or excessive tiredness; the fawn response might look constant connection attempts, writing notes and cards, trying very hard, or distress at any negative teacher attention. Think about the students you work with. Do some seem to get stressed easily? Consider how some of the behaviours you might see in your school might link to the nervous system stress responses.

Regulation is at the heart of so many behavioural struggles at school. When our students are not able to self-regulate, it is very difficult to cope with the day-to-day challenges and highlights of school. It is vital for educators to understand that regulation is learned. As with other elements of a child's education, their experiences before they get to school has a huge influence on what happens when they get to school. We can support students' needs with adults who are attuned and predictable, teaching that is dynamic and engaging, and classrooms that are predictable, yet adaptable, with routine, environment and expectations that support all students in creating the optimal set-up for learning success. Again, it is important to note that these trauma-informed strategies are great for all students and pretty nice for us educators, too.

The body is constantly striving for the balance of stress hormones to achieve self-regulation in a process called *allostasis*. Our stress hormones are constantly adjusting to move toward allostasis, the way that other physiological functions such as our internal temperature, blood glucose and heart rate shift to achieve homeostasis. Allostasis can occur with variability in hormone levels. It is helpful to consider allostasis when we think about our students and the influences on their stress levels. The internal struggle to maintain allostasis can take a toll, and it might be the case that the students who struggle the most with self-regulation are the ones with the highest allostatic load. Home environment is clearly a significant influence on a child's capacity to build the all-important skills related to self-regulation and attention, but we can also see influence in school and pre-school settings. 'Supportive versus negative interactions' (Blair & Raver, 2015, p. 716) with a range of adults and peers in a child's life will impact their capacity for emotional reactivity and regulation, ability to attend and other functions relating to learning. Our body's response to stress has such a significant impact. When the primitive vagus kicks in, the body shifts to a narrower focus, looking for threat (Tronick & Gold, 2020). Consider the way that you might get jumpy when stressed, or experience some noise as irritating – that is the dorsal vagus doing its job.

Big reactions

There can be many reasons why we might come across students having big reactions. When we are attuned to the students in front of us, we can pick up on how they are feeling by noticing or asking about their physical signs that might include fast breathing, chest tightness, clenched fists, clenched jaw, fast heart rate, nausea or butterflies in the stomach, dry mouth, feeling dizzy or feeling hot. Emotional responses might be shame, panic, anxiety, racing mind, feeling overwhelmed, intrusive thoughts, irritability, anger or distress.

We might not always know what causes a big reaction, but certain situations are particular triggers for some students, with sport being a common example. The information coming in via body to brain during sport might include a body that is short of breath and heating up; it might include people yelling and bodies rapidly approaching others. In another context, these messages coming from outside of us might require a neuroceptive response that says 'danger!', but even in the appropriate context of a game of soccer, for example, a student might indeed have a danger response, which might then result in associated behaviours such as violence. What might happen next is what occurs when a heightened nervous system encounters another nervous system primed for a fight response, as many of our students are – it creates a reactive response and the chance of a fight situation is very high. So, the process goes – student enacts a threat response where there is no threat, whoever they are interacting with has a corresponding threat response, student is vindicated in having their initial threat response and conflict occurs. This can be conflict with another student, a teacher or any person nearby, and can be triggered by sport, a board game or even a mathematics lesson. When teaching students about the way our bodies work and pointing out how close feelings of excitement and fear are or how anticipation can tip over into anger, students are better placed to learn how their own reactions work and where they might find regulation tricky.

Fear can be a big trigger for a reaction and, as we know, teachers sometimes, and perhaps often in the past, use fear as a class control strategy. I distinctly remember teachers I was afraid of. They may have raised their voice enough to frighten a room of students into silence and then used silence itself, with a particular facial expression, to reinforce the students' feelings. That sense of fear or apprehension can be maintained with non-verbal signals and the relational aspect of the classroom can see an adult essentially holding students hostage with fear. An educator might not even be consciously aware that they are doing this, for example, they may not be thinking about their face at all.

These experiences will be different for every student in the room. A student who has experienced fear of a parent will be very attuned to a teacher's anger and might hold their response internally, while a student who has not had these experiences may be initially shocked before talking to a trusted adult about the experience, allowing an opportunity to process what it felt like, put names to the feelings and be validated.

It is worth noting that removal of affection or attunement can also cause a fear response. When a child has had the experience of a parent who uses withdrawal as punishment – maybe isolating the child in a room or refusing affection and attention – this will trigger a fear of abandonment because it is abandonment. Ignoring behaviours that are undesirable while acknowledging pro-social behaviours and offering comfort when needed will not illicit this response, but the complete removal of all acknowledgement risks sending a student to a very frightening place.

When we are dealing with these big responses, we are aiming to bring regulation back. We need to proceed here in an orderly fashion, starting with safety first, of course, and moving toward bringing a student down from their heightened state, before continuing with strategies until we find something that works (we will explore behavioural interventions in later chapters). While there is no universal fix, it is important to remember that without getting students back into their window of tolerance, or at least closer to it, we have no hope of connecting to their thinking brain. We are dealing with pure instinct and, as Venet (2021) says, we have to be wary of 'punishing students for their survival skills' (p. 37). After a big blow-up, when interventions have taken place effectively, a sense of safety has returned and the state has shifted, you might expect to see some physical and emotional shifts like easier breathing, heart rate coming down, body twitching to release the tension, even crying, laughing, yawning, burping, farting or coughing (Stanley, 2019). This is the body moving back to proper functioning.

When hypo-arousal is the go-to for signs of stress, we are doing the nervous system equivalent of using a sledgehammer to bang in a nail. Ideally, when stress hits and then recedes, we are engaging the ventral parasympathetic system to put the brake on our sympathetic response and bring on some calm to return us to equilibrium. However, when exposed to chronic stress, it might be that the dorsal parasympathetic freeze system is more efficient to stop those sympathetic responses. In this case, we overuse a system that is designed to keep us alive in the most dire circumstances, or, indeed, make the anticipated trauma or death less painful. The use of this system can be seen to be 'a substitute for genuine regulation' (Kain & Terrell, 2018, p. 142) and using it in this way shifts the window of tolerance down so that it likely operates in a near constant state of freeze, or something akin to freeze.

It can become such a go-to that the first sign of a hyper-response causes a hypo-reaction. This does not work in a classroom. Students in a hypo-state are not tuned in, not fully present and not able to take in information the way we need them to at school. However, students who live in this state can also fly under the radar – they may look really calm, not be any trouble in the classroom and, aside from the fact they don't get their work done, be great students. As the Australian Child & Adolescent Trauma, Loss and Grief Network (2016) states, 'We need to learn what distress looks like when it is not messy and noisy' (p. 10). Students in this state may not even be aware that they are in a state. This may feel like what is expected of calm, but it may be something closer to not feeling anything at all.

It is worth reiterating that this freeze state is the most desperate of states. It is associated with early experiences where the child 'views other people as the source of – not the solution to – her stress states' (Kain & Terrell, 2018, p. 142). Regardless of what we know or do not know about a child's history, we should be looking out for those students who often seem checked out or vague, the ones who give no trouble but also take a long time to complete work, or perhaps demonstrate that they didn't understand what they were supposed to do. It is so easy to skip over these students, or to perceive them in a particular way, or use phrases like *in her own world* and *daydreamer* when really what we are witnessing is a survival response.

I worked with a student who spent a great deal of time engaging dorsal parasympathetic physiology. This was the kind of student for whom teachers used descriptors like *vague* or *away with the fairies*. In our conversations the student disclosed a very rich inner world and a wild imagination. Sometimes, from an adult perspective, it was hard to identify what was real and what was imagined. We worked on some strategies to move out of this state, including a tissue with essential oil to engage the sense of smell. We engaged in some drawing activities together, leaving space for chat with no judgement about what was being said, and the student had space to check out. Most of all, though, we just did the work of every day, creating a space at school that is safe, kind and caring. We were able to talk to the parent, offering the supports needed. A few years later, they were a student who was engaged in learning, who had caught up academically and was now a regular contributor in class. The work may still take a while to be completed, but they now know this about themselves and can work on the skill of completion.

This is an example of how the nurturing impact of school can reach the whole family and can slowly shift a child's reliance on a physiological response that is not ideal and, once that is addressed, can work on academic intervention to catch them up.

Learning: cognition and executive function

There are many ways in which early adverse experiences can impact learning. We know that brain development is impacted and this can see a range of learning issues arising. Issues with cognition, working memory, remaining present, feeling connected, increased social stressors and negative self-narrative can all make learning more difficult. The behavioural ramifications of trauma interfere with learning; relational struggles impact connection with educators and peers; and hyper-vigilance means it is hard to maintain focus on teacher instruction. In focusing on the impact of early adversity on cognition, we are considering the ways that children acquire knowledge, through their mind, their senses, their memory and their experiences to understand concepts and think critically.

Executive function is the term we use to refer to the higher-order brain functions required for metacognition and behaviour regulation – learning and learning behaviours. Executive function describes the brain function required for tasks such as organisation, planning, flexibility and forward thinking. It is the linking of the brain functions of working memory, which allows us the capacity to take in and retain information; mental flexibility, which allows us to respond appropriately in different situations; and self-control, which is required for us to resist impulses (Center on the Developing Child, 2011; McLean, 2018).

As higher-order cognitive skills make use of the prefrontal brain regions, executive function relies on the lower brain function being in place. Executive function is essential for building cognitive skills as well as social skills. The Center on the Developing Child (2011) states:

> *Children aren't born with these skills – they are born with the potential to develop them. Some children may need more support than others to develop these skills... Acquiring the early building blocks of these skills is one of the most important and challenging tasks of the early childhood years. (p. 1.)*

It is clear that for those students who have not had their early needs attended to, the impact on their learning will likely be significant. For us at school, we need to remember that we might need to be building skills that we would expect to already be present in our students, and for those students who missed out on a pre-school education, this will be especially vital.

What happens in these early years sets the scene for later learning and development. For those students who need extra support to develop these skills, we need to be attuned to their needs and ready to teach.

With school we often don't see children until they become our students at age four or five. The work of pre-school is so very important and the impact of attending quality early learning is visible in the classrooms that support students in their first years of school. What we do when they get to us is also vital. We might see significant discrepancies in ability, but this is also where we have the best opportunity to reduce the academic gaps between students. The fact that traumatic experiences can impact a student in ways that will be demonstrated in their academic achievement does not equate to these students being unable to learn, but rather is an indicator that 'schools need to do more to understand their needs and design instruction that meets those needs while prioritizing a sense of safety' (Venet, 2021, p. 36).

Students who are supported to build their working memory, their cognitive flexibility and their mastery over their impulses will build the skills needed for success in both the social and the academic arenas.

Language

Language is one of the most significant things that can be impacted by trauma, which then goes on to influence comprehension and communication. The impact covers both expressive and receptive language, and can delay the onset of language for a child (Eigsti & Cicchetti, 2004; Jennings, 2019). Language can also be impacted by a parent's lack of capacity to spend time in those 'serve and return' interactions with a child – perhaps because of long work hours, being a sole parent, having their own language deficits or caring for a large family. I have seen the impact of parents and children not sharing a language and missing those rich language experiences at home for a variety of reasons. Regardless of why, when students do not have a broad language experience, they have no capacity to learn language comprehensively, which will significantly impact learning. Learning language can also be impacted by a child living regularly in fight, flight or freeze mode. In these states there is no capacity to take in complexity, rather, only the basics are filtering through, the prefrontal cortex heading offline to make way for the parts of the brain associated with survival.

Memory

Memory is vital for learning. As we explored in Chapter 2, many parts of the brain play a role in memory formation and retrieval, and memory is impacted by trauma and chronic stress in a range of ways. While smaller amounts of stress might sharpen our memory, when we are under significant amounts of stress, our brain is busy with the focus on safety, reducing capacity to recall and lay down memory. The skills required to be able to develop sequential memory occur when events occur for the child in a way that is routine and predictable. Those living in states of chaos never get this, as Jennings (2019) states, 'For trauma-exposed children, early memories are encoded episodically, as a collection of random events, rather than as a coherent, linear narrative' (p. 35).

When it comes to learning, we benefit from a great working memory. Our working memory is the one needed to hear an instruction, and hold it long enough to carry out the task. Working memory is always the starting point for long-term memory. Multiplication tables are a good example of this – we begin using our working memory to recall the multiplications, we use strategies to help us remember, we might repeat after a teacher, however, with multiple repetitions, the information makes its way to our long-term memory. How many repetitions this takes will be dependent on the individual brain. Thinking about reading a new text, we would make use of our working memory to hold the ideas in the text and then combine them with other ideas to create the meaning. For students with a very poor working memory, this can make reading harder and 'The likelihood that something will be read, understood and learnt (i.e., be encoded into long-term memory) depends in substantial part on the ability of working memory to adequately process and integrate new information into existing schemata' (Smith et al., 2021, p. 218).

Long-term memory is, as far as we know, unlimited in its capacity. It is not quite permanent, as we can lose things that we no longer use through the process of pruning or degeneration. Having poor working memory goes on to impact long-term memory. Without the capacity to hold the information in the first instance, there is no opportunity to go on to create long-term memories.

As we've discussed, implicit memory is very involved with trauma, especially for the very young. Implicit memory is feelings and senses that are unconscious. They can pop up at any time and hijack the brain. This can impact our students in ways that are confusing to us and to them. As described, we might see students triggered by sounds, smells or the way someone looks or talks. Students may take a long time for school to become a safe place, as they lay down new implicit memories that don't see them stuck in a state of confusing responses to what we think is a benign situation.

Schemas

Schemas are groups of memories or ideas that are organised together and live in the long-term memory. The grouping together can include knowledge of rules, patterns or systems, for example, number systems. Schemas are built through repetition and recall. Schemas can also be related to the self and can be negative or positive. Early experiences lead to particular self-schemas or self-narratives. Schemas become automatic, the way we can recite the alphabet or count to ten without thinking. We can build on these automatic processes to create more complex schemas. We build schemas using our experiences and knowledge, and for students who come to us low on background knowledge, we will find that this will impact their comprehension of texts (Smith et al., 2021). All students come to school with beliefs built by their early experiences, and it can take a long time for them to realise that there are a range of experiences that people can have, and that their truth might not match other people's.

Hidden memories

When implicit memories exist, they can make themselves known via triggers. This is most likely to occur when in a heightened state but can happen any time. Memories surfacing in this way are likely to be somatic and emotional, and may not feel like a memory at all – while the body and mind are essentially reliving a trauma, there is no recall of the trauma. It feels to that person that the fear is happening in the present moment, though it is actually a reliving of a past experience. The study of PTSD was a catalyst for learning about the impact of triggers and flashbacks. A classroom example is a teacher's raised voice, where a student may have a big response, yet be:

> *Unable to understand that the response they are having relates to the threat of harm posed by the raised voice of an abusive parent that is in the past, and not the non-threatening raised voice in the classroom in the present. (Australian Childhood Foundation, 2020, p. 30)*

In our classrooms, these reactions can look like behavioural issues. Sometimes we are able to identify what the trigger is, sometimes the trigger continues to elude us. In one instance we had a student who had very big reactions to death of any kind. A dead bird in the yard caused huge distress to this student, what appeared to be a disproportionate response to an admittedly sad moment. In discussing this incident with the student's mother, she alerted us to the fact that the boy had been present when his twin brother died, a fact we were not aware of but which made sense of his response in this and other situations.

It can be very hard to identify what the trigger for a student might be. They might be linking two things that are not logically connected, meaning a song or a smell can elicit a feeling that is connected to a person or an experience. For example, the song that plays at my school every lunchtime will likely stick in the students' heads as connected to this experience for years to come. The opposite can occur, too, so that one might not make a connection between two things that belong together. For example, a student might experience an ongoing belief that they are bad at mathematics and feel anxiety around mathematics without ever linking it to a shame-inducing experience of getting an answer wrong after being called on in class. Sometimes it seems very clear to us as adults why a student is having a response, but our logic does not ring true for the student at all. These linking or unlinking of feelings and events and senses happens to all of us – sometimes we are aware of it and sometimes we are not. We might notice this happening to students in a way that seems inexplicable to us, particularly when dealing with dramatic behaviour.

A student we worked with in Prep would have huge meltdowns, the kind that meant the rest of the class needed to evacuate the room. There were tears, yelling, fists on the floor, distress, snot, spit – the works. They were, to staff, entirely unpredictable and very upsetting. There seemed nothing anyone could do except be present, calm, keep the student safe and wait for the end. This student remained with us for their primary school years, and these responses eventually slowed and then ceased all together, but we were never able to ascertain what the trigger was. It might have been a sound, a smell, the tone of the teacher's voice or any number of things, but the student didn't know and nor did the staff, just the powerful unconscious. In a situation like this, the trigger generates a response, so when this happens multiple times, the cycle of trigger and response is reinforced and the link becomes stronger.

Focus and concentration

Cognitive load theory

Cognitive load refers to the amount and complexity of information existing in our working memory at any given moment (Paas et al., 2020; Smith et al., 2021; Sweller et al., 2019). As Sweller et al. (2019) identifies:

> *Its basic premise is that human cognitive processing is heavily constrained by our limited working memory which can only process a limited number of information elements at a time. Cognitive load is increased when unnecessary demands are imposed on the cognitive system. If cognitive load becomes too high, it hampers learning and transfer. (p. 262)*

When the cognitive load is too heavy, learning is impacted. Cognitive load is made up of the information coming in about the task at hand, as well as any unrelated information or external sensory processing, such as aspects of the task, the classroom environment or thoughts in the learner's head (Paas et al., 2020). It is easy to see how busy classrooms or student worries or complicated instructions might impede a student's learning, regardless of any history of trauma or adversity. So consider a student who is being bullied or has strong sensory triggers and what that may do to their cognitive load. As we go on to explore interventions, we will look at ways that we can reduce cognitive load for our students.

Impacts of traumatic stress

For those exposed to traumatic stress, the baseline of regulation can be altered, producing a starting point of hyper- or hypo-arousal which, in turn, impacts concentration and cognitive load capacity (Australian Childhood Foundation, 2018; Craig, 2016; van der Kolk, 2014). This shift in concentration capacity can exist for a short time, such as with exposure to a single experience that has impacted the nervous system, like a car accident, and makes sense in the context of responding to threat, rather than taking in information. However, when the stressful event is not singular but repeated, the nervous system has a more long-lasting response, becoming set-up for threat detection and response.

Maintaining student engagement is a significant goal for all educators. When teaching students who have experienced trauma or adversity, it can be particularly difficult. There are lots of reasons why students might not feel engaged and motivated such as: fear of failure; the work is too hard; the work is too easy; family belief that education is not important; other areas of life being overwhelming; or a sense of self not being aligned with being a learner. These are all things that can be addressed by adaptable educators offering a dynamic way to engage with the curriculum.

Paying attention

Trauma symptoms can look a lot like ADHD symptoms in our classrooms (Siegfried et al., 2016). When we see students displaying difficulty concentrating, being easily distracted, being restless and disorganised or not seeming to listen to us, we might be looking at a student with experience of early adversity or one who has ADHD. It can be very challenging for a student who experiences these characteristics to maintain their concentration levels and for teachers to keep them engaged.

We might see students presenting with inattention that could be a result of hyper-vigilance or of dissociative qualities. We could see sensory-seeking behaviours such as tipping a chair back despite being asked not to or rolling on the floor or constant noisemaking. Those symptoms of toxic stress that cover internalising, externalising and sensory-seeking behaviours can present as inattention and hyperactivity (Siegfried, 2016; Thomas, 1995), which adds up to a student who finds it difficult to demonstrate attention and focus in class. In addition, working memory and cognitive load will also be contributing factors to a student's attention, plus sleep, nutrition and other elements relating to their daily care. Being on high alert is also very likely to impact a student's capacity for focus and concentration. The Australian Childhood Foundation (2018) states:

> *...instead of following the natural rhythm which sees stress hormone level peaking in the morning and gradually wearing down during the afternoon and early evening, stress hormones in traumatised children can stay high constantly through the day. This contributes to limited attention span and difficulties with concentration. It also means that these children may experience eating and sleeping difficulties, which further impact on their capacity to engage positively with learning opportunities. (p. 37)*

Whether or not we think a student has ADHD or is responding to their stress, trauma or adversity, the way we approach our interventions will be similar.

Engagement and motivation

When students are engaged and motivated, the capacity to do their best work comes naturally. Many of the behaviour supports we put in place can support these barriers, but there are other things to consider, too. When educators are attuned to their students and create a dynamic classroom, students are much more likely to be engaged with the learning, and educators will be aware when steps need to be taken to support engagement.

The capacity to be motivated comes from a combination of brain structures and begins from the beginning of life (Center on the Developing Child, Harvard, 2022a). These brain structures work in a way that encourages us to repeat experiences that have felt good, where we have received positive feedback in the form of brain chemicals like dopamine. Young children can be motivated to learn and explore because that is what they are wired to do, to move to and from their secure base, safely discovering more and more. This is ideally encouraged by positive feedback from supportive caregivers that help frame these experiences as positive. As children get older, peer feedback might play the role that caregiver feedback once did. Children who did not experience responsiveness from a caregiver, or who did not have positive experiences from their explorations, might not easily experience internal motivation (Center on the Developing Child, Harvard, 2022a). As educators, we play an important role in supporting our students' motivation and engagement in their learning.

Divided attention

During very stressful or traumatic events, removing a focus on what is happening is a common and logical coping strategy. It may involve focusing on something else going on or something else to look at or going into imagination or, more extremely, dissociating. It can be a very useful strategy, but it can have the impact of removing cohesive explicit memory, while not being able to do the same for implicit memory (Australian Child & Adolescent Trauma, Loss & Grief Network, 2016; Kezelman & Stavropoulos, 2020).

Chatting to a student one morning during a teacher-requested check-in, the student recounted that their parents had been fighting before school. When I asked what they had been doing while this was happening, the student said they had been watching the television in their room, re-enacting fierce focus on the television. Divided attention was a strategy that had clearly been used before and offered some degree of protection from the content of the fight, just not the emotion surrounding it. While they had tried to protect themselves, they had still been impacted, evident in the behaviour and demeanour noticed by their teacher on arrival.

As shown in the example, implicit memories of being present while parents are fighting are sticky. They will impact regardless of the adaptive strategy of divided attention, which may protect from the content and mean the explicit memory of the experience won't stick. The implicit memory of the event, however, may become intrusive, causing flashbacks to elements of the experience, including some of the most challenging aspects such as the desire to flee or the experience of feeling paralysed with fear.

We know that divided attention or dissociation are strategies often called on by children as they are more likely than adults to be in a situation that they cannot fight or flee their way out of. This impacts memory, as discussed, but can also become a physiological response to all stress, which has a significant impact on learning as school life is full of stressors. What might be a simple moment of discomfort for other students, might become a dissociative moment for a student with this type of survival physiology, leaving them unable to take in the classroom information that might otherwise become an explicit memory. Consider the challenge of speaking in front of the class and the anticipation some students might feel, perhaps fixating or panicking for hours or days before, resulting in those students not taking in other classroom learning.

Conclusion

Trauma and adversity cause many impacts and these impacts follow children to school, the playground and the classroom. This can look like poor behavioural choices, like sensory avoidance or sensory seeking, or like checking out or acting out. It can be seen in cognition, emotion and motor skills – the impact on development is global. It can influence concentration, cognitive load capacity, skills acquirement and motivation. As we continue through this book, we will delve deeper into ways that we can mitigate these effects of trauma.

7

SAFETY, RESILIENCE AND SENSE OF SELF

In this chapter we take what we have learned about trauma, brain development and neuroscience, and look at this through an education lens. Schools are well-placed to address issues relating to trauma for many reasons, and some of the most significant impacts schools can have are on a student's sense of safety and their sense of self. Schools can offer predictability, stability, boundaries, safety and a place to belong. Consider the amount of time we get to spend with our students. In Australia, we likely have a student at primary school for over 1,300 hours each year. For some students, during term time we get more (awake) time with them than their families do. This places schools in the unique position of being able to provide a therapeutic environment, even for students living with daily trauma or adversity. School is compulsory and while this does not mean that all school-aged children attend all the time, it does mean that we are likely to have access to children more than any other system or network.

For some students, school is the one place they go aside from their home, so when home is a difficult place, school has the opportunity to offer safety and care. Since our core business is education, when things get in the way of learning we are obliged to attend to these. While mental health, housing, physical health and family violence are not part of our core business, if any of these are getting in the way of a student's education, we need to know what to do, because this is how we equitably provide education to all. It is also how we offer students positive relational experiences that can leave them with a lifetime of increased resilience. A thirty-year longitudinal study of 'high-risk' children identified the power of 'a bond with at least one adult in the family or with one adult in the community' and that 'safe passage through the tumultuous years of adolescence is often attributed to creating positive alliances with significant non-parental adults such as teachers and other school staff' (Wolpow et al., 2016, p. 16). The authors went on to state 'Thus, schools are in an ideal position to provide students and their families with the social processes and mechanisms that foster resiliency' (p. 16).

The great thing about embedding student wellbeing practices and operating with a trauma-informed lens in schools is that the interventions serve all students well. The universal interventions to support the behaviour and learning of students who have experienced adversities are interventions that will help any student build the skills that will support them with their learning journey and their life journey. All students, at some point, will be going through a tricky time – parental separation, loss of a loved human or pet, family relocation, social struggles – and the interventions for a trauma-informed school will provide them with the skills to cope and recover. Through the relationships with educators, students are exposed to 'adults who model appropriate relationships and who treat them with respect and kindness' and who can work to 'meet students' unmet developmental needs' (Brunzell & Norrish, 2021, p. 30).

Safety

A sense of safety is vital for learning. Consider your own capacity for learning while feeling unsafe. As explored earlier, our nervous system dictates what is safe and what is not. We may in fact *be* safe, but that does not guarantee that we *feel* safe. When we don't feel safe our body responds, sending us into a sympathetic or parasympathetic threat response, neither of which are conducive to learning or connecting with others.

Consider a time when a frightening thing happened to you – maybe a car accident, a near miss of some kind, a loss or a shock – and think about what happened in your body and how long it took to get back to your usual state of being. We become heightened or even dysregulated when having a response to not feeling safe and it takes a while to recover. So for our students who live in a state of feeling unsafe, it will be almost impossible for them to be in an optimal learning state. This feeling of not being safe might not come from being exposed to violence, but can be as simple as having an unpredictable or disengaged parent. Children are wired to seek connection and nurture from their caregivers and when this is disrupted, they do not experience the co-regulating required to achieve a sense of safety.

As Jennings (2019) says, 'The first order of business in building a trauma-sensitive school is safety, creating a safe environment for all concerned' (p. 68). We always need to be wary of the idea of a *safe space*, a term used rather frequently. A sense of safety lives within a person and, as discussed, it is a sense that is often arrived at unconsciously. What is a safe space for one person feels threatening for another. An individual's threat response can be activated by the sound of a voice, the smell of perfume, the sound of a school bell. I worked with a student who had a huge reaction to the fire alarm, even with warning that it was a practice. This student literally sprang off the ground and into the arms of a teacher on first hearing the sound. As it happened, we knew that the student had been in a dangerous situation with a real fire, so this reaction absolutely made sense. I am sure that it would be a fairly common response for anyone who had real life experience with an alarm, or even anyone for whom loud noises were a trigger. This is an example of a response to a situation that we can attempt to mitigate. Obviously, we could not stop fire drills, but we could give this student forewarning and allocate a special job so that the student had a clear focus and an active role to play. Three years after that first experience, the student was enjoying the important role and not displaying fear, which is not to say it was not being experienced, but rather was manageable. We can't always find ways to eliminate a sense of not being safe, but we can support our students in their experiences and attempt to minimise the impact and offer them a sense of control in the situation.

Teaching and projecting safety

We empower students when we *teach* safety. Because what does feeling safe mean, anyway? When we incorporate the language around safety, and the physical sensations of feeling unsafe, we give students the knowledge and the language to tell us when they don't feel safe. Teaching these protective behaviours may also alert students to times outside of school when they are not feeling safe.

Similarly, a school staff member might hear students talk about a lack of safety in other areas of a student's life, and it is important for trauma-informed schools to have a process regarding how to deal with disclosures from students. As distressing as it is, receiving disclosures can be a sign that a school is doing something right and that students feel safe.

A significant consideration for educators and trauma-informed schools is the way that adults communicate. In his book, *Permission to Feel*, Marc Brackett (2019) talks about research that has identified how facial expressions are filtered through an individual's perceptions to mean that neutral faces might be perceived as faces in fear by people with anxiety disorders; perceived as angry for students exposed to parental fighting; and for students who experience irritability these neutral faces are more likely to be read as hostile or fearful. So, when we communicate to our students, we can impact them greatly without even realising or intending, just with our face.

It is reasonable to think that the biggest source of fear for a child is adults, whether conscious or unconscious (and probably the case for us adults as well). As we've discussed, other people are most frightening when they are unpredictable. We can support students' sense of safety by keeping ourselves and our routines as predictable as possible. What this means for trauma-informed schools is that change should be reduced as much as possible. For all of our students we can offer predictability as the path to mastery and confidence, because when students know what to expect and know what the routines of the day are, they can take part in them, can accurately anticipate what is coming next and can reduce their cognitive load to be able to better focus on the learning for the day. In my observations, teachers quite like routine, too, so predictability as a path to a sense of safety is not hard to create in a classroom.

Attuning to our students

A trauma-informed teacher is watching out for students who do not feel safe. They are alert to the clues that a student might be offering, looking for those who may appear hyper-vigilant or checked out. When we attune to our students, it leads to an ability to read their emotional state and respond appropriately.

A young student who had recently lost a parent really struggled with their emotions and connecting to others' emotions. The student would often misinterpret the feelings of their peers. In great distress one day, we tried to establish what the problem was. The student articulated that they were sure that a peer was thinking negative things about them, interpreted from the peer's face. This kind of experience is indicative of the power of dealing with significant distress. It took considerable convincing to reassure the student that they didn't know the thoughts of the other and that they could only find out by asking. The recovery for this student was years long, but with time and care from the educators around them and their family at home, and communication between the two, they improved their skills in interpreting expressions and did not continue to misinterpret others as thinking negative thoughts.

Anxiety in its most adaptive form protects us from danger, but for those who are a bit more anxious or whose sympathetic nervous system is very active, the internal alarm system is like a smoke detector over a toaster. Think about what increases anxiety and consider what might trigger a student's anxiety at school. A trauma-informed teacher will be ready to adapt as necessary, being aware that some things will be triggers for some students. For example, for students living with an unstable home life, books about the fairy-tale version of home may well be de-stabilising or confusing. It may be the same for other aspects of life, for example, any description of what is typical will absolutely not be typical for many students. As educators, we need to be aware that the students in our care are diverse, their experiences are varied and they will bring their past into the classroom. These varied experiences may not be represented in the curriculum materials, but teachers do have the power to maintain a trauma-informed lens to adapt to meet the diverse needs of students, providing a base of understanding and a sense of stability and safety. As suggested by the title of this book, a sense of safety is at the forefront of a student's needs, and for some, it can take a very long time to experience school as a safe place, if ever.

I have a cat with a curious habit. She always wants someone with her while she eats. She leaves her food, finds a human and directs that person to her food, then begins to eat it. Confused by this behaviour, I did some research and discovered it is for safety. She wants us to keep watch, so she can eat knowing she is protected. School is like this for some students. We, the adults, keep watch so they can feel safe and get on with daily business, knowing that they can relax, that someone else is watching for danger.

Building resilience through social-emotional learning

> *Resilience is defined as the capacity of a system to adapt successfully to challenges that threaten the function, survival, or future development of the system. (Masten & Barnes, 2018, p. 1)*

When we talk about resilience, we're talking about an individual's capacity to cope but also their access to support from areas such as family or community or other cultural contexts. We are thinking about adaptability when faced with change or adversity. In their book, *Nurturing Resilience*, Kain and Terrell (2018) define resilience as 'the ability to achieve positive outcomes – mentally, emotionally, socially, spiritually – despite adversity' (p. 3). Resilience is born of one's temperament, learned traits and the environmental context – family, community and broad societal and cultural contexts (Kain & Terrell, 2018).

Some protective factors that promote resilience include relationships that are supportive; a sense of having control and efficacy; capacity to self-regulate and adapt; and access to faith, hope and culture (Kain & Terrell, 2018; Masten & Barnes, 2018). You can see from this list that the people who are most likely to come up against repetitious adversities are possibly the least likely to have the protective factors required, existing in a context that denies access to this protection and requires more resilience. Resilience is influenced by genetics as well as environment, and school can provide an environment from which resilience can be built.

There are, of course, many elements of building resilience that schools are not able to influence. In researching school starters who had been exposed to neglect or abuse and their strengths and resilience, Armfield et al. (2021) identified that predictors of resilience in this context '…were being older, not having an emotional condition, and being read to at home. Risk factors were being male, living in rural or remote areas, having a physical or sensory disability, or having a learning disability' (p. 1). Though there are things we cannot control, just being armed with knowledge can help us to support our students.

However, many of the protective factors are things that we can influence. As noted earlier, a single stable adult can support the building of resilience (Center on the Developing Child at Harvard University, 2020). This means that through the school environment, we can work to build these relationships with those in our school community. We can support families, we can know where to refer on when appropriate, we can support students to access mentoring programs or extracurricular programs and we can even be that adult.

Schools can support with other protective factors as well, such as positive relationships with peers and adults, physical exercise, stress-reduction practices, building executive function, teaching protective practices, information seeking and help seeking, reframing negative experiences, building optimism and hope, and building skills around self-regulation and coping strategies (Armfield et al., 2021; Center on the Developing Child at Harvard University, 2020). Schools are now much more aware of the ways that these areas can support learning outcomes, so there is more of a focus on building social-emotional skills that sit alongside traditional academic skills.

The trouble with resilience

Qualities or traits like perseverance, grit or resilience are to be encouraged, for sure, but the whole context needs to be seen. We can make a simple assessment about whether or not a student is resilient, perhaps they cry easily, or get clingy with teachers. However, what we can't always do is understand what else is going on that might be contributing to this apparent lack of resilience. Perhaps the student who struggles with minor setbacks has not had breakfast, was up all night listening to parents fighting, has to care for a younger sibling, and school is the place they can show their vulnerability or where they reach their cognitive load capacity.

This is why the narrative around resilience and other areas of positive psychology can be a problematic one. When living with chronic emotional or physical struggles, we increase our risk for experiencing more stress because we are feeling all the things that come with a chronic condition, such as powerlessness or helplessness, which builds over time, 'leaving us with ever-dwindling inner resources for coping with our ever-growing allostatic load' (Stanley, 2019, p. 199). When we have students who live with a constant state of stress, their capacity to cope is greatly reduced as they operate constantly depleted. The question of resilience is often framed as though we all are on equal footing, however, we need to use our differentiation and scaffolding skills to offer the most support to those who need it most, regardless of apparent resilience. As Kain and Terrell (2018) state, 'Resilience is often hard won for those who have faced severe early trauma' (p. 228). A trauma-informed school assumes complexity in a child's life.

I often think about students who, before reaching the school gate, have had to deal with things like – to use some real examples – witnessing a horrific act of violence on the way to school; witnessing a drug deal; avoiding the dog that the dealer uses as protection; or averting eyes from the stain in the lift that is a record of a stabbing… All these things, with no adult there to help them manage their feelings, sees a student cope as best they can in the moment and head to school as planned. After one of these experiences, a student then might have a wobbly moment when they can't seem to get a mathematics concept, they are rude to the teacher and walk out of the class. A lack of resilience! Not enough grit! Compare this student with the one who had a delicious breakfast, a warm car ride, a chat with a parent and was escorted into the playground with enough time for a kick of the footy before school starts. This second student also has trouble with the mathematics concept, but perseveres, asks for help, tries again, and success! What perseverance, we say, what resilience! Gorski (2019) identifies this issue with ideas of grit and resilience, saying:

> *We should be instinctively suspicious of popular educational approaches that often detour us around equity with a deficit approach. For example, presuming we can resolve racial inequities by simply teaching students of color to have grit is like presuming we can resolve climate change by teaching coastal communities to swim faster. It shifts the onus of responsibility away from schools and onto the very youth who are cheated out of equitable opportunity—and who, due to this cheating, often already tend to be quite resilient. (p. 59)*

This quote and my examples illustrate the issues with celebrating and labelling character traits like grit, perseverance and resilience without considering the complexity. I think it is important, that while we do promote these worthy attributes, we are careful to not blame students who are victims of inequitable societal structures for their own battles because of this inequity. If we don't acknowledge these barriers, we are not serving our students well. As we work hard to teach perseverance, effort and resilience, let's also work hard to reduce inequity where possible and highlight it where we can. The idea of everyone having the same opportunity for success is a great one, but let's not pretend that success comes as easily to each individual.

Resilience research

Interest in resilience has continued to grow (Masten & Barnes, 2018) and we can expect that this will continue as the links between resilience and success in life is reinforced. The global impacts of climate change and pandemics mean that none of us will be immune to dealing with stress and adversity to some degree. Looking into resilience research, Masten and Barnes (2018) examined in depth the protective factors that lead to a child having the capacity for 'adapting to challenges as they grow up in families and communities' (p. 6). They make the comparison with research into family resilience and note that the protective factors are very similar whether looking at family resilience or individual resilience. The key factors for resilience, common across cultures, were found to be:

- a caring family and good parenting
- a sense of belonging and close relationships that promote emotional security
- a sense of agency and self-efficacy
- a positive sense of self
- optimism and hope and a sense that life has meaning
- routine and collective ritual
- connection to a school and a community that functions well.

When it comes to resilience intervention, Masten and Barnes (2018) found that the research identifies three key strategies:

> *Reduce or mitigate risk; boost assets or reduce barriers to promotive factors for child health and development; and nurture, mobilize, or restore as needed the fundamental and powerful adaptive systems that generate capacity for resilience over the life course. (p. 8)*

So where does all of this leave us in schools? Perhaps we can see that not only are schools well-placed to offer trauma-informed practices, but also to be 'resilience-informed' (Masten & Barnes, 2018, p. 10). Like so much of our trauma-informed work, we are looking at reducing risks and barriers and building capacity with nurturing interventions that build on what already resides in our students.

We will look further into the ways that schools can introduce whole-school or classroom social-emotional learning programs in subsequent chapters, but it is worth touching on here because the bottom line is that trauma-informed schools will have some kind of social-emotional learning program. The key aspects are that these programs will build students' skills when it comes to understanding their feelings and those of others, which we could consider at the heart of resilience. Knowing that feelings and emotions are transient, and that with bravery we can move through and past tricky feelings, is central to being able to cope with challenges. Trauma-informed schools recognise that learning about emotions is essential, that building a broad emotional vocabulary is valuable and that students will benefit from having the skills to read others, to know their own tendencies toward emotional expression, to understand the link between emotion and behaviour, and to know how to regulate and respond.

Sense of self

We develop our self-concept through the early interactions we have with our caregivers. (Jennings, 2019, p. 24)

We all carry a narrative about ourselves and we share this with others. As adults, we will have experienced many reinforcing messages about who we are, and we may have ideas about ourselves that come from a source that is no longer remembered, but likely began in our family of origin. This working model of who we are is created from a very young age.

At school we meet fullyformed young people with a sense of themselves created by experiences which may or may not be positive. When interactions with caregivers generate feelings, there is an integration of inner and outer life being created. Children co-narrate these shared experiences with caregivers. However, when caregivers struggle to allow certain emotions in themselves, they do not share these tricky emotions with their children. This results in these emotions not appearing in the child's narrative, making these emotions a challenge for the child to feel or understand (Cozolino, 2014), as though they form no part of the self.

We have talked about the positive impact of a family's stories – that in sharing cohesive narratives, parents are giving children the gift of seeing things from multiple perspectives and of understanding context. It is essential for our students to have these skills: it supports them with comprehension, with perspective writing and with friendships and relationships at school. Parents overwhelmed by their own narrative end up with incoherent and disjointed stories, and where there is a chaotic family history, a lack of clarity or existing unprocessed parental trauma, we will see this played out in our students. For students coming from a family where there is no cohesive parental self-narrative, it is unlikely they will have a strong and positive sense of who they are (Siegel, 2010a). Teachers can help to re-tell a narrative in a more cohesive way (Cozolino, 2014).

Our self-narratives create a kind of feedback loop as we filter all our interactions through this idea of ourselves. Self-narratives born of trauma also have a way of being strengthened over time. Consider the student who believes there is something fundamentally wrong with them, has this reinforced by parents and then brings this idea to school with them. In having this core belief, or narrative, they become drawn to hang out with another student who treats them poorly. This is recognisable, in a way, reassuring in its familiarity. In maintaining friendships like this, the idea that they are deserving of poor treatment becomes reinforced with each experience and is synchronous with home. However, if this student should be approached by a teacher or a kind student, they are thrown. It is not familiar, it doesn't feel right and perhaps the student then seeks to sabotage this relationship or experience. They might actually feel more alert with a kind teacher, than one who seems displeased with them. However, if the message of being worth something is coming from multiple sources at school, due to the whole-school approach that is embraced by all staff, the messaging of 'not good' can be slowly questioned by the student. Further, if the narrative of 'good enough' is introduced frequently enough to become predictable, a new story can be created.

The universal trauma-informed interventions we can engage will benefit all our students, regardless of their life experiences. We all live in a society that can be damaging to our sense of self in a range of ways, particularly for those people who do not conform to the dominant idea of who is typical. Not fitting this mould means you are less likely to see yourself represented in politics and other positions of power, advertisements, celebrities and generally in the public eye.

Statistics can be disheartening when we are working with students who have experienced a great deal of adversity. However, as educators we must maintain a core belief in our students' ability to find success regardless of their background and we must take responsibility for ensuring the possibility. This is a difficult line to walk because we also need to accept sometimes that we will let students go from our school in difficult circumstances and simply hope for the best.

I worked for many years to support a student who had experienced a range of early traumas. Placed in kinship care with a guardian trying their best, this student played out the impacts of trauma every day at school. They challenged, fought, ran away and refused learning. Along with my colleagues, we used all our resources, skills, care and compassion to support the student. There was improvement, though not as much as we all wanted. Their guardian made the difficult decision to change school so the student could start fresh. It was incredibly hard to see them go, to release the desire to intervene and help, and to trust that everything would be okay. Many of us thought about this student often. We heard various stories that did not make us hopeful, but as the years passed, we began to hear more positive stories. Eventually, we saw the student again, looking very grown up and capable, still with the same guardian and doing okay. It was a delight to be reunited, but it is important to remember in education that we don't always get access to an outcome. We can only hope that when we provide the optimum environment for students, we are offering the best that we can while we have them. We water them while they are in our garden, to quote a colleague, and we trust that the growth happens and continues to happen.

Conclusion

Educators are important. We can be that adult that offers safety and positively reflects back our students to themselves. When we give students a sense of safety, their growing and developing brain allows it to move between alertness, relaxation, vigilance, co-regulation and learning within the context of connection to another. When we teach social-emotional learning, find ways to reflect students' experiences, and teach skills of coping and help-seeking, we are building our students' capacity for resilience. As we attune to our students, we offer a healthy connection where the experience regulation, essential for learning, can develop and grow.

8

RELATIONSHIPS

Because of the interwoven nature of arousal, neural plasticity, and learning, the regulation of anxiety through secure attachment is one of the most powerful tools in a teacher's repertoire. (Cozolino, 2014, p. 70)

Any educator who has been accidentally called Mum or Dad by a student will be well aware of their role as a kind of school parent, clearly demonstrating the importance of our relationships with individual students. What power these relationships with students we have. Safety is experienced relationally, just as feeling unsafe is. When a student has not experienced safety with an adult, educators have the opportunity to provide this vital experience. The learning that happens at school happens relationally, whether that is within a class group, between students or between an educator and a student. When these relationships allow a student to feel comfortable, to feel seen, and to have themselves reflected back to them in positive terms, we are really contributing to the best possible outcome for them.

Early experiences as relationship models

Some of our students will have 'disrupted working models of relationships' (Jennings, 2019, p. 29). For these students, their blueprint tells them that people cannot be relied on to keep them safe. Their sense of who they are is what they have seen reflected in the adults around them and when those adults are deliberately or unconsciously rejecting, the student may feel unlovable. They might have deep ingrained shame and a fragmented and confused sense of self that has been impacted by periods of active fear, distress or dissociation.

Emotional and physical damage from a caregiver in the early years is a path toward developmental trauma, however, positive relationships are huge factors in later resilience. A child with an abusive caregiver might have someone else in their life – an aunt, a cousin, a teacher, a coach – providing them with a steady reflection of themselves as worthy and lovable. The power of this has been demonstrated to be a significant protective factor (Masten & Barnes, 2018; National Scientific Council on the Developing Child, 2015). The interplay between risk factors and protective factors is complex, and risk factors and damaging early relationships can cancel out the protective element of positive early relationships. It's fair to say that a damaging early relationship, regardless of how many positive relationships exist, is likely to leave a scar. But we must remain clear that the power of positive early relationships is also life-changing.

Students with unpredictable adults in their lives will likely have highly attuned neuroceptive skills and will have them activated much of the time. For some students the forty-one weeks or so at school might not be enough time for them to learn to trust or anticipate what will come, or know that they can trust what reception they, or the class, will reliably receive. However, for staff who maintain a predictable manner of engagement and a predictable response to behaviour, it is absolutely possible. When, as a whole school, we prioritise relationships with and between students (and each other), and have the aim that all adults relate in similar ways, being predictable, respectful and fair, then it is likely that the positive impact on students will be exponentially increased. When we all work to the same end, we give the clear message 'at our school, you are valued, you are respected, you are worthy'. Kain and Terrell (2018) explain:

> *It would not be an exaggeration to say that a strong sense of connectedness is one of the best ways to prevent developmental trauma, and one of the remedies that should be brought in to play for repair of early trauma. (p. 22)*

Connectedness is vital to combat early trauma.

What we see at school

Lack of reliability in people around them can result in students who misread social cues and may be fearful or angry around authority figures.

Behaviours associated with spending lots of time in hyper- or hypo-arousal can be seen in the classroom. We all spend some time in these states, so at times we will recognise these in our students and ourselves. We know the impact of exciting events like a school concert, or special visitors, or of scary events like a big storm – we see hypo- and hyperactive students all the time. We also know these states can be contagious, so will often find ourselves dealing with a little coterie of somewhat dysregulated gigglers, for example. The difference between a student living with chronic stress and one without might be found in how regularly they are in a stress-induced state, and the ease or difficultly they might find in returning to a state that is ready for learning.

I was spending time with a student once, who had come to me after having a meltdown in class. We drew what had happened, talking through the events that had led to the big reaction and what happened after. This student demonstrated a range of behaviours consistent with early adversity and was in the class of a gentle, caring, softly spoken teacher. In recounting what had happened, the student told me that the teacher had yelled in response to the meltdown. This seemed unlikely so I probed a bit, asking what was it that the teacher had yelled? The student replied with words to the effect of 'I can see that you are really upset, would you like to spend some time with Bec, because that often helps?'. Even in sharing what the teacher said, it was clear that these are not words that get yelled, and yet to the student it absolutely felt like yelling. Perhaps the gentle care was so unfamiliar that there was no blueprint to explain what had taken place.

Attachment in school contexts

When they are lacking, we want to 'increase students' relational capacity and attachments' (Brunzell & Norrish, 2021, p. 35). Trauma-informed schools can use knowledge about attachment to understand that when teachers have strong and caring relationships, students' engagement as well as their social-emotional and academic learning will be supported (Brunzell & Norrish, 2021).

Under some conditions 'the school and the people in the school can serve as alternative attachment figures' (Jennings, 2019, p. 48). These relationships are different from family relationships and are not surrogate versions but can operate in a way that supports students to 'develop new models of relationships and new models of the self in relationship to others' (Jennings, 2019, p. 48). It is important to note that positive relationships are a significant protective factor, and we can be that protective factor. As Brunzell and Norrish (2021) highlight, studies are clear that 'strong student-teacher relationships are associated consistently with enhanced school motivation and improved academic performance' (p. 124).

Attachment theory can help us to understand why student–teacher relationships are important. Connections between students and adults in schools can be powerful, and it does not need to be a classroom teacher connection, a student might naturally be drawn to an education support staff member, an admin staff member or their physical education teacher. Schools should be able to honour these naturally emerging connections and allow space for students who need to connect with their special person at school. It is our job to be so good at what we do that we can counter any negative relationships, if that is what is needed, and to strengthen the positive relational experiences that already exist.

For those staff who are not always in the classroom, working in wellbeing or intervention roles, for example, they can be in the lucky position of being an extremely predictable and reliable person for a student. Without the relentlessness of the classroom, and needing to maintain a relatively calm demeanour all the time, non-classroom staff can often have greater capacity to be a point of contact for students who are struggling. For classroom teachers in schools that allow students access to wellbeing staff at any time, this can be a relief.

It can be hard managing our emotions in a busy or overwhelming classroom. Students read us all the time, looking for incongruence. We need to be internally attuned as well as attuned to our students. As Brunzell and Norrish (2021) say, 'If we try to mask moments of irritation or frustration in disingenuous ways, students often detect how we truly feel through their highly attuned neuroceptive capacities' (p. 132). It can be confusing and leave a student feeling uneasy and mistrustful when a mismatch is sensed.

When we tune in to ourselves and our students, we are doing the important work of co-regulation. I have witnessed a teacher co-regulate a whole class with use of a range of strategies – a quiet voice, genuine connection with individuals, adapting moment by moment, selecting an engaging strategy to draw students in. It's like magic! We cannot fake it, though. We are far better off, as are our students, taking a teaching moment and stating how we are feeling and how that is going to influence our behaviour, for example: 'I am feeling frustrated right now, so I am going to have a drink from my water bottle and take some deep breaths before I talk with you.'

By naming an emotion, we model to our students and we also reduce its hold on us (that's an example of 'name it to tame it' again (Siegel, 2010a)). We need to be regulated to co-regulate. When we can manage this, what a great relational gift.

Peer relationships

One of the most robust findings of the wellbeing literature is that social connectedness is related to psychological and physical health. (Brunzell & Norrish, 2021, p. 125)

Adults in a trauma-informed school must model the kinds of relationships they want to see students enacting with staff and with other students. Teacher behaviour influences student behaviour, with Jennings (2019) stating, 'Besides serving as a model of social behaviour, teachers influence classroom social dynamics directly and indirectly' (p. 57). Research has identified that teachers can have an impact on the 'social status patterns of their classroom, such as peer norms and status hierarchies, and social affiliation patterns such as informal peer groups and friendships, which can dramatically affect the classroom climate' (Jennings, 2019, p. 57). So, all you meddling teachers who want to control the social nuances of the classroom, go for it! The research demonstrated that teachers who were active in managing friendships and behaviours positively impacted students' behaviour patterns (Jennings, 2019). The more attuned the teachers were, the more pronounced the impact.

We want our students to be able to read people effectively and to be able to connect and respond. Students exposed to frightening or unpredictable people will likely struggle with peer relationships, and for those with significant attachment issues, the struggles will be huge. With a hyper-sensitive attunement to emotion that might be a risk to them, these students are likely to perceive negativity from their peers, even when it is not there. We want to support accurate perceptions and we may need to scaffold student friendships to get to this point.

I spent lots of time with a student who had a simultaneous desire and fear around close relationships. This led to very rocky friendships and very confused students. This student would give gifts, affection and attention to friends, but also be likely to turn on them, say that they had done something hurtful, write mean notes or even become violent. This kind of emotional whiplash with friendships is very reflective of a disorganised attachment style. Love and fear all wrapped up together.

We need to be mindful that one response to unhealthy early relationships can be proximity seeking. A student might seek out connection with adults in an indiscriminate manner. This can be challenging and quite difficult to navigate. It is important to remember that we are modelling healthy relationships, and this means modelling appropriate boundaries at the same time that we are maintaining a connection and demonstrating care. This boundary setting might include high fives instead of hugs, or reminding students that we need to ask before touching someone and being mindful of personal space. When we do this for students who are proximity seekers, it can feel unkind, but it also might protect them from an adult or child who could take advantage of them and reminds them that our bodies belong to us. When physical affection or attention is required by students, we should be asking ourselves why and reiterating what healthy boundaries look like.

We might have a student who is particularly attached to us, and it can feel lovely to have a student say you are the favourite, or the only one who understands them, but it is important to consider when a student might need more (Venet, 2021). Perhaps you are a secure base from which they can explore, perhaps to work more on cultivating a positive relationship with a staff member from their class, or seeking out a peer friendship. Perhaps they need an external referral to provide them with more than one person with whom to connect.

Unconditional positive regard

We don't have to like or love all the children in our care at school, but to be the most effective at our jobs, it is important that we have unconditional positive regard for them, and for their families, too. A term coined by humanistic, person-centred therapist Carl Rogers, *unconditional positive regard* is used widely in therapy and social work, but is very applicable in trauma-informed school relationships. It requires seeing an individual as whole and as separate to their behaviour, thoughts and feelings. We don't have to support or like the behaviour of someone to have unconditional positive regard for them. Similarly, we don't need to share social, political or religious beliefs.

Separating students from their behaviour is vital and a gift to them and yourself. For relationships between staff and students to be therapeutic, they must begin from the basis that each student is worthy of the kind of care a school can provide, and specifically, the kind of care that an individual adult at school can provide.

Knowing what we do about the structural inequities that exist in our society, it is important to dig a bit deeper when you find yourself judging a student or family. Might there be a reason why a student's clothes are not clean, or why they don't say 'please' and 'thank you', or why they always use a loud voice? When a school considers that they are enrolling a whole family, not just a student, we can work to connect with the whole family. When we know what opportunities are out there in our local community, we can better support our students in a range of ways, even encouraging community connections for students and families and links to external supports where they are welcomed by the family. In all these ways and more we see students and families as more than their behaviour, more than what is on the surface and instead as a whole unit, in the context of our school and a broad society.

I worked with a family once where the parents had a fair bit going on. Their kids would often end up in the wellbeing room, angry or frustrated or using fists to solve a problem. The family eventually received a housing move to a bigger place, and when they left, one of the parents said to me, 'I came to this school not knowing what to expect. You looked after my kids and you supported me. I have never once felt judged. I can't tell you how much that means to me.' This was an incredibly moving moment, leaving me with such a sense that we had done right by the family. This parent's trust and feeling of not being judged worked to support the students, too. When parents feel safe at school, so will their children.

Unconditional positive regard is also helpful when it comes to maintaining our boundaries with students and avoiding paternalism or enacting a saviour complex. It means we can start fresh each day, detaching a student's behaviour from our sense of them. I have seen incredible demonstrations of this – teachers who have been injured and abused by highly distressed students, able to come back again (after some time and with support of colleagues) to view that student through a lens of unconditional positive regard. Take opportunities to reinforce with students that your care for them is not based on their grades, their punctuality, the way they look or the things you have in common – it is just unadulterated care. Brunzell and Norrish (2021) state, 'It is important for every teacher to identify and reflect on the students who make it difficult for them to hold unconditional positive regard' (p.135). This is an important point, we can reflect or seek support from others to question what might be being triggered in us when unconditional positive regard is hard for us.

Again, consider Siegel's (2010a) strategy of 'name it to tame it'. Be honest when some students push your buttons – it happens to all of us. Though we might like to think that we approach all students equally and are blank slates, we all know this is not the case. It does not mean that we can't be fair in our approach, but to be fair requires honesty with self (and others) about those students that you struggle with. Schools with a culture that make space for educator honesty around their own struggles with students, set up a situation that facilitates unconditional positive regard. In fact, a recent study by researchers at a Victorian university (Russell, 2022) trialled a model of reflective practice for teachers, who met in peer groups twice per term to reflect on one experience and respond to a series of questions about that experience:

> *Prior to attending on the day, participants complete a structured series of questions which encourages them to think of an experience they have had, how they reacted to it, the assumptions they made, the meaning of the experience, and how this was influenced by their own circumstances (such as their own prior experience and biases). They are also asked to explore how this experience might be perceived by another person involved. (Russell, 2022, para. 8)*

Peers responded with questions of their own, asked in a non-judgemental way. The study found that participating in these reflective circles resulted in increased wellbeing of those involved. By sharing those things that challenge us with and taking an approach of unconditional positive regard, we can all benefit.

Having unconditional positive regard also trains us to look for strengths. Once you start looking, you'll find they are easy to spot. I remember a young student who had shoes that rubbed and were painful, as they did not fit correctly, and who regularly had blisters. This student had taken their socks, folded each one back down over the heel, then back up to the ankle, to provide an extra two layers of protection. I remember my immediate response was one of sadness – why weren't those little shoes the right size? Who had neglected the child's needs? – but it was pointed out to me that the student had found a clever way around a problem, using such ingenuity.

This is a great example of the dangers of my initial reaction – I probably wanted to go and buy new shoes for the student. This saviour mentality reflected my position of power and influence and served to negate the life-force elements in the child's life; of familial love, individual ingenuity and pride in achievement that this student had without any help from me. That is not to say that we might not find ways to help families who want support from a school, but here, when seeing the student in a strengths-based light, we see a clever solution. When holding the student and the family in unconditional positive regard, we sit equally as people all making the best of what we have.

Shame and fear

Shame can send any of us into a trigger response. For those who have been frequently shamed, that feeling can rise easily and will be enmeshed with a sense of being to blame. Adults use shame against children often and shame remains in present in education. Children will wear shame like a dunce's cap, visible or not. Consider a student having their misdemeanours spoken of in front of a class; stopping a class to highlight misbehaviour; calling on the student you know was not listening; giving a particular student a lengthy lecture on behaviour – all of these things are not providing an opportunity for learning, but instead are to a greater or lesser degree using shame to 'teach kids a lesson' rather than actually teaching.

Now, before you feel shame for having done any of these things, it may well be the case that some of these strategies will simply embarrass and a student will be able to correct their behaviour and move on with limited impact. For those brought up with a strong sense of self and ability, and the knowledge that making mistakes is natural, that sense of shame will not hit in the same way as it will for someone who has been shamed regularly. Kain and Terrell (2018) explain, 'Healthy shame should be time-limited, and followed by reconnection and reconfirmation of belonging' (p. 172). What happens after using a shaming strategy in a school is of utmost importance. Once again, attunement will allow you to know when a student feels shame, and if shame has occurred, there is the opportunity to reconnect in a more positive way. Students will need guidance and correction, but it will be more effective if a connection has occurred first – the principle of connection before correction.

These feelings can produce a sense of defensiveness that can be hard to be on the other side of, especially when it looks like aggression or disinterest or rejection. Learning to identify signs of shame can be helpful when it comes to interpreting a range of behaviours.

For students with learning difficulties, the shame can be substantial. I remember a student who had lived with a fair bit of adversity and also had some learning difficulties. They were a lovely kid, really personable and easy to connect with, but really struggled to try something when failure was possible. 'Not doin' it!' the student would loudly proclaim. This student was relentlessly encouraged, small wins were celebrated with family and leadership (who doesn't love a Principal's award sticker?!), and relationships were built. The student became braver, learning happened, effort and persistence and growth were named and a virtuous cycle ensued. Years later, the student tracked down the teacher and sent a message saying, 'Thank you. Without you, I would never have learned to read'. This story reflects the power of countering shame by reframing a student's sense of themselves. It is possible.

Relationship-centred teaching leaves room for authoritative teaching, but by being the leader and not the tyrant – authoritative and not authoritarian. Obviously, you can choose to rule with fear, and it may look effective from the outside, but it is important to clarify, is this how you want to work with students? What do you want your legacy to be? When educators look back and reflect that they never would have behaved in such a way as students do these days, the answer to why not is generally because of fear. Fear does not facilitate learning, but it can control behaviour, temporarily.

Conclusion

Schools are here to support children to learn. Not all students arrive at school with the same skill set or the same advantages. Schools should be a place where this does not matter. Educators in schools are adaptable and can meet the needs of whoever is in front of them, particularly when they work as part of a committed team. When we consider the ideal environment for a brain to develop, what is important alongside physiological support are relationships. Through practical measures and the power of relationships, we can create a place where safety and security exist for students, providing them an internal and external learning environment.

9

CLASSROOM STRATEGIES FOR SUPPORTING STUDENT BEHAVIOUR

There are so many ways that we can support student learning by supporting student behaviour. While, as Brunzell and Norrish (2021) say 'There are no quick fixes for addressing deeply entrenched behavioural concerns' (p. 83), when we understand what might be behind behaviour, our relationships with students improve and when the relationships are strong, the learning is supported. As we prioritise relationships and safety we learn to become more attuned to ourselves, our colleagues and our students, leading to less reactivity and greater compassion and self-compassion. When we can use our trauma-informed knowledge to design our schools and classrooms to be predictable, and yet leave room for an approach that can adapt to our students, we are meeting students' needs and supporting their behaviour.

Teacher strategies

The most immediate, and possibly powerful, strategies that can be used day-to-day in a classroom are relationships, co-regulation and modelling. Paying attention to your face, voice and emotional state allow you to set the emotional tone in the classroom. Those magical teachers who can quieten a noisy class by being quiet themselves are the perfect example. Even if we are not quite able to achieve this, we can set the tone in a class and draw the students in using our relationships, modelling and co-regulation.

Relationships

As we have established, relationships are key to resilience. This means that positive relationships with students in the classroom is a strategy to support student behaviour and learning. Kain and Terrell (2018) state, 'Safety and security are the underpinnings of resilience and are key in supporting the capacity for self-regulation' (p. 9). When you are a predictable person, students will feel safe around you and when you demonstrate your care, they will feel it. Coming to work each day and experiencing positive relationships is also pretty great, too.

Teachers plan each week, identifying what will be taught at what level as well as any differentiation needed for individual students. So why don't we plan how we are going to connect with students across the week? We can do this by including wellbeing in weekly planning, investigating the reasons behind tricky behaviour in the classroom, considering which students may be acting differently and thinking about who we have not had a one-on-one interaction with lately. By doing this we plan to strengthen student relationships and wellbeing and allow space for compassion in the classroom.

Co-regulation

Students are attuned to our emotional states (Cozolino, 2014; Porges, 2017), meaning that when we can provide a class that has us leading a positive emotional environment, we are supporting learning and even changing biochemistry. Brunzell and Norrish (2021) note that 'In our experience, many teachers use co-regulation all the time without realizing it is a strategy' (p. 104). This quote refers to things that educators do, like getting down on a student's level, being side by side, the ways that feedback is delivered with encouragement and, at the right moment, altering breathing and voice to reflect calm.

Co-regulation is such a powerful tool but it does require us adults to maintain our own regulated state, which can be a challenge. Sometimes students might be violent, or abusive, as they recreate previous experiences, or a sense of self that they live with and this will cause a reaction in the adults around them. It is so important for us to know what is behind behaviour to retain our unconditional positive regard and to not take it personally. We need to control our reactions, because it is likely that our own instincts will also be fight, flight or freeze. It is also vital that we forgive ourselves when we fail at this.

We are not always in control of the way we impact each other. While we might deliberately alter our voice or breath to support a student to become calm, we can also unwittingly escalate a student and they can escalate us. We are not immune to the impacts of others' nervous systems. Dan Siegel talks about 'interpersonal neurobiology' to describe the ways in which our brains interact and impact each other. We will all have had the experience of being exposed to anger, possibly the anger of a stranger or anger not even directed at us, and know the way that it impacts us – potentially heightening our awareness, causing physiological changes such as increased heart rate. We might even start feeling angry ourselves. The same response can occur from being around someone sad – we might find ourselves welling up with emotion. Both dysregulation and regulation are 'contagious'. In education, this provides us with the opportunities and risks of being an educator – the chance to positively impact young lives and the risk of burnout, or vicarious trauma, which we will look at more closely when we look at educator wellbeing in Chapter 13. All the regulation work we do with students, we need to do for ourselves, too.

It is worth noting that if we are working hard to be regulated, we are not actually regulated. We need to match our actual feelings to our face, our body and our words because as humans our social engagement systems will pick up incongruence and it can be unsettling. When we moderate our voice to show calm, our face to show care and connection, and our body to be in an open stance, we are sending clear messages to those around us that we are safe and predictable. When working with a small group or one on one, you might even notice that those around you will match your tone, maybe even match your breathing. This can also work with a whole class, capitalising on existing relationships, coming together in a regulated state.

Modelling

As classroom models we always have the option of naming it when we are not in a regulated state. This can be more powerful than remaining regulated all the time! By naming it, we are normalising, we are 'naming to tame' and demonstrating that often the first step to self-regulating is being aware that we are not there in the moment.

The incredible power of relationships, co-regulation and modelling can be somewhat understood as a product of brain cells called mirror neurons, described by Olson (2014) as the way that 'Students resonate with teachers in a seemingly magical dance of synchronicity' (p. 118). The initial discovery of mirror neurons occurred when researchers working with monkeys noticed that the same circuits of the brain became active when a monkey reached for food, as when the monkey observed a person reaching for food. Just pause to consider that for a moment because it is rather momentous. By simply observing another, mirror neurons help us to experience what others are experiencing. Anyone who has ever been face to face with a small baby, watching them as they try to mimic our facial expressions will understand mirror neurons, or anyone who has watched any thrilling, edge-of-seat feat of daring or skill might remember the feeling as though it were us having the experience. When it comes to mirror neurons and classrooms, Cozolino (2014) identifies that students learn not just from explicit teaching, but from watching educators.

Students can learn as much from watching as listening. They do as we do, not as we say, so we have to teach by doing. Model what you want to see from your students, so don't use shame or fear unless you want to see shame or fear being used in your classroom. Again, it is important to repair when you slip up, remembering that you will slip up since you are not perfect. Just like the students, educators will learn by making mistakes. Sometimes you will be modelling in reverse, taking your own good advice and following the instructions you set for students, so remember to check in with yourself the same way we hope students will be able to check in with themselves. Check in with feelings and bodily sensations, talk about what is happening for you when you are not 100 per cent, or if you are feeling frustrated, or tired. Take part in class relaxations and the check-ins, too.

There is a strong history of use of power in schools that naturally trickles down to student use of power. With a significant focus on bullying in schools, knowing what it is and how to stop it, it is vital that adults in schools also don't behave in ways that use power to control. While we can't always control what happens at home, we can be the models at school, and adult use of power over a child is how bullies are made. What this means for us is that we need to model to our students what positive relationships look like, and know that we may be countering what students have previously been exposed to. We model this in the ways that we speak to students, what we do when we do feel frustrated or cross and how we communicate with other adults at school. Provide many opportunities for your students to see what a healthy interaction looks like.

We can also consider ways in which we might pass on some unconscious and unnecessary modelling or projection. In schools we are often controlled by a bell – we can't eat when hungry or go to the toilet when we need to. This is a situation that can be considered dehumanising, the denial of our body's needs. As Venet (2021) says:

> *As teachers, we sometimes then pass the dehumanization we feel along to students by attempting to control their bodies, too, such as limiting their bathroom access, requiring students to sit a certain way, disciplining them if they do not walk in straight lines. (p. 59)*

It is worth reflecting on the purpose of classroom tools such as standing in line and sitting with legs crossed. We need to check in with the students we have and ask ourselves if they are all benefitting from these tools, considering different bodies and varying capabilities. These simple classroom approaches might be tricky for some students who struggle to self-regulate their disappointment if they are, for example, not at the front of the line or who need a bit of movement in their body to enable listening. When the back of the line is used as a punishment or consequence, no one wants to willingly be at the back of the line and then the problems at the front of the line persist.

Instead, let's think about what we really want from our students and give them the appropriate skills. We want to feel listened to and respected as we speak with a student or a class, so perhaps we want to teach what respectful listening looks like. We want to ensure all students feel safe and not impinged upon, so we teach about body bubbles and care with one's body. Perhaps then, rather than requiring students to place their body in only one way, what we ask for is a respectful, listening body that does not touch anyone else.

Teacher strategies overview

So, to recap, the power a classroom teacher has to positively impact students with relationships, co-regulation and modelling can be harnessed with strategies such as:

- paying attention to your face, voice and emotional state
- increase student feelings of safety with predictability

- add wellbeing to your planning
- plan how we are going to connect with students across the week
- deliberately alter your voice or breath to support co-regulation
- model all the key behaviours you want to see from your students
- repair when you slip up, name it, apologise when necessary
- model to students what positive relationships look like
- think about requesting the outcome you want, such as respectful behaviour, rather than one rule for all bodies, such as lining up or sitting with crossed legs

Predictability and routine

When students know what to expect in class, we build their self-efficacy and reduce their potential stressors. Some students might be happy to roll with whatever is happening, but most often, students who live with any unpredictability or daily stress or anxiety will love knowing what is coming next.

Class routines

Having a classroom routine is a really simple thing that most teachers are likely already doing. The more this routine is embedded and reinforced, the better! Strategies for sharing the routine, such as a visual timetable, are important. For your students who have a poor working memory or who struggle to focus, being able to refer back to a picture of what is happening now and what is happening next can be very grounding.

I was in a junior classroom that had their visual timetable on a whiteboard which enabled a big tick after each session was complete. I have also seen some schools that take away each picture after the session is complete, storing it until next time. Schools might even take the opportunity to go through the routine in the morning, practising words from whichever language they teach.

Morning routines can include photos of which adults are in the class that day. With many staff working part-time, it can be helpful for students to know which faces they will see. When there are specialist classes, it is also a reminder of who will be taking those classes. This can also provide a nice moment to introduce any educators who might be filling in for the day.

Rhythm and routine promote a sense of safety and belonging. Having really clear routines recorded somewhere for when alternative people are taking a class can make things much easier for the fill-in teachers and for the students. The idea is that the more we can remove change and increase predictability from students' school lives, the more likely they are to feel safe and confident.

Music can also help with routine. A morning song, a packing-up song, a song to come in from breaks – lots of opportunity. Music can act as a cue to promote a behaviour, as well as being something that can help to regulate. Music can be used at any time – relaxing music to calm, or focus music when work is being done. Other vocal cues can be used, too, like the classic teacher call and response. Music can help to support transitions, which is beneficial as this is often a particularly tricky time for students who are regularly dysregulated. Reducing transitions is ideal, but not always practical.

Checking in

Alongside a visual timetable you might have a check-in opportunity. This might be all the students' photos ready to be moved from 'away' to 'present' as they arrive, or a chance to place their photo or name beneath some images or emojis to show how they are feeling as they arrive. I have seen this work incredibly well for students to let teachers know they may be feeling a bit wobbly without needing to say anything. It is an opportunity to promote compassion and empathy, too, knowing who might be raring to go and who might be still warming up or need a bit of extra support from an adult. In my experience students don't feel shy about sharing in this way, but it is, of course, worth considering that it might be a bit public. If this is the case, there might be another way to support students to share. I saw a senior year class do this very well. They spent a short time journalling each day and had an agreed way for students to identify if they did or did not want their daily entry read by a teacher. The students used this opportunity to share many things relating to what was going on for them in all areas of their lives. I also worked with a PE teacher who did a check-in at the beginning of class and again at the end, supporting the students to note the impact of different types of movement and exercise on their bodies and feelings.

Differentiating routine

There are also times when an individual student might require their own routine. It might be inside or outside the classroom. I worked with a student who would come to school late most days. Before the student headed to class, they would come into the wellbeing room, conveniently located close to the front entrance and ask, 'Who is my teacher today?'. The class had two teachers job sharing and one day a week began with a specialist class, so it was a very fair question. This student did not mind who would be at the front of the class, but it mattered to know before entering the class, and thus the creation of a routine that filled the space of the not knowing. Other students might like to start the day with a personalised check-in or might like to take responsibility for a daily job to build extra reliability into their day. Some students might even require a more extreme version of the visual timetable, breaking each hour up into smaller increments to be ticked off, or having activities divided up into smaller tasks to help with working memory issues, or to create many opportunities to experience success.

Key strategies for predictability and routine

When it comes to promoting a sense of safety and reducing cognitive load, your predictable classroom will be a winner. To recap, strategies might include:

- daily predictable routines
- beginning the day the same way each day
- visual timetables that show the day
- photos of which adults will be in the room that day
- ticking off as things have occurred, so it is clear what is coming next
- individual student timetables where needed, broken down into small increments
- a check-in opportunity
- songs to represent routines like packing up, coming in to relax after play

Regulation supports

There are many class resources available that support sensory needs. With the rise of knowledge and diagnoses of conditions like ASD and ADHD has come increased resources that support common sensory characteristics, many of which overlap with early trauma and adversity. These might include resources that allow for constant movement like a wobble cushion to sit on, small handheld toys to fidget with, weighted toys or resistance bands that can wrap around chair legs to be kicked or flicked during class.

It must be said that many of these things are not helpful in a classroom, and my rule for fidgets is that they must be silent, not dangerous if thrown and not so interesting that everyone wants it. Unfortunately, this rules many things out. It is the perennial struggle finding the perfect fidget toy!

When using toys and other resources, we need to do some teaching around how and why they are used, supporting students to be able to name the state they are in and move back within their window of tolerance. There is a very useful framework from which to teach the basics of various nervous system states to students – Zones of Regulation (Kuypers, 2011). The Zones of Regulation framework was developed by occupational therapist Leah Kuypers in 2011. You can find resources online or in the curriculum resource. The basics of this framework align colours to different regulatory states, so that the green zone is our optimal, regulated learning zone where the feelings might be calm, focused or happy; the blue zone is associated with feelings like sadness, tiredness or boredom; the yellow zone is associated with feelings like silliness, excitement or worry; and the red zone is associated with feelings such as frustration, anger or elation. Categorising these various states of regulation means that students can easily describe what they are feeling, without searching for the right word. Using the Zones of Regulation framework, students can create a list of strategies that work for them. This can also work well with education about the different strategies including the use of fidgets.

Lots of classrooms now have a calm corner – perhaps a tent, or a class library, or just a pile of cushions – that a student can be in while they continue to listen to the teachers (ideally). This is a space that a class can create together, saying what they would like included and sharing ideas about what helps them to feel calm. A calm corner can also cater to sensory needs, including items such as noise-cancelling headphones, things that feel nice or a fidget toy. It is often the case that the students who make silly noises while in class are actually the ones who are struggling with the noise levels (Department for Education, South Australia, 2019), so they are great candidates for headphones. Most of the low-cost available headphones I have used work really well – they don't take away all the noise but soften it, so voices can still be heard but the general hubbub of a classroom is reduced somewhat.

Whole-class sensory strategies can include opportunities to energise, or to calm. Often schools will have a calm time across the whole school, using meditation or other calming activities such as colouring or just sitting quietly. This is best used after break times when it is likely that students will be hyper-aroused after the unstructured play and running around of recess and lunch. It is a really nice time when across the school, each class has relaxing music or sounds playing and students come in knowing it is a silent time, but also an opportunity to check in with an adult if needed. It is worth noting that this time does not work well for every student and it might be that someone will always need to be sitting up at a table or might need another adjustment. For students who find it difficult to feel safe, lying down with closed eyes may not bring a sense of safety. Alternatives to assuming a meditation pose might be calm colouring, knitting or finger knitting, or creating shapes with shells or buttons or other small things. Simply taking slow breaths together can be another whole-class calming strategy.

Energising strategies are the classic brain breaks of which dancing is often a favourite. Simple games can be good energisers, like musical statues or partner games that involve moving around to bring some energy back into a classroom after a period of sitting. Singing can also be a great brain break, even singing a counting or times tables song. Coming together as one voice is a great way to create a sense of belonging, too.

Classroom staff can get to know their students' regulatory needs, noting what might be a trigger, or what might work to calm. Often this will be clearer to us than it is to a student, but we can support them to notice, and learn about themselves. By weaving sensory activities throughout the day, students' nervous systems are pre-emptively or responsively calmed (downregulated) or energised (upregulated).

Some regulation strategies that we can use to support our students include:

- learn to spot the range of ways that your students demonstrate they are in fight, flight, fawn or freeze
- reduce triggers such as multiple daily transitions
- use Zones of Regulation cards to help students identify their own responses to each of the zones, and what helps them get back to the learning zone
- learn as a class how to use fidgets
- movement breaks
- keep regulation tools available, and visible around the room
- share your strategies with all adults who work in the classroom

- repetition reduces cognitive load – the same pack-up song, the same routine etc.
- brain breaks that can be accessed by individual students, such as a hallway obstacle course

Tuning in to bodies

With the youngest students in our charge, and sometimes with older ones, too, a beginning point for teaching the tuning in we are talking about is interoception. That vital internal sense that monitors our sensations such as hunger, body temperature and the need to go to the toilet is not something all students come to school with. For a student who is overly attuned to danger and fear, other sensations might take a back seat and be harder to recognise, sometimes including sensations of comfort and safety.

Many of the students we work with who have behavioural and self-regulation struggles have never been taught these important skills. Supporting students by identifying what can be seen from the outside can help them tune in to what is happening on the inside. Noting to the class who missed their usual snack break that they must feel hungry and then commenting on how they feel better after they eat, would be an example of this, as would pointing out to the sweaty student that they will feel better when their jumper comes off. Beginning by teaching students to tune in to sensation is a path to actively teaching the link between emotion, what it looks like on faces and bodies and what it feels like in us. This can help us when we are trying to get to the bottom of what is going on for a student. And by sharing these learnings with each other, students learn about themselves and also come to understand that reactions and responses are different for every person.

For children to develop a good ability to accurately detect both safety and danger using their neuroception, Kain and Terrell (2018) identify that they require three things: reliable experiences of a sense of safety; caregivers who can help regulate and understand responses; and consistent feedback from peers about how to interpret experiences. We can offer all of the experiences at school. We can teach students to notice their behaviours and learn about what drives them. Students and staff can all be taught to recognise the early signs of dysregulation to better anticipate a significant disruptive dysregulated response.

Interventions for regulation

There are so many regulation interventions available as we increase our knowledge and understanding that we all have differing sensory and regulation needs. Many offering designed to support individuals with a particular diagnosis can work well for many students and educators, too. Interventions can include:

- calm corners
- fidget toys, weighted items, resistance bands
- wobble cushions or wobble chairs
- Zones of Regulation tools
- handheld things that are soft or feel nice to hold, soft toys
- noise-softening headphones
- post-break relaxation
- movement breaks
- singing
- teaching students to tune in to sensation
- highlighting what you notice regarding a student's interoceptive state

Mindfulness

Bringing mindfulness into a classroom does not need to be complicated. There are many resources to support doing this, but the key does seem to be the educators practising it. A recent trial in British secondary schools found that the impacts of teaching a mindfulness program was no better than a quality social-emotional learning program (Kuyken et al., 2022). However, when teachers were taught the program in order to bring it to the students, their own wellbeing improved (Kuyken et al., 2022). The main factor behind the lack of impact was that the students did not practise outside of school as was intended by the program, which we might think was to be expected.

However, what we can do in our classrooms is bring everyday moments of mindfulness in, creating a shared practice of noticing. The benefits are likely to complement a quality social-emotional learning program, and in fact social-emotional learning programs often do include mindfulness because of the significant benefits.

We can define *mindfulness* as a state of '...nonjudgmental awareness of moment-to-moment experiences' that has the capacity to 'reduce stress, and promote less reactive, more reflective decision-making and behavior' (Center on the Developing Child at Harvard University, 2022, p. 13). It goes along well with social-emotional learning because applying a mindfulness practice can lead an individual to tune in to 'thoughts, emotions, and bodily sensation. This helps us notice the subtle feelings that signal the onset of an emotional reaction' (Jennings, 2019, p. 121). In this noticing, there is no judgement, which in turn supports a compassionate approach to self and others (Jennings, 2019). Can you tell I am a fan?

Mindfulness in the classroom includes providing frequent opportunities to pause and take a moment, a breath or tune into a sense, perhaps stopping to create silence and then listening to see what we actually can hear, or silent eating so we can fully experience taste. More specific activities might be yoga or another deliberate movement practice. It is vital to be aware, as mentioned, that some students might find elements of mindfulness triggering, and it is always important to offer alternatives. We can't know what will be a trigger, but we can observe and be curious about resistance from students to try to establish what the issue may be. We will look more at mindfulness when we look at educator self-care, but it is a valuable tool to consider using yourself and with your students. It is also worth keeping in mind that if you don't use it yourself, it may not be valuable to use with your students.

Belonging

When students feel a sense of belonging, their behaviour is positively impacted. Classrooms can have shared ways to recognise and acknowledge students. I have a colleague who gives out 'bonuses'. Giving someone a bonus is a whole-class activity and involves the class saying loudly and in unison 'Bonus!'. As the recipient of a bonus, I can tell you it feels pretty special. This works in two ways as both the giving and receiving makes for a sense of community and belonging. Another teacher I worked with had a rotating student of the week who had their photo and a biography put up on the class door. Other class teachers would end the day with a 'three As' circle, giving every student and classroom staff the opportunity to offer an appreciation, an apology or an 'Aha!' moment. Being part of these circles was always a meaningful experience and students took it very seriously. It was an opportunity for teachers to discover the things that were important to the class and to promote class cohesion, too.

Simple things like birthday calendars or personal strengths displays help a class to see everyone represented. In fact, photographs of the students being their best can be very strategic as it creates an ongoing positive reminder of whatever it is you want to promote. Displays of student work, quotes from class members about learning and name labels on student resources can also support a sense of belonging. Group projects where the class work together to support others are also great strategies. Any routines that are unique to the class help, too.

Remembering to acknowledge students in class supports their sense of belonging. A simple thumbs-up or other acknowledgement in a student's direction for a contribution or recognition of effort can feel great for a student. Using names regularly and giving students who knew the answer an opportunity to give themselves a pat on the shoulder can facilitate a sense of being seen. Some students might need more of this than others. It is likely you can think of a student who needs more teacher attention and acknowledgement than others. This can be tricky and tiring, but consider ways to work this into a lesson, perhaps walking around the room with a pen and adding a tick to acknowledge progress in that student's work.

Bringing student voice into the classroom can be very effective to support belonging. Allowing students to have an opinion in how things work is important, as is tailoring teaching to the students in the class. In *Attachment-Based Teaching*, Cozolino (2014) talks about creating a sense of being a bonded classroom community (he uses the word *tribe*, I prefer not to), and the sense of belonging this can create. One idea Cozolino shares is of having students, at the beginning of the school year, write about a time they experienced teaching (from anyone across any topic) that worked for them and a time when teaching did not work for them. The students then share these moments as a class. From this, the whole class gets a sense of how they prefer to be taught and what does and does not work well. The same idea can be considered for individual strengths in the class by noting who has strengths in what areas. Again, as a class this paints a picture about where the strengths lie and, more individually, who can be called on if a certain strength is required. I saw this work in a colleague's classroom, where a student could add their name to a list of people who could tie shoelaces, so others who could not knew who to go to, to get help – promoting strengths and help-seeking behaviour and as an added bonus reducing the time the teacher had to do up shoelaces!

Many classes also make class agreements together. This will work in many ways – creating ownership, being a point of reference for undesirable behaviours, helping to keep everyone accountable and building education around respect and inclusion. I have worked with teachers who facilitated classes to write their own Acknowledgements of Country, an important teaching moment about First Nations perspectives and an opportunity to create something together that is then read out each morning.

Strategies for belonging

There are so many opportunities to promote a sense of belonging in a classroom. When students have a sense of what it means to be in a particular class, things that are unique to that group, they are able to feel a part of the group in a way that can be very powerful. Classroom teachers can establish individual and group pride and cohesion in many ways that might include:

- a unique way for students to acknowledge someone
- class projects that help the school or other people
- displays that include student names, photos or work
- a regular way for teachers to acknowledge students
- establishing as a group how the class prefers to learn
- creating a display that highlights individual and group strengths
- lots of opportunity for student voice, and naming it as such
- creating a class agreement together
- crafting an Acknowledgement of Country and reading it each morning

Supporting learning

Earlier, we looked at the impacts of trauma and adversity on executive function and memory. There are many strategies that can be utilised in a classroom to support student learning. Like so many strategies in this book, they are good for all students, and even adults. When we aim to make the process of comprehending and retaining information easier, everyone benefits.

Music and movement

If you are someone who listens to the lyrics, you likely hold the lyrics to a very large number of songs in your head. Ads are the same, even when you haven't heard a jingle for decades, it can come right back to you. And you can probably remember the moves to any dance you learned, as soon as you hear the music. Experience highlights to us that when we use music or rhythm in our learning, it strengthens our memory. Multiplication tables are a perfect example of where we recite with rhythm, use repetition and learn collectively, supporting our memory and tapping into our sense of connection and belonging. I have been lucky enough to witness a class of six- and seven-year-olds singing a song together that begins with zero and counts to a melody, moving all the way through to the 'big numbers' ('The Big Numbers Song'). As students sing along to a video, they are looking at numbers like ten thousand while they name the number, working with visual recognition, repetition, singing together and building on their existing counting skills. The students love this song and it is a delight to witness (and quite a catchy tune, too).

Some use of music and movement can be to learn a specific thing, as in the case of multiplication tables or a days of the week song, and some can be to learn a learning skill such as paying attention or controlling the body. Movements that cross the midline, for example, with a hand going across the body to touch the opposite side, is improving gross motor skills, which in turn support attention and working memory (Kline, 2020). In fact, all physical movement is working to build the nerve-cell networks that are essential for all learning (Kline, 2020).

Some examples of music and movement that can support building learning skills include:

- Simon says
- days of the week or months of the year sung to a tune
- copying complicated rhythms (clapping, clicking, drumming)
- create a tableaux or freeze-frame scene
- robot/controller (one student mirrors the movements of another)
- 'I say, you say'
- singing in rounds
- dancing or following dance moves
- yoga poses
- use of breath
- slow motion movements

Learning environment

We should be aiming for a classroom environment that promotes calm. In education there are trends that often leave teachers not as in control of their classroom environment as they might like to be – think open-plan, clean walls, anchor charts, bright colours, no colour, windows that open, big classrooms, small classrooms, team teaching, single teacher classrooms.

A large study (Barrett et al., 2015) broke down the relevant factors in classroom influence on learning to three things: naturalness, individualisation and stimulation. Some elements of naturalness like light, sound, air quality and temperature are all very important, but may well be out of the control of individual teachers. However, providing a classroom that promotes a sense of ownership and community with connectedness to the rest of the school (individualisation) is entirely possible. This focus also allows teachers the opportunity to talk with students about what works for them, bringing in the important student voice.

When it comes to stimulation, it might be a case of experimentation. Teachers need to consider students' sensory needs, including understanding that they can change depending on a range of factors. When there are stimulating things in the environment, cognitive load is increased and this can negatively impact the taking in of information. In fact, closing our eyes (removing visual stimuli) has been shown to help when trying to retrieve a memory, and even just looking away from the surroundings can help working memory (Paas et al., 2020).

Searching for the right amount of stimulation, without causing overstimulation, will require adaptability. Our relationship to our environment can be led by our emotions, but it can work the other way, too, as 'Colour research shows room colour has an effect on both emotions and physiology causing mood swings that can have an impact on performance' (Barrett et al., 2015, p. 121). It is likely that finding the balance will require a bit of trial and error.

When it comes to visual supports, lanyards can also work effectively, when a teacher can have a range of visuals at their disposal, around their neck. This is standard practice in special setting schools, but work so well for any student who is easily overwhelmed, or who has English as an additional language, or benefits from getting information in a visual format. A visuals lanyard might include visuals for toilet, stop, quiet, break, food or anything else that can happen in a day.

While it might be impossible to meet the needs of all learners, there is capacity for teachers to introduce elements into their classrooms that support students to be engaged but not overstimulated. If all classrooms had access to natural light and views of nature, that would be the ideal, but there are also other factors more in a teacher's control. Here are some suggestions:

- removing excess visual noise
- neutral or warm-toned colours
- different areas in the classroom for focus time and self-directed learning time
- displays that include images of students, and student work
- anchor charts specifically relevant to the current unit of study
- visual timetables
- visual reminders of ways to help calm and focus

Sense of self interventions

There are many interventions that build a student's sense of self that we can use in classrooms and across schools. Happily, many practical strategies that are supportive for students' positive identity building are also academically beneficial, too.

Strengths and appreciations

The classroom provides so many opportunities for students to share their self-narrative, building it up as they produce more and more work in this area. Personal strengths work can be so powerful here. Character strengths or personal strengths use stemmed from the *Values in Action inventory of strengths* (VIA-IS) that has been scientifically validated (VIA Institute on Character, 2022). Researchers identified twenty-four character strengths that sit under six categories of virtue that are universally used across cultures and belief systems. They have developed a test that can ascertain one's strengths, including a test for children over ten.

When students focus on their strengths and abilities, they are reminded that they are capable. Conversely, when things are difficult for an individual, the reminder that each person has differing abilities can help a student remember that things can be achieved, even when they are not immediately easy. It is helpful, and honest, to identify that each person finds different things easier or harder.

Building a sense of self

Lots of classroom learning can support the building of a positive sense of self. There is a great crossover with literacy providing lots of opportunity for classroom teachers to integrate self-narrative into classroom learning.

For students who are part of any marginalised group in our society, it is vital that they are able to see themselves represented in our curriculum. Classroom teachers have capacity to collate materials that will support the diversity of their students to see themselves represented, and for students who might fit a dominant culture to see diversity. When we represent our diverse society in the curriculum materials, we support all students. And for those students who are under-represented when it comes to academic success, it is essential. In the simplest of concepts, 'you can't be what you can't see', a quote attributed to Marian Wright Edelman in the film *Miss Representation*, but used in a range of settings. We have an obligation to show all students that success is available to them and we need to believe it, too. As Fricker and Fricker (2022) state, in reference for First Nations students, 'Our children need to see themselves reflected in their schools. This includes flags, acknowledgement plaques, art works, library books and other ways' (para. 16).

Family narrative

Family narrative can be extremely powerful, too. I remember a class where students were asked to go home and talk to an adult about their experience of school. This was a class where most of the students had parents born outside of Australia, many with interrupted schooling themselves and with a refugee or migrant background. The stories that came back were fascinating to the students, most of whom had never asked these questions of their adults. Those who wanted to, shared the stories with their class, facilitating lots of conversation. Remember, though, not all students would have a positive experience with this activity, especially if the adults were not able to engage, or if they had schooling trauma. But in this case, it worked beautifully, often encouraging the sharing of parental self-narrative that had not previously been shared – such a powerful thing, and as previously noted, a pathway to a child's wellbeing.

Inner narrative

Studies have demonstrated that the use of self-talk allows children to better self-soothe (Siegel, 2020, p. 350), and when self-talk is positive and encouraging, it supports a positive sense of self. This can be taught as a strategy that can be used often, and in teaching it, we can also support students to notice when their self-talk is negative and to flip the script when this happens. Rather than 'I can't do it', a student might be encouraged to reframe the story to be 'I can try, even when it is hard'.

Writing tasks can also support students' inner narrative. Adhering to the basic premise that emotions are better out than in, a great activity might be journalling to practise handwriting while also providing an opportunity to work through a problem. Similarly, writing for no audience can help with stress. Interestingly, there is research that has demonstrated that doing a quick expressive writing task before a test can improve test performance, giving students the opportunity to release worries around failure (Paas et al., 2020).

Effort and success narratives

In a study of high school students about stories of success and failure it was identified that a focus on effort and competence building, when narrating stories of both success and failure, was linked with students who demonstrated higher goal persistence for several weeks and went on to receive better grades (Jones et al., 2018). What this tells us is that it is important to support students to create positive narratives about their successes and their failures with reflections that focus on the effort and the learning, even when the learning is learning what to do differently next time. The learnings from this study align with Dweck's (2015) growth mindset theory. It reinforces the idea that with effort comes growth and reminds students that they are capable of producing different outcomes based on their input.

Sense of self strategies

Strategies to build a student's sense of self to support learning can include:

- students can identify their strengths, the strengths of others and their strengths as a class
- classroom display of the students' strengths so that there is a constant reminder there for individuals
- photos identifying what happens in class, with individuals doing things that they might find tricky, as a reminder to them that they can do it

- acrostic poems, popular for decades in classrooms because they allow a child to celebrate themselves
- focus on effort so students recognise what it feels like, and link it with growth
- have students identify what led to success, what they did well and the effort they put in, supporting 'the idea that they are capable protagonists in their own lives' (Jones et al., 2018, p. 77).
- have students acknowledging any positives that have come from failure, including lessons learned, to build students' sense of their own competence, even in the face of failure
- have students interview their families
- create whole-class positive talk catchphrases
- journalling

Play

Sitting still, paying silent attention to a teacher, and focusing on abstract concepts are unnatural acts. (Cozolino, 2014, p. 160)

I do love the use of the phrase *unnatural acts* in the quote above. Particularly in the early years, schools can often be places where we are training our students to go against what their developmental level is. With pressure from parents and from education departments, many schools do not feel able to dedicate time to play as part of learning.

Play provides many varied opportunities to build social skills and skills associated with learning. Play with others supports the consolidation of executive function skills. When students have dedicated time for social play, like dress-ups and pretend play, they are building language and social skills in a low-stakes situation. When students build these language and social skills, they increase capacity to comprehend and to express themselves. In fact, studies have linked vocabulary in pre-school with both social and academic capacity in primary school (Yang & Purtell, 2022). Even from very young, children's pretend play can be quite complex, allowing for the practising of the skills of effective social communication and working memory, as well as cognitive flexibility. When students struggle with this kind of play, it can indicate that they require more scaffolding to be able to continue to build their executive function skill set. Students who are able to participate well in free play will likely also participate well in classroom learning.

Playing games with classmates also supports many important skills that help students with self-regulation and behaviour such as turn taking (inhibitory control), regulating with peers and working memory. Physical games can be great, too, for remembering the rules, quick decision-making and self-control, which can all be built during games like tiggy or dodgeball (Center on the Developing Child at Harvard University, 2022). I recall a student discovering the rules page in a board game, astonished that such a thing existed, making us realise that for this student, even the concept of a board game was foreign.

Playing learning games in the classroom can support student skill-building as the adult scaffolding can be significant as students learn the game, but then be removed.

Strategies to include play

- use games as reward for periods of 'hard work time'
- set up a 'game show'
- games hour weekly, offering a range of board games
- use dice or cards in numeracy lessons, teaching turn taking and collaboration
- in junior grades have a room, or corner of a room, that is for pretend play, with equipment relating to the curriculum, such as a shop when studying a money unit
- have students design their own game
- include role play and performance such as joke-telling
- use games as brain breaks
- have fun with your class

Whole-class game ideas

I have always been astonished at how much students enjoy a game, even when it is quite basic. Here are just a few, but there are an innumerable number out there.

- The game called Rock is a favourite, where a few students work silently to try to make all the other students, who are standing in a line, laugh.

- Silent ball is like magic, where something is thrown from student to student, in silence, with students 'out' with a bad throw or bad catch, the game getting progressively harder, perhaps standing on one foot, or catching with just one hand.
- Guess the number, just by identifying whether it is higher or lower.
- 21 – in a circle, beginning with number 1, students count on by 1, 2 or 3 – if you have to say 21, you're out!
- Charades.
- Shopping list – where each student adds to a list, needing to remember the list as it grows.
- Sausage – where one student is asked questions by the others, and must only answer 'sausage' without laughing.
- Rock, paper, scissors, using various words, and played in groups.
- Musical statues.

Hope

Hope is something that is essential when we are dealing with all students, but particularly the ones who are communicating via challenging behaviours. As we have established, students follow our lead, so it is vital that we hold hope for the future of these students. How, you might ask, when sometimes they have everything going against them including the system we are working in? It can indeed be extremely challenging and it is important to consider that we don't always get to see the impact of our positive interventions. But we are always laying the foundation for the future.

When we think about promoting hope, we can consider both the internal drivers and the systems and community around the individual. Colla et al. (2022) reference 'the importance of broader system influences in the emergence of hope' (p. 8) as relevant to the way that hope arises. Our schools can facilitate hope in us and our students or can negatively influence it. We can consider the combination of internal and external resources as equally important and go on to do our best with supporting both.

Referencing research by Colla et al. (2022) identify that 'high hope individuals actively seek the support of others in working toward their goals but are also likely to support the goal pursuits of others that serve to strengthen social bonds' (p. 10). This idea helps us to focus the promotion of hope around achievable goals, including wellbeing goals as well as the classroom aims of working together, supporting each other and sharing strengths and goals as a class. The balance of high expectations, optimism, hope and a solid knowledge of the impacts of trauma and adversity is quite a balance. But it is possible, along with a few hiccoughs and tricky days.

As always, these lofty ideals of how we operate with our students comes with the caveat that we will not always be able to do it. Sometimes things feel too challenging and that is okay. We need to make room for our own uncomfortable feelings when they come up and in giving them space, often we will be able to put them to bed and come back fresh for another go. When we are unable to come back fresh, or unable to see a way through for our challenging students, it is not a tenable situation.

Conclusion

We have such a powerful opportunity to holistically address the struggles of our students. With knowledge, we can begin to see that behaviour is always a form of communication. We can see the links between motor skills, cognition, memory, physical and mental health, behaviour, stress and life experiences. When we support our students to build their capacity when it comes to recognising the messages their bodies give them, it helps them to learn how to regulate, but this is definitely not a quick fix. Again, it is important to point out that we are not just talking about children who have experienced abuse or neglect, but also those who have experienced things like the loss of a parent, medical trauma, parental mental illhealth, who might live with their own mental health challenges, or who might just have a very sensitive temperament. Helping children learn about their bodies and their feelings, how to ask for help, to self-regulate and recognise when they feel safe or unsafe is a skill set that will benefit any student and promote a wonderful school culture.

There are so many reasons why children's behaviour is challenging, and none of the reasons are that the child is bad or unteachable. It is the responsibility of educators to find a way to educate, to meet the student where they are at and to teach at their point of need. Educators working with students who have challenging behaviours need to be supported to support the student. Students need a team around them, sharing the learning journey. With time, understanding and a plan, a student's academic and behavioural skills will grow and they will flourish.

10

BEHAVIOURAL STRATEGIES FOR INDIVIDUAL STUDENTS

Our schooling system was not designed to be tailored to individuals, but we can find ways to do just this, creating spaces that feel safe and enjoyable in the process. Here, we will look at some of the things that can positively impact an individual's behaviour.

It is important to note that we always need to begin with the strategies mentioned in the previous chapters to build safety in classrooms and in relationships first. For some of our students, all our skills and strategies will fall flat if we don't understand what the student is really communicating to us via their behaviour.

It is also worth noting that we all bounce around with our energy levels and while it is very useful to know how to bring ourselves back to our window of tolerance, it is also normal and expected to move outside that window at times.

Responding to student behaviour

Responding to a student who is behaving in a way not conducive to learning can occur in different ways, but there are two main approaches we can look at as ways that we often use, either beginning with the brain, or beginning with the body – sometimes referred to as *top down* or *bottom up* (Brunzell & Norrish, 2021; Ogden et al., 2006; Porges, 2017; Teicher et al., 2016).

Top down

Attempting to engage a student's thinking brain is top-down regulation. Top-down regulation means working with cognitive capacity to alter behaviour. We often start with connecting with a student's brain by appealing to a student's better judgement. We might try to engage with what we know of them by saying things like, 'Come on, I know you can make a better choice', or trying to plead or bargain to squeeze a little more from their capacity, 'Only two more minutes on the floor, then we will get up'. We may try to engage some empathy, 'You're making it hard for those around you to learn', but essentially what we are doing is connecting with a student thinking-brain. In some cases (for minor infractions from non-traumatised students), this will work, although generally, not in the moment.

When a student is hyper-aroused, their needs are to calm and return to equilibrium. How easy it would be if students would simply respond to our requests at times like this, or even to their own thinking brain. As one student said to me, 'I tried to tell myself to not do it, but I did it anyway'. Similarly, Brunzell and Norrish (2021) state, 'Time and time again we witness students who struggle through the school day because their own bodies are unable to do what their minds tell them to do: to sit still, listen, and complete the learning tasks' (p. 86).

Top-down regulation strategy examples include:

- teaching the Resilience, Rights and Respectful Relationships program
- social-emotional learning
- social-emotional skills such as recognising emotions and intensity of emotions
- check-ins (in classroom)
- teaching interoceptive skills
- explicitly teaching the link between bodily sensations and emotion
- restorative justice approaches
- reset conversations

Bottom up

The opposite of brain-based strategies to help with regulation are the bottom-up approaches that begin with the body. These strategies might include inviting a student to go for a walk; having the whole class take a brain break; time in a class reset space; or accessing sensory toys. For students to understand their behaviours, their brain and their nervous systems, we need to use bottom-up approaches to shift states of extreme dysregulation before we can attempt to engage a top-down approach. Ideally, we will use both approaches and help a student to learn their own strategies.

Bottom-up regulation strategy examples include:

- kinetic sand or play dough
- calm colouring
- meditation or calming music
- creating a rhythm with body like clapping or patting thighs
- singing
- bouncing a ball
- dancing, running or aerobics

It is important to remember that these strategies might need to be used for students who are hypo-aroused, too. These students may be harder to spot, but are just as detached from their learning. For these students, energising activities are going to be what helps them move to being present.

Using both bottom-up and top-down approaches together allows an in-the-moment response, but also provides opportunity for a reduction in the need for future adult intervention. Our aim is to move toward self-regulation with less reliance on co-regulation.

Individualising approaches to regulating

At my school some years ago we began a process that supported students to have meaningful conversations with an adult about what was getting in the way of their learning and what they could do about it. We called these conversations 'resets'. Brunzell and Norrish (2021) make reference to a similar idea with their 'triage conversations'. These conversations are an opportunity to look at what went wrong and why, and what a student could do to prevent it from happening in the future by building the relevant skills. In having this time to explore behaviour, a student builds their capacity to understand themselves and to build strategies that work for them, now and into the future. Identifying the strategies that work for them can help a student create a personal toolkit.

The strategies might need to be about dealing with anger, or improving focus, or working on staying present. Building these skills may well take a long time. The conversations might also be happening to support a student during a hard time. There have been many occasions where a student came to have a chat every day for months. I have heard the suggestion (many times) that they just want to get out of class, which begs the question: why? My experience is that students want to be in class with their peers and their teacher, unless something is getting in the way. In one example I had a student spend time with me every day after they had lost a parent. Although we didn't talk about that loss specifically, the time together was therapeutic and the student eventually reduced, then (mostly) ceased the visits.

In another situation a young student had lots of trouble containing impulses in class so often needed a break. The visit was often suggested by a teacher, and the student and I would talk about how to build the skills to be able to tolerate longer times in class. Again, over some months, possibly a year, these visits reduced and subsided, until I would be seeing the student in the halls and feel compelled to check in to find out how everything was going because I missed our regular catch-ups. For each student, the intervention lasted just as long as it needed to.

The information gained during resets can be used in behaviour support plans and shared with families. The reset conversations are not a place for judgement, but a place for compassion, understanding and practical support. They are not punishment. Resetting within the class space is often ideal, but not always possible. The calm spaces in a classroom provide this opportunity to reset without the adult guidance, but for those students who need greater support, a reset can work really well.

For an intervention like resets to work, a whole school needs to be on board. A person, or people, need to be available and shared expectations need to exist. Teachers need to have the opportunity to refer students out for a reset and students need to be able to negotiate with teachers about a self-referral. Sometimes, if the student–teacher relationship is a priority, the better approach might be for the classroom teacher to have the opportunity to support the reset, while a wellbeing person is in the classroom with other students. All of these elements can be negotiated when it is a whole-school approach.

Responding to incidents

Sometimes a student is so distressed or angry or in a trigger response so severe that their behaviour is a potential danger to themselves or others, or they might be behaving in a way that is frightening to those around them. This happens in all schools and it is important to know how to respond in the moment and afterward. Seeing a student in distress can be incredibly difficult, and when we witness extreme anger or violence, we are seeing that distress play out.

One of the most distressing and profound moments I have had at school was witnessing this kind of extreme behaviour in a student. I mentioned this student earlier, the one with a parent who said they were 'the bad one' – no coincidence, I am sure. After the student stopped their screaming and lashing out, they collapsed into the arms of a teacher. The teacher held the student, rocking instinctively and making soothing noises, while the student sobbed. I don't think anyone present will forget that image. What a reminder of the power of educators who can bring such generosity of connection to a situation and provide a safe haven for a student who has experienced great adversity.

When you are the adult present during an incident, it is vital that you maintain your own self-regulation or sub out (if a colleague is available). You can use vocal tone, face, body and breath to support regulation and thus co-regulation. Speak calmly, attempt to regulate your breathing, and think about maintaining a face that demonstrates calm and connection (Harris, 2016).

Remember the phrase 'Connection before correction' (Siegel & Bryson, 2011), regardless of what the student has done. First, we connect and only when the student is feeling safe, comes the opportunity to talk about what happened. A sense of safety might come from the location you are in, the proximity you maintain, your calm voice. A friend or staff member might help. Attempts to redirect and re-engage the student include re-engaging the prefrontal cortex – the thinking brain. Sometimes a student will respond to a question that is easy to answer like, 'Can you see three red things?', 'What is your sister's name?', 'Can we count backwards from 20?'. To offer simple choices can also help return a student to calm and safety (Australian Childhood Foundation, 2018; Harris, 2016).

Recovery is so important. You, the student and any others involved will have had a rush of stress hormones. Staff members affected should take a minimum of ten minutes of time away from students. Affected students need to have a quiet place and a staff member with them. Taking time out for affected staff members is a strategy for the prevention of burnout, as it allows the nervous system to begin to calm and for the affected staff member to ascertain what it is that they need. More time may be required and it is important to take as much time as needed. We might need different things depending on the day, the week, the student involved. Consider this recovery time a wise investment. Missing a small amount of face-to-face teaching time at this stage can prevent lots of time being missed at a later time.

Debriefing is an important part of the process, as it has been shown that debriefing supports staff to leave an incident at work and not 'bring it home'. An incident report might provide an opportunity for a written debrief, or to tell what happened as someone writes it for you. It might feel right to talk about the incident to a colleague, someone who was also present, someone from your wellbeing or leadership teams, a friend at work or even someone from employee assistance if you have access.

When you have had to deal with a confronting incident, allow your response to come. Know that it might be distress, anger or any other emotion. Know that it is typical to have an emotional reaction to a child, adult or family in distress. Acknowledging where there is inequity in a situation is important, as is recognising that you are not in control of others' circumstances, but that you are contributing positively as an educator.

Differentiating behaviour supports

Behaviour that disrupts the learning process must be addressed without exception, but also without disrupting the students' connection with the school community. Exclusionary policies such as suspension and expulsion only reinforce students' feelings of rejection and low self-worth. (Jennings, 2019, p. 90)

Like all teaching, the teaching of behaviour needs to be differentiated. If there is one thing to take from this book and into your classroom, it is this. If we practise zero tolerance or one rule for all, we are punishing those students who have not learned the skills we want them to have. We would never do such a thing with teaching academic skills. We don't simply teach everyone at the same level and then punish those who do not get it right. There is plenty of evidence to demonstrate the zero-tolerance approach to violence in schools, popular in America, did not work (Brunzell & Norrish, 2021; Greene, 2014). It did, in fact, disproportionally negatively impact students of colour and students living with disability.

What punishment does is fulfil a desire to punish. It is much more about the adults involved than about the student, as Lewis (2015) states, 'After all, what good does it do to punish a child who literally hasn't yet acquired the brain functions required to control his behavior?' (para. 13). A particularly helpful intervention is for the educators in a classroom to have access to a list of all the students in order of age. This can be very helpful, particularly in the younger years, but really across all year levels, to be reminded that one class can have students born over a year apart with similar expectations placed on them. Our students will all be developing at differing rates, based on experience as discussed, but also based on age.

Having logical reasons for challenging behaviours does not mean that there should not be consequences for behaviour, but they should be natural consequences – many of which happen as a matter of course, and our role might just be to point them out. Restorative conversations mean confronting the impact of one's behaviour on others; cleaning up messes made is a natural consequence; spending time in more controlled environments when looser activities prove too much of a challenge provides opportunities to practise skills in a safer environment.

Individual approaches

The use of behaviour support plans that include information about a student's background and about where we believe tricky behaviours are coming from can help with differentiating behaviour supports. When we see behaviour that is harmful or not appropriate, we can look at what we know about a student to make a guess about where such behaviours might be beginning. We can identify which behaviours we would prefer to be seeing and pinpoint the skills that need to be built for that student to have a chance at demonstrating the behaviours that will help them to feel a sense of belonging. Once we know what skills a student needs, we can start to make a plan to build them. When designing a behaviour support plan you might want to consider adding relevant history, a de-escalation plan, a functions of behaviour chart, what has already worked and what staff might like to try. It is always a work in progress.

Sensory profiles can also be useful. If you are lucky enough to have access to an occupational therapist, they can assist in creating a sensory profile. If not, you can create one based on your own observations. It is so helpful to know what a student's sensory needs are and how they can be met to facilitate a sense of calm and safety. The student I mentioned back in Chapter 5, who was often at the back of the class rolling on the floor, had clear proprioceptive needs. Because it was important to them to have the pressure sending signals to the brain to meet these needs the teacher did not stop this behaviour, but rather made sure the student was in a place on the floor where there was space and that it did not interrupt any other students. Gathering data about sensory seeking or avoiding can help us get to know what will support our students.

One reason that individual approaches are so important is that it means we can approach a student holistically, looking at their wellbeing and academic needs together, identifying where there might be a crossover.

There is strong evidence that links behavioural challenges to speech and language challenges (Carpenter & Drabick, 2011; Curtis et al., 2018; Greene, 2014). This makes a great deal of sense when we consider the impact of not being able to communicate easily. Other conditions that impact communication or comprehension or impulsivity can all also lead to behavioural challenges. It can be very useful to investigate different contributing factors of a student's struggles through resources such as language assessments. A student who has been exposed to early-life adversity in the form of inadequate parental attention might come to school with a small vocabulary. This in itself is a barrier to expression and comprehension, likely leading to times when communication occurs in the form of behaviour, rather than words. For students who have not been spoken to much, and not participated in the 'serve and return' style of communication that parents and children often engage in, they have not had the opportunity to gain the speaking and listening skills that are essential, and expected, at school. These missing experiences can occur for families living with high stress, with parents who work long hours, where older siblings play the role of surrogate parents, or where parents and children do not share a first language, as sometimes occurs in families with a migrant or refugee background. Any of these scenarios would need to be taken into account and students supported accordingly.

Interventions

We have touched upon a range of interventions that support individuals' behaviour, schools can tailor their interventions to suit their student cohort, but here are some options:

- remember that behaviour is communication
- assume students have complex lives
- keep a list of students ranked by age

- facilitate restorative conversations
- teach, don't punish
- work on individual skills, one at a time
- create individualised behaviour support plans
- create individualised de-escalation plans
- access speech and language assessments
- build student sensory profiles
- have a mentoring program, offering 1:1 time
- build a student's emotion vocab
- make use of visuals to identify emotions

Structural inequity

As we explored earlier, the inequity that we find in our society exists in our classrooms and schools and has a detrimental impact on our students. As educators, we have an obligation to do all in our power to both mitigate the impacts of inequity and to fight against it. When it comes to behaviour support, this can take many forms. To reiterate what has already been said, we need to see children holistically, which includes the consideration of social inequities like racism, poverty, homophobia and transphobia, and ableism. In Chapter 1 we looked at the way that living with these kinds of inequities and discrimination can create a state of chronic stress, makes the impacts of other traumas worse and may play out in a student's behaviour. Behaviour is communication and a student who is carrying the burden of chronic stress and trauma will show us with behaviour, if not in words.

Schools are relentlessly judged on academic outcomes rather than academic growth or pastoral care. Schools lacking high academic results are deemed as underperforming, resulting in targeting teachers for extra training with the perception that this is where the issue lies. When asking a young colleague, about to graduate as a teacher, how she was finding the Department of Education's online behaviour support training, she said it was good, but it did assume that there was a high-functioning class with only one student who was struggling with behaviour. What she felt was missing was information about how to triage behaviours in class when there are multiple students struggling, potentially setting each other off. We still work with an understanding in schools that the vast majority of students will be able to cope with the day-to-day business of sitting and listening, interacting calmly with peers, following instructions and being tuned in. However, as I have laid out, it is more common to have some schools with a statistically higher number of students with behavioural challenges than we'd expect.

The myth of educational equity

Although we know about the impact of early adversity, it is fair to say that it is up to individual schools to address the ways that trauma and adversity play out via behaviour in schools. Trauma often does not factor in the running of schools, except as an add-on or where individual schools prioritise the work. As Alverez et al. (2016) state:

> *The ways in which trauma is recognised and acknowledged in schools may disallow certain experiences to 'count' as traumatic experiences. In particular the dominant view of trauma invalidates other forms of trauma, and, in particular, the ways that factors such as race and poverty influence trauma. However research indicates that when a person is subjected to any conditions situations or events that produce high levels of stress, trauma is more likely to occur. (p. 29)*

This quote points out that ongoing and systemic experiences of discrimination are often not recognised as traumatic, and yet, as we have identified, the kind of chronic stress that is the result is very likely to eventuate in a traumatic stress response. The fact that much of the 'minority stress' experience is built into systems is an important factor that can make it difficult for those in the dominant culture to identify.

Though schools are funded with a model designed to compensate for students who may need additional support, based on factors such as family income and language background, anecdotal evidence would suggest that when a school services a neighbourhood where the majority of their students live with adversity, the cumulative impact means that this additional funding support is not enough. Added to this is the way that some schools deal with challenging behaviours, namely to remove the students from the school. This happens often and adds to the imbalance between schools, as some become known for supporting students with high behavioural needs, and thus take on students who have been expelled from other schools with a zero-tolerance approach.

Interventions for individuals

As we have identified so far in this chapter, one-size-fits-all approaches just don't have the nuance required to meet the needs of the wonderfully individual students we have in our classrooms. Each student comes to us with their own life experience, attachment experience, pre-school educational experience, sensory needs, physiological make-up, etc. There are many interventions that can apply to individuals; here are some we have touched on:

- 'resets' or similar, allowing students to have specific skill-building interventions designed for them
- classroom list of all students in age order
- behaviour support plans
- de-escalation plans
- sensory profiles
- pointing out natural consequences
- restorative conversations
- use of comics or drawing to demonstrate perspective taking
- social stories
- bringing educators together to discuss a student holistically
- language assessments where appropriate
- educators understanding the impacts of systemic harm

Measuring growth

The growth of trauma-affected students can be hard to spot. When the huge focus for a student is just being in the school environment in a way that works for them, you might not see the growth where you would traditionally look for it. I am a big fan of celebrating the small wins. Keeping regular student notes can be really helpful, and looking back can be illuminating when we don't notice the day-to-day changes. It is so important to pause and reflect.

When students have behaviour support plans, there is a clear opportunity to set simple goals and return regularly to see how progress is going. These plans are a very helpful way to measure growth in the tricky area of behaviour. They can involve the student and parents as well as relevant school staff, so that goals are meaningful and relevant and celebrations of growth can be shared. Other growth measures need to be relevant to the student. You might use a measure such as the *Wellbeing, stress and distress questionnaire* (Government of South Australia, Department for Education, 2020) to look at the growth and shift in a student's behaviours and feelings. There may be other scales that might be appropriate. You could even use students' drawings to show shifts in how they view themselves or their connection to school. You might also have school measures, such as how often a student needs to check in with an adult regarding behaviour skills or attendance data, or perhaps how frequently they require tools that you have in place such as use of a calm corner. You can work with a student to look at goals that are meaningful to them, while maintaining an approach that highlights that all growth is to be celebrated. It is also important not to be hard on ourselves, or our students, when we don't reach a goal.

Rebecca Eanes (2022) states, 'All emotions are data' (para. 12). We want our students to feel good. We want to reduce the instances of those tricky feelings that can lead to behavioural struggles. Practising tuning in to feelings allows us to track how we are going with making school a safe place for a student and we can monitor our own feelings, too. We can learn from our emotions and we can teach with our emotions. We want our students to be attuned to themselves and others, so we should model it. Getting into the habit of regular emotional check-ins can help with looking at how we are tracking day-to-day.

Conclusion

Differentiation is essential to good teaching practice, and when we get to know our students really well, we can support their learning by supporting their regulation, too. Each of our students comes to us with a history and with a current living experience. The more we can notice what is going on for them as individuals, as well as meeting whole-class needs, the better chance we have at creating an equitable classroom to meet the needs of all.

Of course, we all get dysregulated. One of the most powerful things an educator can do is to understand their own regulation. As the quote attributed to Socrates states, 'To know thyself is the beginning of wisdom', and educators are supposed to be wise! By knowing ourselves, we can better support our students to know themselves, we can model, we can teach, we can bring compassion, and we can bring an individualised response to each of our students.

11

EMBEDDING A WHOLE-SCHOOL APPROACH

Educational equity is the work of ensuring that all students have access to a high-quality education and the resources they need to be successful in school. (Venet, 2021, p. 11)

Throughout the second part of this book, I am working with ideals. I know that schools are busy places, at the whim of departmental policies, education trends and the wishes of those in leadership roles. I believe it is important to maintain an idealistic view of how things should be and then do what we can. As Venet (2021) says, we should start where we are and work within our sphere of influence. I have explored a range of interventions in the previous two chapters that can be used for whole classes and for individual students, and I hope that feels empowering for educators. Being able to make a classroom feel safe and nurturing, or having a relationship that can facilitate those powerful, life-changing moments with students and families is something that an individual teacher can do.

The next two chapters is where we get to dream about whole schools being able to commit to trauma-informed practice and embedded student wellbeing practices. While this may not be the case in your school, know that each move you, as an individual or a team, make toward the ideal is an important step in the right direction. Individual teachers can make a difference, whole schools can make even more of a difference and 'Sometimes teaching itself is a life-changing intervention' (Venet, 2021, p. 157).

Environment and culture

School gestures like appreciation days or meditation sessions are meaningful when they are accompanied by a genuine commitment to staff mental health. School staff members should feel okay to identify when they need a mental health day, they should feel able to express their feelings to each other and to leadership about things that are happening at school, and broadly in the education system. Leadership should be available to hear, with an attitude of unconditional positive regard and compassion, what is going on for staff. Without this commitment, any teacher appreciation morning tea is going to leave a bitter taste. Leadership should also talk to someone else themselves, and in some states, this might be built in as a principal support, but in many cases it will be up to individuals to seek their own access to reflective practice opportunities.

The culture of a school will likely be evident in everything that happens at the school. A school that values relationships will demonstrate this in all interactions, a school that values all educators will have a more harmonious workforce, a school that puts students at the centre of decisions will have students who feel valued and a 'vibe' as soon as you enter. A school operating with compassion and unconditional positive regard will be palpable to visitors.

Schools that wish to truly have a culture of embedded student wellbeing can keep it front and centre. Link to your wellbeing policy in job ads, put students at the centre, even when that might seem to require more work or not always align with departmental policies. There are so many opportunities in schools to put our students at the centre. When I visited a secondary school that had no school uniform, the Assistant Principal identified that he was never willing, when working at a school with a school uniform, to have a conversation with children about their 'inappropriate' socks when instead he had the opportunity to ask them how they were going. Taking all the moments available to have positive interactions with students sets the tone at a school and models to everyone what the school values. Appropriate socks, however, sets a tone that is entirely unrelated to student wellbeing.

Individual schools can create their own rituals and routines and can collect data to support this. School culture, like family culture, can be individualised to support the individuals that create the collective. At my school I have collected years of data that looked at student wellbeing interventions.

It was fascinating to note that while the need for interventions differed based on a range of things – for example, our building was renovated while we remained inside and it wreaked havoc on students' and staff nervous systems – the pattern of our terms and our year was more or less the same. I could overlay the line graphs of years and see a pattern. What is it exactly about Term 2, Week 3, I do not know, but it was always a tricky one! The years that we experienced many lockdowns messed up my data collection, but it will be interesting to see what the following years look like and if we return to our former patterns. Having this information, taking the pulse of a whole school, allows us to see ourselves as a whole and to note our collective, shared experience.

High expectations

Maintaining high expectations for students gives the message that we believe in them and their ability. In some instances, we might need to honestly share feedback with students, letting them know that certain aspects of learning might indeed be harder for them. Being clear that different brains and different nervous systems can make school easier or harder acknowledges that individuals are different. While acknowledging the additional difficulties, we can approach their learning honestly, while continuing to demonstrate our high expectations and encouraging aspirational approaches by the students.

Relationships

A whole-school approach to embedded student wellbeing will receive the bonus of embedded staff wellbeing. As mentioned in the previous chapter, student and staff wellbeing go hand in hand. When the relationships at school are attuned and predictable, when staff know themselves and their own nervous system, and there is a culture of openness and honesty, then you have a great place to work and a great place to learn. Education is a challenging environment. With competing demands from parents, students and education departments, and the judgement of policymakers and the media, it is important that schools are places where educators feel safe, seen, heard and cared for. When we commit to positive relationships across a school, it benefits absolutely everyone within the school. Bringing our whole selves to school can place us in a vulnerable position, but it can also make our workplaces richer and extend the life of our careers in education. Staff should never feel that they can't ask for help, nor should they feel that they are enacting policies that harm students or families.

When we are asking our students to show us and each other respect, we need to model that. While it has not been traditional for adults in schools to treat students with respect and unconditional positive regard, it is essential if we wish to embed student wellbeing. When we can apologise if we get something wrong, express how we are feeling or extend all the common courtesies to our students, we can expect to see these ways of relating reflected back to us. One rule for adults and another for students is, when it comes to respect, not appropriate. Every moment is a teachable one.

Families and community

Families can be such an asset to schools and to students. When we work together, we can achieve great things. Engaging families can be challenging, but it should be something that a school maintains a focus on and does not give up on. Of course, many of our parents arrive at school with their own histories of adversity, and possibly with negative (or no) school experiences, too. School might not feel like a safe place. It is not our role to judge, but to welcome them as fellow educators and to support them to see themselves that way, if they don't already.

A large global study on parental engagement in education identified that 'across the world, parents and caregivers uniformly want to be engaged in their children's education – regardless of education level or socio-economic status – but did not always know how' (Winthrop, 2022, para. 5). Many parents reported feeling shut out of their children's schools. Just because you invite and welcome parents, does not necessarily mean they will feel welcome. Similarly, if they don't come, it doesn't mean you should stop asking. When we remain open and with a stance of unconditional positive regard, willing to be attuned to families' needs, adaptable and willing to persevere, we can make significant changes.

I know of one school that had stopped holding parent–teacher meetings because they said no one came. With a new Principal and a new approach, they began again. Early on, very few people came, but the school persevered. They ensured there were plenty of interpreters, they were adaptable and made it work when allocated times were not adhered to. They ensured parents were able to meet with teachers whenever they came. Teachers were friendly and welcoming and did not talk down to parents. Ten years later, almost every student had a caregiver attend, and the ones who couldn't make it were given alternative options, including holding the meeting in the yard over a walk for a parent who did not feel comfortable coming into school.

Face-to-face meetings give the opportunity for staff and caregivers to come together to talk about the students. At these meetings we do need to share information, but we also need to listen. Really engaging families means hearing what they have to say, understanding their aspirations for their children, understanding where there are barriers and really understanding how we can work together in the service of our students.

When families live with stress and adversity, schools are in a unique position to build relationships. We might see parents or caregivers more than they see anyone from any other organisation. It can be very helpful for wellbeing teams to have knowledge of where families could be referred to when they ask for support, and how the referral processes work. Warm referrals are ideal, when we know the person at the other end of the referral and we can vouch for them. If we are able to provide a safe enough environment, we might be lucky enough to gain the trust of families so that we can learn how we can offer support, and also hear the ways that family members might wish to engage or participate at school. These ways don't need to be anything traditional and schools should be open to a range of ways that parents might engage.

Avoiding retraumatisation

It is vital to understand that schools can easily be traumatic places, retraumatising vulnerable students and family members. Schools should ensure that any trauma-informed or student wellbeing approach is known well by every staff member, so that every single interaction at school is as safe as it can be for students and their families, no matter who it is with. Those staff in a school who are the welcomers, at the reception or front desk, need to be part of this approach. They are vital. Often these staff in schools have a multitude of jobs and deal with a range of frustrations, yet by remaining calm and inviting they can set the tone as a family's first engagement with a school.

Curiosity, joy and exploration

Schools can reject the traditional use of fear of punishment or shaming and instead commit to a focus on curiosity, joy and exploration (Cozolino, 2014). This antidote to fear and shame can be facilitated by compassion-engaged educators.

A whole-school approach should educate staff about what is effective for students, and it is important that any educators who might be inclined toward strategies such as shame question why it might be a go-to for them, and what they can replace it with. Educating staff about the impact of their behaviour can support the elimination of fear and shame strategies. A school culture that embraces curiosity, joy and exploration provides many opportunities for student-led learning, as well as for positive coping strategies. When we can be curious about what is going on for us, rather than judging, we are on the way to acceptance of ourselves in all our complexity.

Reducing trauma for families

Family members are vulnerable to experiencing fear and shame in schools, too. For family members living with adversity, there can be a power imbalance when dealing with school administration. Things like having to discuss payments or needing to fill out forms when literacy is an issue can generate strong emotions, even when staff members are kind. Schools should consider all the ways that they can communicate their care and lack of judgement about these things. So often families have to approach schools to ask for help, but help should be something that is advertised as available and easy to access, whether that is financial, or other supports.

Caregivers might have had terrible experiences in their own education settings and school could easily be a trigger for them. Perhaps popping in to chat with the Principal is not a big deal at your school, but for a parent who remembers violent encounters with their childhood Principal, they may be very reluctant or even have a trigger response to being invited in. Bringing ourselves to parents is one way we can reduce the chances of school being retraumatising. Wandering out at the end of the day with the students, being available for a casual chat, a hello, getting to see the younger siblings or just being present for families can be a really lovely end to the day and also a gentle way to connect, especially as this is an opportunity to share a positive story about their child.

Big transitions

While we have talked about the multiple transitions that occur in a school day, and the way they impact students, here, we will look at the really big transitions that happen for our students.

Some primary schools don't have a culture of linking with local kindergartens or secondary schools, and some schools do it really well. Being able to do a warm handover for our students can be so valuable, we can help students and their families to feel safe when we know the names and routines at the place their child is coming from or going to.

Transition to primary school

Lots of primary schools now have a comprehensive transition program for pre-schoolers. This usually occurs in the latter part of the year before they transition to beginning primary school. This is a great start to school, providing the opportunity for students to get a sense of the school, the staff and the routine. These programs also give us educators a chance to meet our new families, to make ourselves known and to begin building those new relationships. If we are committed to being a school that supports families, this is a great opportunity to show this off.

I have been part of a transition program that, when working at its best (able to be staffed, unaffected by lockdowns) involved the pre-schoolers working with two educators, while the wellbeing and community staff connected with parents. This meant everyone had the opportunity to meet and conduct an informal interview. This was the perfect set-up to start the following year with existing positive relationships.

Working with local Kindergartens can provide opportunities for children to come to school for a visit in their Kinder year. When cohorts move together, Kinders and schools have the opportunity to share wellbeing programs. For families living with adversity, individualised transitions that include lots of support and information sharing can support this big experience.

Transition to secondary school

The transition to secondary school could do with a lot of work. Students at an age with potentially poor reasoning skills and high risk-taking tendencies head off to a new environment that provides them with a false sense of student independence. While our twelve- and thirteen-year-olds should indeed be experiencing more independence, it is also vital that they are well supported by the adults around them.

Primary schools can help with as much preparation as possible for this tricky transition, explicitly teaching the skills that will be required at secondary school, such as reading a diary and a timetable, adapting to multiple subjects each day and managing homework from all of them. Allowing time and space to discuss fears, concerns and exciting feelings, too, can also support students to feel more ready for secondary school.

Schools might run an in-house transition program, or might partner with a secondary school, or a youth service to talk through these preparations. I have been involved in these programs and the student feedback is positive, particularly when we have been able to bring in some early secondary school students to share their experiences. The school setting change is significant and the concerns students have are not always what we might expect. Having students who have recently been through the experience can be so illuminating.

Good relationships between primary and secondary schools are important, too, as well as appropriate information sharing, with the student at the centre, ensuring that important student information is not lost between schools. Parents might also like to be supported with the transition to secondary school, including with things such as knowing how to access financial support, understanding new systems around communication with school and other things.

Intervention teams

Embedding student wellbeing across a school is an opportunity to look at both academic and wellbeing interventions together. I have been part of an intervention team that included leadership, a speech pathologist, an intervention teacher and student wellbeing staff. When we look at students holistically, we can see the areas where they might struggle and the areas where they are strong. We can also potentially have some insight into how to bring families on board.

This intervention team I belonged to was actually born during a COVID-19 lockdown, in an attempt to do our best to ensure students were getting what they needed (to the best of our ability). A benefit of online learning was that we had more time to meet. We decided to continue to meet once school was back face-to-face. It is helpful for each of us to know what the others are doing with individuals or groups of students. It is also the case that one member of the team might have an insight that could be really useful for another team member. While it is the case occasionally that a student might have needs in just academics, or just wellbeing, it is still helpful to bounce ideas for these students around.

An intervention team might meet weekly, fortnightly or a few times a term. The size of the school, and thus the team, might be an influence here. It is helpful for the meetings to have structure so that general intervention issues are discussed along with the opportunity to talk about individual students.

It can be helpful to have a big picture view – what does a multi-tiered system of support look like for literacy, numeracy and wellbeing? How do we decide who gets the precious intervention time? This is an opportunity to have those thorny ethical discussions about allocation of resources. For example, what about the student with terrible attendance? Do we allocate them more time due to need, or less because they don't turn up? How do we measure our success? A team approach is important here, knowing that the data makes sense across the school. For individual students, an intervention team provides a chance for a group of people all invested in the same outcome to consider what the best approaches will be. We can share insights since a strategy that might work in wellbeing intervention might also work in literacy intervention. It can also be very powerful for students to know that we talk about them and are unified in our caring.

By coming together with our knowledge that wellbeing and academic success are intrinsically linked, we can share our approaches and support students in a range of ways. We can also help to keep each other accountable, ensuring we access evidence-informed interventions. A recent literature review by the Australian Independent Schools Association, looking at a range of approaches to wellbeing in schools, identified that whole-school approaches that make a use of a team-based approach were the most effective. They also point to 'the need for key facilitators to be approachable and unambiguously interested in the students' wellbeing' (Runions et al., 2021, p. 2). In addition, they identify that approaches need to be able to be tailored to the school community, an important role for the team. When we can come together to help our students, things do seem more achievable.

Equity and addressing structural impacts

> *Education is not an equalizer... children's future economic success is more strongly related to that of their parents than to their own educational attainment. When we repeat the false narrative that anyone can succeed if they just pull themselves up by their bootstraps, kids blame themselves for a lack of success. (Carnevale et al., 2019, p. 165)*

We may have come a long way since Mr Smith in my Year 8 maths class wouldn't let me do the extension work because I was a girl, but there is still a significant way to go. While conversations around gender inequity in education have improved, those around the inequities of class and race still leave us with plenty of work to do. Sexism is discussed in schools in a way that class and race are not and, in most schools, homophobia and transphobia are also not topics for discussion. This is an example of how institutions can be harmful. By not naming these elements of our society, we gaslight those people impacted as though no harm is occurring contributing to minority stress and all the implications of this.

As educators, I would argue that we have a moral imperative to address inequity in a range of ways. As Dudgeon et al. (2014) point out, 'An institution can engage in racist practices without any of its members being individually racist' (p. 15), and so while our individual approach is important, we are still working in a system that in most instances, in most schools, engages in harmful and discriminatory practices. When schools acknowledge and address this, they go some way to creating an environment that is moving toward equity.

Definitions of *trauma-informed* are generally focused on meeting the needs of those already impacted by trauma. Venet (2021) suggests that it is important that we shift this notion to include a focus on the causes of trauma, not just the impact. When we are only reactive, we neglect and fail to look at the ways in which the structures that we participate in, including education, perpetuate and even cause trauma. As she succinctly states:

> *When we recognise that trauma originates from both inside and outside of schools, we realize that it is not simply our job to respond to trauma or to reduce potential triggers inside of school. Instead, we become key agents in ending the trauma that happens within our schools and our education system. (Venet, 2021, p. 9)*

Equity data

Every three years in Australia a national survey, the Australian Early Development Census (AEDC), is completed, looking at school starters and their degree of capacity across five domains: physical health and wellbeing; social competence; emotional maturity; language and cognitive skills; and communication skills and general knowledge. This data is useful when it comes to investigating equity as it looks at specific cohorts of students across the country. What it tells us is that:

> *Children living in the most socio-economically disadvantaged communities are twice as likely to be vulnerable on one or more AEDC domains and three times more likely to be vulnerable on two or more domains compared to children living in communities with high levels of socio-economic advantage. (Commonwealth of Australia, 2022, p. 7)*

The 2021 report also highlights that the impacts of the COVID-19 pandemic in 2020 hit hardest in communities that have the least. This is unsurprising and certainly something that was anecdotally very clear at the time of remote learning. For children from a language background other than English, the report saw them with the highest rates of vulnerability in the domain of communication skills and general knowledge, and for Aboriginal and Torres Strait Islander children, the data showed that in 2021, 34 per cent were on track across all five domains, as compared to the national average of close to 55 per cent.

It is vital to reiterate that our society is where inequity is born and flourishes. We cannot blame families for the barriers that are in place in society, and we must see it as part of our role to know, name and push against the inequities that our families and students live with. We can do that in whatever way possible as individuals, considering what we ourselves live with and what our capacity is. However, we must be careful to ensure we are not placing an undue burden on the educators in our schools with lived experience.

Alvarez et al. (2016) identifies some ways that less recognisable race-related experiences in schools contribute to trauma, these include; students not seeing themselves represented in the curriculum or seeing themselves perceived negatively in the curriculum; a lack of validation with regard to a student's experiences; and low expectations. These experiences can all have huge impacts on an individual, especially when that individual is not part of the dominant cultural group in the community they live in. As Alvarez et al. (2016) point out, 'These traumatic race-related experiences may result in trauma symptoms comparable to more recognizable events, such as sexual abuse or natural disasters, but within school contexts, these experiences may be unrecognized or unaddressed by educators' (p. 31).

This will be the case for all students who are not represented, or are represented negatively, in the curriculum: those with disabilities; those who are sex, sexuality or gender diverse; or those who are part of non-dominant Faith communities. Educators and schools play a vital role in teaching diversity, and appropriately representing our society in the curriculum they deliver. We often hear arguments that home should be the place for children to learn about diversity, often from those whose beliefs might contravene legal understandings of what equality and discrimination is. However, I would argue that home is the place for families to share their opinions and beliefs, but school is where we teach broadly and factually.

The results of inequity

The data around NAPLAN and parental occupation groups is clear: 'The proportion of students at or below the national minimum standard is considerably greater for lower parental occupation groups than for higher groups. The effects of students' backgrounds are still strongly evident in Year 9 reading levels' (Masters, 2018, para. 13). What's more, 'The most advanced students typically begin (and end) the school year five to six years ahead of the least advanced students' (Masters, 2018, para. 9). While this information is not a reason to lower expectations, it is a reason to increase scaffolding and supports. Schools that predominantly service low-income areas are less likely to have school counsellors, multiple specialist classes, after-school activities, excursions and camps, and active 'parents and friends' committees who fundraise for such educational luxuries as air-conditioning. While our state departments and our Federal Government do offer additional funding to support students who are likely to need it, it is inadequate. We need to be aware of our role as educators in systems change, local change and individual change because '...inequity in schools can cause and worsen trauma' (Venet, 2021, p. 27).

First Nations, and other students of colour, along with students living with a disability in Australia are disproportionally likely to be suspended or expelled, at the same time as they are more likely to be targeted for inclusion policies (Graham et al., 2021; Rudolph & Thomas, 2023). Rudolph and Thomas (2023) note that, "Education both actively excludes (through suspensions and expulsions) and tries to include (through inclusion policies, programs, and pathways)" (p. 110), but that each of these approaches, and those who are affected by these approaches, situate the educational mainstream as 'white, heteronormative and able-bodied' (112).

Our education system shows us that it is inequitable again and again through evidence such as who does well in NAPLAN; who experiences the most suspensions and expulsions; who we are not engaging well enough; and which groups are more likely to school refuse. Educators within school may not have capacity to change the system, but by arming ourselves with knowledge about who is not well served by it, we can use this knowledge as power to move some small way toward mitigating the impacts of educational inequity.

Teacher judgement is encouraged, and in fact required, in schools, and this judgement is a powerful tool that can be discussed, moderated and used with regard to equity, as it is with literacy or numeracy. Leadership in a school can support whole-school learning about impacts of poverty, racism, ableism, family violence, and homophobia and transphobia to better serve the students who are more likely to be impacted by the inequitable system we work within. By doing so, a whole-school approach to equity can be embraced.

Addressing and highlighting barriers

Many of the barriers for our students are rooted in structural inequity and it is part of our job to speak up and act where we can against the structures that stand in the way of student success and educational equity. It is my opinion that in this search for equity, we scaffold and differentiate in class and we agitate as members of society. This might include speaking up within the schools or education departments we work for. It might be writing letters to a minister, or it might be highlighting existing inequity in conversations with the people around us. As always, we can work within the spheres of influence we have.

There can be a sense, politically and in the media, that teachers are to blame for the academic outcomes of students, with little regard for the impact of other aspects of a student's life. This tendency to see areas of life as siloed – education, health, housing, employment – rather than as intricately connected is very common in many countries. For teachers working in areas that see high instances of community violence, poverty, unemployment, housing stress and racism, they inevitably understand how much better things could be for some of our families with appropriate resourcing. It is clear that living with a lack of appropriate supports and the daily stressors of inequity means some families are doing it tough.

Another factor, when it comes to structural inequity, is that there is also often an impact on access to student supports. For example, for students to receive consideration for a learning difficulty, a diagnosis might be required. Receiving a diagnosis might involve many months on a waitlist, a couple of thousand dollars, travel requirements for appointments or technological accessibility, since the services are not available evenly across the country. This is not accessible to everyone and not accessible through our supposedly equitable education system in all states. In fact, access may even differ across regions in one single state. A recent headline in *The Sydney Morning Herald* identified that 'Sydney's wealthiest suburbs claim the most HSC disability provisions' (Carroll & Gladstone, 2022). The inequity demonstrated by this headline is something that all educators should be rallying against, regardless of the demographics of the school they work at. It is our job to break down the barriers to equitable access to education and to highlight the inequities when we can't. For those students with extreme behaviours and mental health concerns, timely access to specialist services is very difficult, and depending on where you live, close to impossible. This is an inequity that should be highlighted again and again.

Schools can note where they fall in the spectrum of access to services, and how their student socioeconomic data compares with other Australian schools. Remembering this information, and not falling into the trap of believing that education is accessed in the same way, is vital for a trauma-informed school. What schools choose to do with the information they have about their own school is then up to them, but worth investigating.

Child development is rarely seen as a public issue by policymakers or the general public (Shonkoff & Bales, 2011). It is traditionally viewed as something resting entirely with family as an individual issue. When we consider the future of our students, we should be thinking in a societal way: what we, as educators, can do to ensure our students have the future they want, and how we are contributing to the greater good of society by ensuring we do not add to the inequity that exists across our society. We should be thinking about how we can mitigate the impacts of educational inequity. For those of us who hold greater power in society due to our race, religion, sexuality or ability, educating ourselves about inequity we have not experienced is important, and rewarding, and will have an impact on all the students we work with.

Conclusion

In this chapter we have looked at lots of elements of a whole-school, trauma-informed approach. As I stated, individual educators can make a life-changing difference to their students, but when a whole school works together, the impacts grow exponentially.

Schools are challenging and stressful places to work. We can't change the inequity that exists to create educational barriers, but we can push against them, and we can name them and highlight them. We can work within our sphere of influence to support all of our students. In my experience educators are driven by their commitment to the students, and in many cases to the families, too. When we can work toward making school a place that is safe, caring and compassionate, we are really showing our commitment to those students and families.

12

HOW WE TEACH WELLBEING

Curriculum violence is the result of classroom content and pedagogy that harms students intellectually and emotionally. (Venet, 2021, p. 32)

In the previous chapter we looked at the ways our school culture and engagement practices can positively impact our students and families by embedding wellbeing. Here, we look at teaching practices and programs, and how we can use them to help embed wellbeing across a whole school. When a school shifts focus from outcomes and rankings, to effort and growth, it can immediately demonstrate to students that we see them holistically and not simply in comparison to their peers. When we bring growth mindset, teaching empathy, and a focus on social-emotional learning together, we get the outcomes we really want – student learning growth.

Effort and growth

With a strong focus on effort in the classroom, and the promotion of the belief that all children are capable learners, students experience reward for what they are contributing to their own learning, not for a perceived pre-existing level of intelligence. (Harris, 2016, p. 26)

Learning isn't always easy. Teachers often note that students love those worksheets that we might refer to as 'busy work', but why? Because it is easy. Being unchallenged can be relaxing and comfortable. Learning is often uncomfortable, and especially hard for students who live with a great deal of discomfort and tricky feelings already. We need to find ways to support students to push through the hard parts of learning. We might call this the learning pit, roadblocks or a learning curve. Students need to have the ability to not equate the challenge with their actual capacity. Having a focus on student growth means that we are able to look at the ways in which individual students' learning happens. If we are solely focused on the endgame – for example, is a student 'at level' and the answer is either yes or no – that really does a huge disservice to all the students, and their teachers, who have grown their learning with effort. When we can track learning growth without having the same goals for a whole class or year level, but instead for each individual student, we can show students the results of their effort and encourage the growth to continue.

So much of what we do in schools uses a deficit model. We have students focusing on their goals, perhaps keeping a mathematics or literacy goal sitting on their table. When students achieve their goals, we don't always have time to celebrate as the pace in schools is a cracking one and it is straight on to the next goal. We need to assess, we need to grow learning and focus on learning goals, which cannot be anything other than a deficit model as we constantly focus on what has not yet been achieved, where the gaps are, what still needs to be imparted into the brain of the student, ready to take more in.

Individualising goals

There are ways that we can shift the focus toward effort somewhat, including the use of that powerful word – *yet!* Students can be reminded that learning goals are almost always guaranteed to be reached with the simple formula of effort and focus. This reinforces how vital it is for student learning and goals to be 'just right' for them as an individual, regardless of their starting point. When we take into account what might be impacting a student, including living with trauma, it might be that their goal is just working toward feeling safe at school. There is an explicit expectation that a classroom teacher will have the capacity to differentiate their teaching and learning goals to cover the spread of abilities in their class, and this involves making the work achievable. This might involve students working above or below the expected level, but for students to experience both success and learning growth, the learning needs to be achievable. As 'Australian research shows that achievement can be spread over five to eight year levels within a single class' (Goss & Hunter, 2015, p. 1), that is no mean feat. When it is successfully done, however, students are able to see their progress as they meet each goal.

The use of individual growth data can be very helpful, so that rather than ranking a student against their cohort, they are ranked against themselves. The strong focus on NAPLAN does the exact opposite of this. In classrooms we have the capacity to keep the focus on individualised data and finding the most strengths-based ways to share this information with students.

For students who might struggle with concepts around goals, strategies mentioned earlier can be employed. Charts with visuals and capacity to tick off can be used to break down larger goals into chunks, for example.

Growth mindset

Naming a child as smart is not helpful. It does not acknowledge effort and can impede their learning as time goes on. Framing success as a personality trait identifies the success or failure as not being linked to learner strategies such as perseverance and stamina – those things that require effort – and instead sees the outcome as a given, reducing the motivation and effort of the student (Mueller & Dweck, 1998). However, it is important to note, and Dweck (2015) herself did, that the equation is not always as simple as effort = growth. This is a straightforward way to talk about growth mindset, but we must acknowledge that for some students, they can put in lots of effort and still not grow. There might be many reasons for this, and it is our job to find out just what is standing in the way. Part of learning growth involves investigating why learning might be a struggle. Effort is an important part of the puzzle, but so is recognising what else is happening in a student's life, as with one young student I worked with who feared failure, having been told they were dumb. Time might be required to establish a growth mindset for students with fixed beliefs about their ability, whether negative or positive. Educators must acknowledge effort, but also be ready to investigate what barriers might be in place for a student beyond the mindset and be ready to set achievable goals and celebrate small successes.

Making growth visible

The data specialist at my school designed effort and growth bar graphs that each student received at the end of a unit of work. They had the comparison of their pre- and post-tests measuring their growth, and an additional bar that showed their growth as compared to the class average. I clearly remember the day that two of the academically lowest students in the class came to show me their results – they had grown the most out of all their peers! They were so delighted. The motivation that was produced and the opportunity for the adults to celebrate them was so powerful. Were they still the lowest students in the class? Maybe, but it didn't matter, their learning was doing exactly as it should – growing – and their sense of themselves as learners was also growing. The momentum was there for this to continue.

Students come to us with varying experiences of success and we aim to give them this experience based on what is success individualised for them, not pushing to meet an expectation identified by a curriculum authority or a government department. We can use the language of growth with our students, and in showing them their growth, we are showing them that they are learners. Simple things like creating an 'effort graph' can be so powerful for individuals. Schools might have access to a program that can create these graphs, or one can be made simply as I described above.

When these graphs are produced, the teacher can take time to speak with each student individually about their results, linking things like attendance, behaviour or effort to learning. With the students mentioned above, our aim was to build a new self-narrative that saw the students thinking of themselves as learners. Seeing their learning made visible helped with the intrinsic motivation that then went on to support more learning. Rather than a focus on the outcome – who knows the most – a focus on the learning growth allows for more personalised learning conversations to happen.

Model mistakes and celebrate the small successes

It is hard to ask students to be vulnerable with their learning. To do this we need to model it. A mistake on the board can be crossed out, not wiped out, left as a reminder that everyone makes mistakes and this is how we learn. To be process-oriented not outcome-oriented is how we prepare our students for life. It is what we are attempting to do when we are teaching strategies for self-regulation, the same way it is what we are doing when we teach strategies for what to do when we make a mistake in our learning.

Students need to see themselves as learners, and it is possible that not having this view might be the most significant barrier to learning. It is our job as educators to create a learning community and ensure each student feels a part of it. Part of developing a learning community that each student feels part of is to reinforce the notion of the growth mindset all the time. This includes celebrating growth, which can pump up students for whom seeing themselves as a learner and putting effort in might be a new approach to school. We create a virtuous cycle, where the self-perception of self as a learner leads to effort, which leads to growth, which leads to self-perception as a learner! Sometimes, to get this cycle going, we need to celebrate very small successes, and that is okay. It is important that educators follow the growth mindset of focusing on effort and not intrinsic characteristics.

Teaching empathy

Understanding what others are feeling and our impact on others is an important part of learning empathy. When a child can identify that other people feel and think things that are different to them this is referred to as *theory of mind*. Theory of mind is a path to empathy and can be particularly challenging for some children and definitely tricky to teach. Not being empathetic might actually be a protective strategy for a student who is exposed to others' pain regularly and some thought around this is necessary. We also need to consider where students are at in their development, since empathy is only possible at a certain point in a child's development and individuals are all wired differently. As Walsh and Walsh (2019) state:

> *Empathy is a work-in-progress throughout childhood and adolescence and is shaped by a range of factors including genetics, temperament, context, and environment. Empathy does not, however, simply unfold automatically in children. While we are born hardwired with the capacity for empathy, its development requires experience and practice. (para. 5)*

Teaching empathy can help students' writing and comprehension, as well as speaking and listening. When perspective taking is required in learning, students who struggle with theory of mind will likely find it difficult. We can consider building theory of mind skills in literacy classes with a range of strategies, such as:

- in the early years reading books about feelings and relatable scenarios and teaching text-to-self connection
- role play promotes perspective taking
- real-life examples of relatable people

- persuasive writing that is meaningful
- use of cartoons with both speech bubbles and thought bubbles
- sharing student work, demonstrating a range of experiences, thoughts and opinions

Social-emotional learning programs

Social-emotional learning is the process that takes children to the place of understanding the 'knowledge, attitudes, and skills' (Domitrovich et al., 2017, p. 408) that they will need to recognise and manage emotion, build capacity for empathy, have positive relationships, problem-solve and have a positive sense of self. To build social-emotional skills, students will have to engage with cognition, feelings and emotions, and behaviour. Domitrovich et al. (2017) identifies having these skills as 'a multidimensional construct that is critical to success in school and life for all children, including those at risk due to economic disadvantage, minority status, and early emotional or behavioral problems' (p. 408).

There are so many good reasons to employ wellbeing interventions across a whole school – the primary reason being that it is good for all students. Additionally, it promotes a workplace that values the wellbeing of those who work in it. When a whole school speaks the same language, the impact of the intervention is multiplied. All the elements of social-emotional learning are great approaches for all of us, and they support trauma-informed work because they teach the skills needed to be able to cope with adversity, promote emotional awareness and build positive relationships. Not only does this teaching support students' social emotional growth, as the earlier chapters discussed, but much of the work of social-emotional learning (SEL) can be mapped to the curriculum.

Bringing SEL to the classroom

The beauty of social-emotional learning is that it requires no specialisation, just the support of good curriculum materials and professional development where necessary. There is a lot of research to support universal SEL programs delivered to all students by familiar staff. In using the word *universal*, I mean across the whole school and accessible to every student. However, 'Universal is not the same as one size fits all' (Venet, 2021, p. 62) and a good program will adapt to the needs of the students. Classroom teachers have the capacity to adapt so it is accessible to all – they know their students and differentiate across the curriculum and behaviour every day.

Research that has looked at supporting students post-disaster found that students who had access to good-quality universal SEL programs delivered by school staff fared better than those who received one-to-one or small -group interventions delivered by mental health professionals (Cahill, 2021). Of course, this is very relevant to consider after the worldwide impact of COVID-19. The research identified that students dealing with traumatic experiences like war and natural disasters were less likely to develop PTSD if they had access to these programs. In addition, there is research to show that even when students might be needing more intensive interventions, the universal interventions provided positive outcomes. And if that isn't enough, providing a quality SEL program is also linked with improved academic results, reduced bullying, increased capacity for emotional regulation and better school connectedness (Cahill, 2021). There is also evidence to show that teacher–student relationships are improved, too. So, though it might feel as though it is time away from the curriculum, everything we do in these programs supports our students.

Intervention and prevention

The benefit of universal intervention is that it can work both as a prevention as well as an intervention. Students are learning the skills that they need both in the day-to-day, as well as in the future. A good universal program can build the skills of a whole student cohort, which can leave more space for individual interventions we might term tier 2 and 3. If teachers are not needing to intervene with every friendship or sporting issue that arises, they have more time to notice and attend to the student who might need a bit more from them. Another perspective, identified by Domitrovich et al. (2017), is that across a population we have both those dealing with present issues and those who will develop issues at some point. Considering the investment of a universal intervention, we can see that it helps not just those who present with current struggles, but also those who may come across future struggles giving them the skill set to deal with what may come. This means that the outcomes for those that might go on to struggle are statistically more significant than for those currently struggling because over time there will be so many more of them.

The beauty of school-based universal interventions is that almost all children attend school and they do so for a great proportion of their childhoods, so we are perfectly poised to offer SEL with the capacity to improve many young lives. As Domitrovich et al. (2017) identified, the benefits of teaching SEL reach far beyond the years of the teaching, into the world of post-secondary success. What's more, the impacts appear to be regardless of ethnicity, gender (noting studies use the gender binary) and socioeconomic background, with a possible slight favouring of impacts for those from a lower socioeconomic status background. As Domitrovich et al. (2017) note, it can particularly support those living with adversity, without particularly targeting them:

> *There is considerable evidence indicating that both intrapersonal and interpersonal competencies enhance the ability of youth to behave appropriately, avoid risk behaviors, develop healthy relationships with adults and peers, and achieve academic success... This is especially true for children who are vulnerable due to higher levels of behavioral dysregulation or exposure to the numerous risk factors associated with poverty. (p. 410)*

Selecting a SEL program

There are several ready-to-go SEL programs with varying angles, but more or less offering a framework for teaching the skills that we have explored in this book – understanding emotions and our emotional reactions, and building skills to support relating well to others. But when it comes to the most effective programs, we can look to a meta-analysis of SEL programs in schools by Durlak et al. (2011) that identified that the best programs can be described as SAFE: 'sequenced, active, focused, and explicit' (p. 408). These four practices related to having activities that were planned as linked and coordinated; focused on particular skill development; used active forms of student learning; focused on developing skills that were personal and social; and used explicit teaching.

Noting these key practices, it is clear to see how being taught in these ways will benefit our students and absolutely supports trauma-informed practice in schools. Looking at a trauma-informed approach often begins with a focus on helping adversity-impacted students gain self-regulatory skills and build relational capacity. This can be seen as a deficit model with a focus very much on repairing damage already done, seeing the student as requiring fixing, rather than seeing students in a more holistic manner, containing struggles as well as strengths and resources (Brunzell & Norrish, 2021). When we look at a whole student cohort, offering all of them the opportunity to learn the skills and knowledge required to have a positive sense of self, relate well to others and self-regulate, we move away from seeing some students as needing fixing and shift to promoting a positive, strengths-based focus on all our students.

Resilience, Rights and Respectful Relationships

Taking into account the research mentioned earlier, it is clear that we have, here in Australia, a SEL program meeting all the requirements of an effective program, that has been developed to suit our schools, rolled out in Victoria, but accessible to all online – Resilience, Rights and Respectful Relationships (RRRR).

RRRR was written as a primary prevention program against gender-based violence. The program was designed with the knowledge that SEL programs are most effectively delivered by teachers and school staff (Cahill et al., 2019; Domitrovich et al., 2017). The program uses collaborative experiences and encourages students to critically reflect on scenarios relevant to them, as well as broader ideas that offer the opportunity to understand more about the world and their context within it. It practically teaches how to come to solutions, from the simple to the complex. It is a curriculum and a resource, useful both as a universal intervention and as something to be used in individual wellbeing support. It can help in situations such as problem-solving with a group of friends, or being strengths focused with a struggling child. Lessons might include a focus on a topic like coping strategies, or what a rollercoaster of a day looks and feels like, or perhaps investigating how emotions can become bigger and more impactful – building vocabulary and understanding. The lesson plans include role plays and the students love them.

The ideal scenario for RRRR is for two staff to deliver the lessons. I have been a part of this approach, delivering the lessons alongside the classroom teacher and ideally with some education support staff, too. This means that we are all using the same language – we carry this language from class to class, co-teaching the lessons and being a thread that moves through the school. The benefit of more staff in the room is that students can break into small groups to discuss or write ideas down, and the staff can circulate, checking in. The small group work allows students to all have a voice, and for different students to work together. There is so much learning in this. It also means that there is someone available to take a student aside to check in if it seems that the content has brought up some emotion.

The professional development associated with the program is free in Victorian schools and is able to be individualised for schools. RRRR can be delivered however schools want, with some having an RRRR week a couple of times in the year, some having weekly lessons or fortnightly classes across the year, some running it one term or two each year. Schools can use the lesson plans provided or create their own. I know that I chose to make a few changes, but mostly followed the plans provided. One comment I will make is that I wasn't keen on the division of emotions into positive or negative, and I opted to describe some emotions as 'uncomfortable' or 'tricky' instead. Aside from this, the curriculum aligns very well with trauma-informed practice, promoting 'student connectedness, collaborative engagement, critical thinking and the development of positive relationships' (Cahill et al., 2019, p. 137). Most importantly, it is enjoyable for the students, who get to play games, act in role plays and engage in creative thinking.

Zones of Regulation

We have no choice but to work with the Window of Tolerance that a student has. Changing perceptions of safety takes a long time and requires multiple interventions. As always, the most important intervention is creating a classroom and a school that provides a sense of safety for the student. In addition to this lofty aim, we use a range of interventions to support our students to get to know their own nervous systems. This teaching is for life. It is also part of how we create schools that feel safe. When students know what is going on in their body and can articulate it, they feel safer and so can those around them.

As mentioned in earlier chapters, the Zones of Regulation (Kuypers, 2011) framework can be a very useful tool to promote SEL. The framework provides a shared language, a kind of shorthand that allows students to quickly identify how they are feeling – which 'zone' they are in.

When working with the Zones framework, classrooms might make posters with drawings or photos of faces that belong in the various zones, or they might start to investigate the regulation strategies that help them move from red, yellow or blue into the green zone. It is important to note that when we have our trauma-informed lens on, we know that it is not always easy or even possible to move away from a zone. Feeling things is important and our reactions are often beyond our control, particularly for students impacted by trauma and adversity. We must remember to be mindful of this when we use a tool like Zones of Regulation. However, it is part of an important learning journey for students to recognise that emotions do not last forever and we can have an influence on them.

This tool can be used to help students understand that our feelings are our own, that we all feel differently and there are different strategies to regulate. I have seen this used in a behavioural support school, where everyone had a lanyard, including staff, that showed what supported them to regulate when in each of the zones. Both students and staff had created their 'toolkit.' All the information was right there all the time and served to reinforce that strategies are individual. So, while Zones of Regulation is not a complete SEL program with a curriculum plan, it can be a very useful add-on.

Positive psychology and positive education

Positive psychology has made its way into education in recent years, though its origins can be tracked back to the 1970s (Green et al., 2011). Positive psychology is often a feature of self-help books, bringing together aims such as a strengths focus, building positive emotions, shifting negativity bias and improving relationships. The term *positive education* is often used when referencing positive psychology programs in schools and can be described as 'applied positive psychology in education' (Green et al., 2011, para. 1).

Positive education strategies work to boost the individual's sense of self and can also support a sense of belonging and cohesion. We have already touched on some strategies that fit the criteria of positive education and can be used in classrooms. When a whole school takes on positive education, these strategies are applied in *every* class. Staff can even make use of strategies during planning meetings, or whole-school meetings.

Strategies that can be applied to a whole school might include:

- built-in opportunities for student reflection and feedback
- a board or mural in the school that showcases students' personalised affirmations
- a 'secret kindness' activity, where students are allocated someone to show small acts of kindness for the day

- having a shared school goal that involves helping others in the community
- routines that occur during whole-school assemblies
- a way to express gratitude
- strengths displays

Impacts of positive psychology in schools have been shown to include increased enjoyment of learning; positive engagement in school; increased strengths that support learning; attitudes of gratitude, hope and life satisfaction; reduced negative thinking; reduced loneliness; and improved social skills (Brunzell et al., 2016; Laakso et al., 2022; Seligman et al., 2009; Waters, 2011). Positive education and trauma-informed work can complement each other well.

There are a range of whole-school positive education programs in Australia, and many programs that incorporate it, such as the Berry Street Education Model, and RRRR as well as educator wellbeing approaches, and theories such as growth mindset. Some programs will also contain the elements of an effective SEL program.

Positive behaviour supports

While not actually a SEL program, one of the most common schoolwide approaches is the schoolwide positive behaviour supports (SWPBS), or positive behaviour intervention and supports (it has various names). It is worth a mention here as it is so prolific, shares some elements of SEL programs and is promoted by education departments across Australia, the UK, US and Canada.

Based on behavioural science, the focus of SWPBS is on reinforcing 'positive' (desirable) behaviours and replacing 'negative' (undesirable) behaviours with more acceptable ones. Reflecting what is known as 'operant conditioning', the idea is that the results of a behaviour will impact whether or not the behaviour is repeated, so when we hype up a student for desired behaviours, they are more likely to repeat those behaviours. It is a whole-school universal program that begins with identifying collective desired behaviours, examines when undesirable behaviours are happening and identifies replacement behaviours, which are then taught. The emphasis is on being explicit, encouraging, positive and re-directive, with consequences rather than punishments to teach and reinforce desired behaviours. It is a one-size-fits-all approach and comes along with some key schoolwide behaviours that are the behaviours all students are held accountable to, such as 'be safe' or 'be respectful'. There might be an associated matrix of expected behaviours that explicitly identifies what each of these shared behavioural expectations looks like in different areas at school, such as the yard or the hallways. This explicit teaching of what is acceptable is a key feature.

Another element of SWPBS is the three-tiered behavioural intervention pyramid. Tier 1 interventions are universal, Tier 2 might be small group interventions and Tier 3 are often more significant, individual interventions. This can be a useful way to talk about interventions, but we should be wary of talking about our students in a way that can be pathologising, and rather be clear that those Tier 2 and 3 interventions are available to all students, when needed, and do not require diagnoses or labels, particularly around students' behaviour as sometimes occurs, such as 'at-risk behaviours'. When we talk about a 'multi-tiered system of supports', it is important to note that they should be holistic and very flexible.

The act of noticing and naming positive behaviours is a lovely one to be part of. I was part of the introduction of a schoolwide positive behaviours intervention that included the aim of making six acknowledgements of positive things to every one corrective comment. It was a challenge, but also pretty satisfying. This approach led to good feelings around the school with lots of positivity. It also meant that for those students who regularly received corrective comments, they were also getting lots of positive acknowledgement, even if it was something simple like how they walked safely down the stairs. The idea behind this positive approach is aligned with applied behaviour analysis – that challenging behaviours are not changed or actively reduced, rather they are understood with changes made to the environment or experience to reduce triggers, with positive or desirable behaviours replacing them. It is fair to say that when students have experienced significant trauma, this is not going to be enough.

Critiques and trauma-informed adaptations

One of the criticisms of this framework is that it ends up being the most challenging kids who are constantly praised and the well-behaved students not getting enough recognition. However, in my experience, students are sensitive to the range of needs in their class and understand that some students require greater encouragement than others. The flipside of this criticism is that much of SWPBS is not trauma-informed, nor is it always a friendly space for those who are not neurotypical. In my opinion, the usefulness of these programs lies somewhere between these two critiques.

When students are encouraged and staff are focusing on being positive, the school climate becomes one of striving to seek out the strengths in individuals. All these things can be great to be around and it is always a good thing for educators to be looking for the positive. However, it is also helpful at times to have some guidelines, understanding and additional tools to support those students with particularly challenging or violent behaviours.

Our knowledge of trauma and adversity mean that we understand that there is always a message behind behaviour and often a serious reason why students present with challenging behaviours. Because the focus of SWPBS programs is behaviour modification it is, according to Venet (2021) 'fundamentally incompatible with trauma-informed practices' (p. 63). Further, she states, 'Children affected by trauma need an environment that is based on consent, not coercion' (p. 63), which is not what is happening when there is an attempt to alter behaviour with rewards for desired behaviour, designed to support compliance. In addition, who is the one to judge what is acceptable and what is not? Would an autistic student who uses a self-soothing strategy such as rocking back and forth, or hand flapping or foot tapping, be deemed to be doing something acceptable, or would they be encouraged to find a more acceptable replacement behaviour?

Bringing a trauma-informed lens to positive behaviour support sees this support as something that we can offer to all students across a school, thus highlighting the positivity levels in the school, focusing on strengths and care. We do need to offer more than this, though, in a non-pathologising way. Bringing academic and wellbeing interventions together in a multi-tiered system of supports can be a way to avoid seeing it as behavioural interventions, but rather the ways that we need to intervene to produce equitable access to education at our schools.

Sensory and routine-based interventions

Schools naturally have rhythm and routine, and it can exist at many levels and be a focus to support all students, but particularly those who have experienced trauma and adversity.

Whole-school approaches to sensory support should include certain elements that also align with SEL. Sensations and emotions are intertwined.

In Chapter 5 we examined interoception – attuning to what is happening in our body – and teaching or reinforcing this skill is an important part of any sensory-based programs. Indeed, it is an important part of SEL, too, because, as Kline (2020) states, 'interoceptive awareness, self-regulation, and co-regulation are inseparable' (p. 28). So, senses, emotion and regulation skills co-exist to support student wellbeing.

The other important element of students with an understanding and language around senses is that they are then able to describe what their sensory needs are. We have discussed ways to address sensory needs in the classroom, and this can be amended to be a whole-school approach. Imagine a school where all classrooms have a calm corner; access to noise-cancelling headphones; weighted cushions; 'take-a-break' cards for appropriate movement breaks; regular brain breaks; and a language around sensory regulation. Here, a student would gain the skills required to identify their sensory profile and the skills to find out what they need to ensure their sensory sensitivities (or sensory-seeking needs) don't interfere with their learning.

Another benefit to a whole-school approach around sensory interventions is that teachers also work out what their sensitivities are, so they are then able to see what biases they have in their classroom design. Interestingly, recent research has identified that up to a third of people experience some degree of misokinesia – a negative response to seeing other people fidget (Dockrill, 2022). Given the number of fidgeters there are likely to be in any classroom (I couldn't find statistics on this!), a teacher with misokinesia is going to be very frustrated, and so will the fidgeters who are told to stop fidgeting. Coming together to understand how our sensory needs might influence each other is likely to be very helpful and conducive to a positive classroom, as well as trauma-informed and SEL supportive – a worthy tool to add to any whole-school approaches.

The South Australian Department for Education designed a school program called *Ready to Learn* that teaches interoception and includes daily activities to promote interoceptive awareness to support students understanding their sensory needs. Other approaches could include:

- accessing an occupational therapist to help educate teachers and parents, make suggestions about school spaces and offer assessments for individual students
- access to interventions like calm corners and fidgets in every space

- shared whole-school understandings about use of
  sensory interventions
- a sensory room with access to larger sensory interventions like
  trampolines and swings
- sensory spaces outside, such as gardens
- students and teachers creating their own sensory profile

Is it working?

Earlier, we looked at different ways that schools can collect data around wellbeing. Standard measures that your state employs is one consistent way to collect data, or any data collections that are part of a SEL or trauma-informed practice program that you are using would fulfil this role. It might be that you prefer individual data and are able to use standardised measures such as the *Wellbeing, stress and distress* questionnaire (Government of South Australia, Department for Education, 2020), or something similar, there are even apps available to measure wellbeing in schools. Measuring the use of a calm corner, or the number of times students need to reset can be a measure of the degree of dysregulation in a cohort. As I described earlier, I had collected years of data that identified how many resets students were needing. We could use this data to look at cohorts, days of the week, weeks of the term and reasons for resets. This data-collection tool was designed specifically for our school, to see if our interventions were working. We could extract data about an individual student and track their progress. This was not the only data used, however, and it can be beneficial to use qualitative data, too. Making use of something as simple as a shared location for wellbeing notes is, in my experience, incredibly helpful when looking for the stories behind individual quantitative data. We might notice a spike in a student needing support, but when we can tie that to what is going on in their life, with information gathered by various staff members, we have some really powerful data.

Thinking about measuring growth, we have to remember that students impacted by trauma and adversity need time. A long time. Growth can be slow and looking at data can help us to see small gains and to know that they are contributing to a positive trajectory. We also need to understand that for students who live with their adversity ongoing, we might not see growth the way we would hope. However, collecting school wide data can help to know if the approach you have chosen is working for your school.

Conclusion

My whole-school embedded student wellbeing dream sees schools with a robust trauma-informed practice that includes a whole-school SEL program; engaged, passionate, activist staff; families who feel welcome; and a school that acts as a therapeutic environment for everyone involved with it.

Teaching is not for the faint of heart, but when the work serves to holistically support and educate, the impacts are tremendous. A school that can focus on individual students, is able to collect individual growth data, employs visible learning strategies and builds SEL into the curriculum is well placed to educate and impact students for life.

EMBEDDING EDUCATOR WELLBEING

Talking about how we cope is vital. Education is a hard job, as is any work that involves close work with other people. In addition, we often do our work within structures that can feel as though they are working contrary to our aims – a recipe for frustration. We spend many, many hours with our students and our colleagues. Having good relationships with them supports us to enjoy the work that we do. When things are tricky, or when we are tired or rundown or facing additional stressors, we need the internal resources to maintain a positive approach to our work.

As Flook et al. (2013) states, 'Most school-based interventions are designed for students. There are fewer efforts to address stress and burnout among teachers and boost teacher's well-being' (p. 182). There may not be a way to guarantee protection from extreme stress and burnout, but we can create internal and organisational resources in a range of ways, building connected teams, emotionally protective habits, strong boundaries and the ability to recognise when we are responding to others in ways that are not ideal. As we build our own capacity, we are better placed to support our colleagues, students and families and to push against structures we work within when they don't serve our aims.

Impacts of others' trauma

Vicarious trauma

Working in caring professions, particularly where there is stress and exposure to the distress of others, comes with personal risk. Venet (2021) identifies this when she reminds us that 'Vicarious trauma isn't a sign of a bad teacher or a weak person – it's a normal response to the stress that comes from caring deeply for others and witnessing their struggles' (p. 130). As mentioned in Chapter 1, educators can experience vicarious trauma, or secondary traumatic stress, sometimes called *compassion fatigue*. Being deeply impacted by the traumatic stories of another, or by the repeated exposure to trauma that can come in this line of work, can impact educator mental health. These kinds of responses can end up looking a lot like PTSD and, in some instances, will indeed meet the criteria for this disorder.

I have a clear and unrelenting memory of a story told to me by a parent who had suffered terrible abuse. The parent had landed in a place with people that felt safe and I became a trusted support for the family. On occasion the parent would ask me to share the outline of the story to others, such as the social worker who began to work with the family. This was a protective strategy for the parent, who then did not have to repeat the distressing content more than was necessary. I carried that information, shared when requested, sent a great deal of care to the parent and the children, our students, and it felt like the least I could do for someone who had been through so much. It took a toll, though. Many years later, I still have images in my mind that I wish were not there, though the sting of them has greatly reduced. I don't regret being a support for this family at all, but I do note the impact of caring deeply and carrying the trauma of others.

Burnout

The impacts of the contagion of trauma, along with the difficulty of work stressors that might lead to a sense of not being able to 'do enough' or never getting on top of the workload, can lead to stress, which can lead to burnout. In our industry we can face immense pressure to view student achievement or success in an overly simplistic way that doesn't leave room for the complexity of the work. This can be a huge contributor to educator stress. Educators experiencing symptoms such as 'physical fatigue, mental and emotional exhaustion, feeling unacknowledged or unimportant and viewing the people one serves and one's colleagues with apathy or a lack of care' (Kendrick, 2022, para. 16) are likely experiencing burnout. Burnout causes individuals to feel emotionally exhausted, to struggle to care, to feel unable to experience accomplishment in their work and to feel detached from others (Koenig et al., 2018). What's more, burnout negatively impacts student motivation and stress, too (Lever et al., 2017). Burnout stops us from doing our job well, but can also be caused by a sense of powerlessness in our job, by not having the self-efficacy or coping skills to do the job well. Burnout can be something that builds up over a long time, so it is important to know what to look for and to take action if you think you, or a colleague, might be experiencing it.

Prevention

In very good news, creating a trauma-informed classroom will likely act as a burnout preventor (Kim et al., 2021). A study where teachers were trained in a mindfulness-based SEL program as well as trauma-informed practice found significant decreases in emotional exhaustion, and after two years, it was found that there were particularly significant improvements in self-efficacy and accomplishment (Kim et al., 2021).

The strategies we teach to students are the same strategies we can use ourselves. Noticing and naming our own inner state is so helpful, and sharing how we are feeling and responding helps, too. As for our students, educators can also benefit from keeping things predictable, enjoying daily routine, and creating a sense of belonging. Similarly, teaching students the basics of SEL also gives educators daily reminders about their emotional state. This book has highlighted many things that can be done by educators to teach SEL to support trauma-informed practice. There are many reasons to work in this way, and while our focus has been on the positive impacts for students, it is important to note that the impact on educators is also positive and protective.

Judgement, empathy and compassion

While we do deal with many elements of our jobs that remain outside of our control, there are many things within our daily sphere of influence that support us and our students. When I first began working in student wellbeing, I was fresh from studying developmental trauma and was ready to put that together with my previous experience working with parents. I think that, for the first year, I cried proper tears about once a week. They were tears of empathy, of frustration and of despair at the impacts of inequity I saw every day. It took time for me to learn how to create strong boundaries that left plenty of room for compassion and care without undoing me. A wise friend reminded me as I was sharing my difficulties, that each of the students and the adults I was working with was on their own journey and it wasn't my role to judge or change that journey. On reflection, I could see that in situations I was placing my judgement and perspective on, my role was to actually walk alongside, to listen and to offer what I could, not resolve the issues. It is important to note that we can work against inequity, while not judging or discounting the experience that each individual has.

There will be times when we feel caregivers are not acting in the best interests of our students. This includes when the legal guardian is a government department. This situation can place educators in a really tricky position. How can we not make judgements about others when we see our students are not receiving the love and care we know they deserve? The reality is that we will judge, we will feel fiercely protective of students who don't belong to us, though we might use the phrases *my kids* or *my students*, because we feel that connection.

Our relationships with our students are complicated, and our relationships with their families and caregivers equally complicated, if not more so. What we can do to make things easier on ourselves, and to protect from educator burnout, is to practise unconditional positive regard and compassion. Compassion is 'empathy in action' (Aguilar, 2018, p. 199). We don't have to like some of the things that our students deal with on a daily basis and we can even take action to help keep our students safe (in fact, many of us are mandated to). But we also need to consider that generally everyone is making the best of things with the resources they have available to them. This includes the caregivers and families of our students. Compassion and empathy can make it easier for us to deal with situations when we can feel our judgement of others kicking in, as this judgement is not a helpful part of this process.

When we experience empathy, we are feeling the feelings of another. Our heart rate increases as we watch sport, we wince when we see someone getting hurt. As previously mentioned, the neural networks in our brain respond as though it were happening to us. Moving from empathy into compassion includes action, a response to the suffering of another (Aguilar, 2018; Kendrick, 2022). When the brains of those feeling compassion are studied, it is the regions connected to caregiving and pleasure that are activated. What's more, 'neurologists find that when thoughts are directed toward others in compassionate ways, people's minds wander less to what has gone wrong in their lives or what might go wrong in the future' (Aguilar, 2018, p. 201). And if that is not enough to sell compassion, the risk of heart disease, and likely other diseases, can be reduced by practising compassion.

Compassion offers us a way to care and act on our care, without experiencing the suffering that can lead to burnout. There are many ways to practise compassion and to practise creating that burnout-preventing boundary between you and your care for others. A wealth of compassion meditations exist. Simply turning your mind to a positive thing about someone or noting that you wish for them not to suffer can be enough to activate compassion. Doing this for yourself is also very powerful. It may well be the case that you notice you are not that compassionate with yourself, and self-compassion is a vital ingredient of compassion for others.

Relationships

Relationships at school should be fun. We need to experience fun with colleagues and with students, too. It is great when, as a staff, we can practise the wellbeing work we do with students. I have completed the character strengths test with my colleagues, which is always interesting and entertaining. It helps us to know each other better, but also provides an opportunity for a fun meeting – a delightful combination of silliness and appreciation.

Unconditional positive regard is also key in our relationships with our colleagues. Grieg (2018) reinforces the benefits of unconditional positive regard as a tool to enhance educator wellbeing, as well as benefitting students:

> *Deepening the practice of UPR reveals how interconnected the wellbeing of everyone in a community really is. It emphasizes the importance of UPR as both a way of being and as a concept that can be taught to students as they develop an awareness of how they build and maintain relationships at school and out in the world. (para. 9)*

Having and feeling trust and care between educators is an important ingredient for educator wellbeing. As a teacher, the job can be somewhat isolating as generally we work as the only adult in the room. As mentioned, we know reflective practice groups support teachers (La Trobe University, 2022; Russell, 2022), yet while these sorts of peer supervision models are familiar territory to social workers and counsellors, they are uncommon in education. The trial 'showed that peer support in the form of "reflective circles" significantly improved teachers' ability to adapt to classroom challenges with a culture of openness, flexibility and compassion, allowing them to find solutions to complex problems together' (La Trobe University, 2022, para. 5). A set-up along these lines can be formal or informal. It might be a team meeting dedicated to reflective practice within a school, or even a group of people outside of school getting together to improve their practice, while also benefitting their work relationships and their wellbeing. This is a great example of a way that school leadership can help to embed educator wellbeing.

Interventions for individual educators

In thinking about interventions that support educator wellbeing, I considered what has a good evidence base, what doesn't take too much time and what aligns with the work that this book encourages we do with students. We don't necessarily need a whole new range of interventions for educator versus student wellbeing, although we might choose some that are different. The following are a few key interventions that can make a big difference without a big investment of time. I am not suggesting that it is easy to find the motivation to do these things, but if the time and motivation can be found initially, it is likely to breed more time and more motivation.

Mindfulness

There is a reason that everyone seems to talk about mindfulness as the answer to everything, and it is because it is, more or less, the answer to everything. Forgive the hyperbole, but mindfulness has been shown to help stress, anxiety, depression, addiction, eating disorders, emotional regulation and chronic pain, among other things (Aguilar, 2018; Andrews et al., 2013; Center on the Developing Child at Harvard University, 2022; Flook et al., 2013; Jennings, 2019; Kim et al., 2021; Seigel, 2020; van der Kolk, 2014; Williams, 2010). As discussed earlier, mindfulness can be thought of as awareness of our experience in the moment without judgement. Mindfulness can be just a moment or a lengthy meditation. Mindfulness will benefit us if we can cultivate a practice, which does not need to take up a lot of time, but does need to be regular to experience significant benefits. There are lots of apps that support the practice and so many examples online.

One of the benefits of mindfulness for educators is the reduction in those 65,000 thoughts and emotions that can relentlessly batter our minds each day (Aguilar, 2018). Mindfulness offers an observer's approach to these mental events and thus a choice regarding whether or not to engage. This observer approach – when we notice what is occurring in thoughts and feelings – gives us a little space between us and what is going on internally. Sometimes this space is what we need to reduce being caught up, or at times consumed, with our inner experiences (Aguilar, 2018; Harris, 2019; Hayes et al., 2016). This is the key to how mindfulness works, so if there is one thing that you take up, shifting your perspective in this way might be the ideal one. Try saying to yourself, 'I am having the thought that…' rather than getting caught up in the thought, or even better, go one step further, 'I notice that I am having the thought that…'. Be non-judgemental and curious about your uncomfortable experiences. Ask yourself what is happening, with care and wonder: 'I wonder why that student always leaves me feeling so frustrated?'; 'I notice that buzzing in my body that comes with anxiety, I wonder what is going on there?'; 'That wasn't my usual calm reaction, I wonder why I reacted like that today?'.

Educators continuing to be in the moment with mindfulness can expect to move away from habitual responses, high emotion reactions or drama, and toward lower levels of burnout, greater efficacy, clear-headed decision-making and even more compassion (Aguilar, 2018).

Write it out

Long-time writing researcher Pennebaker (1997; 2018), whose research began with personal experience, has many decades of studies, all essentially telling us the same thing: writing about emotionally charged events changes lives for the better. The research highlighted that twenty daily minutes of free-form writing about emotionally charged experiences, not necessarily recent experiences, led to participants' experiencing:

> *Marked improvement in their physical and mental well-being. They were happier, less depressed and less anxious. In the months after the*

writing sessions, they had lower blood pressure, improved immune function, and fewer visits to the doctor. They also reported better relationships, improved memory, and more success at work. (David, 2017, para. 6)

With a link to the benefits of mindfulness, these writers were able to find that bit of space between themselves and their thoughts and feelings. The act of writing filled the role of noticing or observing, without needing to do it consciously. The writers became more insightful about their experiences and their responses. These results make logical sense, and relate to the physical and mental wellbeing link we have explored in this book – the capacity to express and understand emotion to create a clear self-narrative is extremely beneficial. You could do this in a very unstructured way or, if starting is hard, perhaps give yourself a beginning point each day, such as 'My strongest reaction today was to...' or 'If I could change one thing from today it would be...'. You might want to start with dot pointing your day and seeing where a jumping-off point might be. So, perhaps if the thought of mindfulness or meditation is not for you, trialling the twenty minutes of writing could be an approach that suits better.

Strengths and positive psychology

Another approach that works for students and educators alike is a strengths-based focus. As discussed, strengths within a positive behaviour framework can support our students in areas such as self-narrative, general sense of wellbeing and class cohesion. Opting to take on a positive behaviours approach, or finding a way to integrate some of the elements that work best for you or your school has an impact on staff, too. Based on positive psychology, it makes sense that we are more inclined to do those things we are positively acknowledged for.

Building these approaches into whole-school or team meetings takes pressure off an individual to have to remember and to be motivated to commit to this approach. Something as simple as positive self-talk can be really helpful for our state of mind. The trick is to consider things that are true and talk about these things to ourselves. For example, rather than having an over-the-top statement about unrealistic success, we can tap into what we know to be true to frame a statement about success (Anbar, 2021). Consider feeling exhausted by some of the behaviours in your class. You might say to yourself, 'I can use my compassion and unconditional positive regard to better connect with my students'. A true statement can shift the unconscious approach to coming to school. Adding visualisations to your positive self-talk can make it even more powerful.

Our brains tend to notice more of the negative, and this is why deliberately interjecting with positive thoughts and visualisations can help. It makes evolutionary sense that we might be more attuned to the negative, to those things that might lead to us being unsafe, however, it is not all that useful day-to-day. In fact, maintaining a negativity bias supports both anxious and depressed states (Williams et al., 2009). As well as offering positive self-talk, it is possible to focus on the positive moments in your day by setting an intention to notice the joyful moments. We have a suggestable unconscious, so we might as well make it work for us. Moving toward a stance of positivity can boost our self-compassion, which can in turn support our compassion for others and make tricky moments in our days a bit easier.

Thinking about your strengths and those of colleagues can boost positivity, too. Having staff conduct a character strengths evaluation can be a great thing to do together (the VIA institute on character offers a free assessment). Research has explored how people focusing on their strengths can make positive changes in their lives, and the research covers a broad range of people and situations. One study asked participants to discover their top five strengths, and each day for a week, choose a strength and aim to use it in a new way. The results were that participants even after just one week of the practice had increased happiness and experienced fewer depressive symptoms and this lasted for six months (Seligman et al., 2005). There were similar results for the positive intervention of writing down three good things that happened each day and what caused them to happen (Seligman et al., 2005). Some additional findings about a strengths focus were that character strengths work can lead to:

- greater happiness
- acceptance of oneself
- reverence for life
- increased competence, mastery and efficacy
- better mental and physical health
- more positive and supportive social networks
- satisfying, engaging and meaningful work
- accomplishment of goals

- greater engagement and life meaning
- higher work productivity
- increased likelihood of work being a life calling
- less stress and improved coping
- greater academic achievement
- improved close relationships

So, it might be worth your while taking fifteen minutes to undertake the survey and find out what your top strengths are and then put them to good use.

Yawn – sleep enough, eat well and go for a walk

Yes, I know it's boring, but the more you manage to sleep enough, exercise and eat well, the more effective you will be at work and in life. Adequate sleep is linked to resilience, psychological health, clear thinking, healthy eating patterns, greater immunity, reduced inflammation, long-term motor memories and many other beneficial elements of a healthy life (Aguilar, 2018; Noakes & Clifton, 2005; Szoeke, 2022).

While there is not a single rule that works for everyone, loosely we need about eight hours of sleep per night. Sleep is actually legislated in some industries due to the acknowledged link between reduced sleep and error (Szoeke, 2022). Trading off sleep for work is a false economy. If you want to be efficient with your work, get enough sleep. While I appreciate that life does not always allow for eight hours each night, make it your aspiration.

Exercise helps with many things mentioned previously, too. There is a benefit to understanding that, from an evolutionary perspective, conserving energy was very important and so we are not wired to seek out exercise. Even when we know it is good for us, we don't necessarily want to do it. It is the same with food – maximum energy for minimum input sends us to fatty, starchy and sweet foods. Do you notice the craving for these foods when you're particularly tired? When these kinds of food were not so available to humans, it makes sense that we became wired to seek them out. In fact, we get bursts of happy hormones when we eat fatty, starchy and sweet foods (Szoeke, 2022)!

So much of making exercise and eating well work for us is about preparation, thinking positively and making it easy. Doing some research about food can be helpful, but I suspect most of us know what is healthy and what is not.

Having a mindset that is focused on abundance rather than deficit can help with eating well – that is, thinking about all the things that you will eat in order to eat well, rather than focusing on what is on the banned or reduced list. When it comes to exercise, just fifteen minutes a day can increase lifespan by three years and incidental exercise has been demonstrated to be more successful than a focused program (Szoeke, 2022). When we build more incidental exercise into our day, it can become a habit and not feel like a burden. Luckily, in education we get lots of opportunity to build incidental exercise in. We can work with colleagues to add to these incidental moments – perhaps a walking meeting.

Vicarious resilience

I knew a student who handled a range of medical struggles. The student ended up requiring a 'halo' – screws in the scull holding a metal halo in place, with rods attached to a vest that had to be worn all the time. One morning I was sitting with this student, who couldn't participate in the daily morning run with the class, and they said, 'I'm so lucky. Everyone in my family is allergic to something, except me. I'm not allergic to anything.'

I tell this story when I go out to schools to talk about trauma because of the way it is such a perfect illustration of vicarious resilience. So much of our work is challenging, but we are also privileged to meet students who, in spite of adversity, present us with a remarkable approach to life. What luck (screws in skull aside) to have no allergies! We can look for these moments and sit with the power they have to impact us.

While the majority of the research around vicarious resilience is regarding trauma therapists, there is plenty that resonates with the work of educators. Hernandez-Wolfe et al. (2014) state that therapists, 'can be potentially transformed by their clients' trauma and resilience in ways that are positive, even if not pain free' (p. 166). We can think about this in education, too. We can be transformed by our students. If we are doing things right, school is a therapeutic environment for our students and for us. When we work with our students who live with great challenges, there can be both positivity and pain. The complexity of education work is one of the things that makes it so special.

Look out for the moments of resilience you see that might affect you. When you see it, allow it to be something that supports the work that you do, bringing hope, positivity and resilience of your own.

Conclusion

While we often can't alter the structures we work in, we can still work within our sphere of influence to focus on educator wellbeing. One of the best things about trauma-informed practice and educator wellbeing is that if you are doing one, you are doing the other. Strong relationships help students and educators; mindfulness, or tuning in to sensory needs, can regulate all humans; regulated educators support regulated students; and taking a strengths-based approach helps both students and educators. When teachers take care of themselves, it benefits them and it benefits their students. So, if you have a commitment to student wellbeing, expand your lens to include yourself. Do all the strategies you are sharing with students. Most important is the commitment to yourself. Know that you can't pour from an empty vessel. Taking care of yourself is a gift to your students as well as yourself.

CONCLUSION

Throughout this book we have been on a journey. We began with exploring trauma, adversity and their impacts. We explored what might occur in a child's life before they become a student at school. We have thought about our society, the impacts of structural adversity, as well as the way trauma can move through generations, in communities, through families and individuals. We delved into the science of brains, understanding the way that development is impacted from pre-birth by environment and experience, and we explored the way that humans are wired to respond to threat, and what it looks like when an individual lives under the shadow of constant threat.

We have considered schools, the impact they can have and the power of the capacity of educators within them. We have explored a range of approaches schools can take. We explored interventions that can work for a whole class, with strategies that can be embedded into daily routine. We looked at what we can offer when a single student needs more from us.

I hope that even if you are one person in a school wanting to make a difference, you will have identified some things that you can do. My dream is that whole schools are choosing to make education available to all of their students, choosing to embed wellbeing practices in order to increase the equity within their school.

I hope that we never have to hear the phrase 'zero tolerance' again, that we instead bring understanding, compassion and unconditional positive regard to all our interactions at school, even when it is hard. I hope we forgive ourselves and try again when we don't succeed in this. I hope that after reading this it is clear that differentiation is not just for academics, but must also be applied to behaviour, because behaviour is communication, and we need to listen.

We know that the systems we work in can be harmful. We don't experience the will to resource public education the way it needs to be resourced, and educators work within a much less-than-perfect system. While we highlight the inadequacies of the system we work within, and shine a light on the myth of educational equity, there is alwyas the capacity for an individual educator to do their best, which remains so powerful.

I hope that in this book it is clear that a single person can make a difference, even as we know that this impact will be magnified when teams take on the challenge of embedding student wellbeing. The most impactful situation lies in whole-school approaches. Schools can start slow and build up, or even jump right in with a commitment to a comprehensive program.

For those of us in schools, the work of wellbeing – when we can do it in a supportive environment – is incredibly rewarding. It may, and likely will, be exhausting and challenging, but ultimately, it is a gift, and possibly an obligation. It's complex, but when we can meet our students where they are, we can attune to their needs and our own, and make use of the strategies and interventions available to us, with differentiation at the heart. We can embed practices that support positive and respectful relationships, and promote a sense of welcome and safety for everyone who comes to school. It is very possible to do all of these things, while we also care for ourselves.

The commitment is significant. The reward is great. Schools save lives.

REFERENCES

Aboriginal and Torres Strait Islander Healing Foundation. (2013). *Growing Our Children Up Strong and Deadly: Healing for Children and Young People.* Aboriginal and Torres Strait Islander Healing Foundation. https://healingfoundation.org.au/app/uploads/2017/02/Growing-our-Children-up-SINGLES-updated-2015.pdf

ACE Resource Network. (n.d.). *The Science of ACEs: Beyond the 10.* NumberStory.org. https://numberstory.org/the-science-of-aces-2/beyond-the-10/

Agishtein, P., & Brumbaugh, C. (2013). Cultural variation in adult attachment: The impact of ethnicity, collectivism, and country of origin. *Journal of Social, Evolutionary, and Cultural Psychology, 7*(4), 384-405

Aguilar, E. (2018). *Onward: Cultivating emotional resilience in educators.* Jossey-Bass

Alvarez, A., Milner, H., & Delale-O'Connor, L. (2016). Race, Trauma, and Education in *But I Don't See Color: The Perils, Practices, and Possibilities of Antiracist Education.* Edited by Terry Husband. Sense Publishers

American Psychiartic Association. (2022). *Diagnostic and Statistical Manual of Mental Disorders (DSM-5-TR)* (5th ed.). https://www.psychiatry.org/psychiatrists/practice/dsm

Anbar, R. D. (2021). How positive talk can improve your life, *Psychology Today,* 25 December 2021. https://www.psychologytoday.com/us/blog/understanding-hypnosis/202112/how-positive-talk-can-improve-your-life?amp=

Andersen, S. L., & Teicher M. H. (2008). Stress, Sensitive Periods and Maturational Events in Adolescent Depression. *Trends in Neuroscience, 31*(4), 183–191. https://doi.org/10.1016/j.tins.2008.01.004

Andrews, G., Dean, K., Genderson, M., Hunt, C., Mitchell, P., Sachdev, P., & Trollor, J. *Management of Mental Disorders* (5th edition). (2013). School of Psychiatry, University of New South Wales

Anna Freud Centre National Centre for Children and Families. (2023). *Discrimination* https://mentallyhealthyschools.org.uk/ Retrieved 19 February, 2023

Armfield, J., Ey, L., Zufferey, C., Gnanamanickam, E., & Segal, L. (2021). Educational strengths and functional resilience at the start of primary school following child maltreatment, *Child Abuse & Neglect,* Volume (122), 105301. https://doi.org/10.1016/j.chiabu.2021.105301

Atkinson, J. (2002). *Trauma Trails, Recreating Song Lines: The Transgenerational Effects of Trauma in Indigenous Australia.* Spinifex Press

Atkinson, J. (2012). *Educaring a Trauma Informed Approach to Healing Generational Trauma for Aboriginal Australians.* We Al-li. https://www.oics.wa.gov.au/wp-content/uploads/2017/07/Judy-Atkinson-Healing-From-Generational-Trauma-Workbook-We-Al-li.pdf

Australian Child & Adolescent Trauma, Loss & Grief Network. (2016). *Stepping Up for Kids: Understanding and Supporting Children who have Experienced Family and Domestic Violence.* Commonwealth of Australia

Australian Childhood Foundation. (2011). *Discussion Paper 18: Polyvagal Theory and its Implications for Traumatised Students.* https://professionals.childhood.org.au/app/uploads/2018/08/SMART-Discussion-Paper-18.pdf

Australian Childhood Foundation. (2016). *Considering Neurobiological Development, Block One Handout, Graduate Certificate in Developmental Trauma.* Australian Childhood Foundation

Australian Childhood Foundation. (2018). *Making Space for Learning: Trauma Informed Practice in Schools.* https://littlestarskids.org.au/wp-content/uploads/files/MSFL-Discussion-paper-Impact-of-trauma-on-memory.pdf

Australian Childhood Foundation. (2020). *Discussion Paper 3: Exploring the Impact of Abuse Related Trauma on Memory Functioning of Children.* https://littlestarskids.org.au/wp-content/uploads/files/MSFL-Discussion-paper-Impact-of-trauma-on-memory.pdf

Australian Council of Social Service. (2020a). *Poverty in Australia 2020: Part 1 – Overview.* Australian Council of Social Service, in partnership with the University of New South Wales

Australian Council of Social Service. (2020b). *Poverty in Australia 2020: Part 2 – Who is Affected?* Australian Council of Social Service, in partnership with the University of New South Wales

Australian Institute of Criminology. (2011). *Children's Exposure to Domestic Violence in Australia. Trends & Issues in Crime and Criminal Justice No.419.* Sourced from: https://www.aic.gov.au/publications/tandi/tandi419

Australian Institute of Health and Welfare. (2015). *Child Protection Australia 2013–14.* Canberra: Australian Institute of Health and Welfare. www.aihw.gov.au/publication-detail/?id=60129550762

Australian Institute of Health and Welfare. (2019). *Family, Domestic and Sexual Violence in Australia: Continuing the National Story 2019.* Australian Institute of Health and Welfare

Badenoch, B. (Speaker). (2017, March). *A Symphony of Gifts from Relational Neuroscience: How Understanding our Brains can Support Lives of Hope and Resilience.* Neuroscience Training Summit. Sounds True. https://www.soundstrue.com/store/ neuroscience-summit

Baker, J. (2022). Brain study shows children bounce back from encouraging feedback *Sydney Morning Herald,* 2 January 2022

Baram, T. (2022). Predicable and consistent parental behaviour is key for optimal child brain development. *The Conversation,* 22 June, 2022. Accessed from https://theconversation.com/predictable-and-consistent-parental-behavior-is-key-for-optimal-child-brain-development-184300 24/6/22

Barrett, P., Davies, F., Zhang, Y., & Barrett, L. (2015). The impact of classroom design on pupils' learning: Final results of a holistic, multi-level analysis. *Building and Environment,* 89, 118–133

Bentley, J. A., Thoburn, J. W., Stewart, D. G., & Boynton, L. D. (2012). Post-Migration Stress as a Moderator Between Traumatic Exposure and Self-Reported Mental Health Symptoms in a Sample of Somali Refugees. *Journal of Loss and Trauma,* 17(5), 452–469. https://doi.org/10.1080/15325024.2012.665008

Benazzo, Z., & Benazzo, M. (Producers and Directors) (2021). *The Wisdom of Trauma* [Streaming Video]. The Hive Studios. https://thewisdomoftrauma.com/

Bergeron, F.-A., Blais, M., & Hébert, M. (2015). Le rôle du soutien parental dans la relation entre la victimisation homophobe, l'homophobie intériorisée et la détresse psychologique chez les jeunes de minorités sexuelles (JMS): une approche de médiation modérée [The role of parental support in the relationship between homophobic bullying, internalized homophobia and psychological distress among sexual-minority youths (SMY): A moderated mediation approach]. *Santé Mentale au Québec, 40*(3), 109–127. https://doi.org/10.7202/1034914ar

Bernardi, N. F., De Buglio, M., Trimarchi, P. D., Chielli, A., & Bricolo, E. (2013). Mental Practice Promotes Motor Anticipation: Evidence from Skilled Music Performance. *Frontiers in Human Neuroscience, 7,* Article 451. https://doi.org/10.3389/fnhum.2013.00451

Blair, C., & Raver, C. (2015). School Readiness and Self-Regulation: A Developmental Psychobiological Approach. *Annual Review of Psychology*. 2015; 66: (p.711–31). doi: 10.1146/annurev-psych-010814-015221

Blue Knot Foundation and BEING – Mental health consumers Inc. (2021). *Living with and Healing from Complex Trauma.* National Mental Health Commission

Bowlby, J. (1944). Forty-Four Juvenile Thieves: Their Characters and Home-Life, *International Journal of Psycho-Analysis XXV,* 19–52

Bowlby, J. (1969), Attachment. *Vol 1 of Attachment and Loss.* Basic Books

Brackett, M. (2019). *Permission to Feel: Unlock the Power of Emotions to Help Yourself and Your Child Thrive.* Quercus Editions Ltd, Great Britain

Bravehearts Foundation Limited. (2021). *Child Sexual Assault: Facts and Statistics.* Bravehearts Foundation Limited

Bretherton, I. (1992). The origins of attachment theory: John Bowlby and Mary Ainsworth. *Developmental Psychology. Vol. 28* (5) 759–775. https://cmapspublic2.ihmc. us/rid=1LQX400NM-RBVKH9-1KL6/the%20origins%20of%20attachment%20 theory%20john%20bowlby%20and_mary_ainsworth.pdf

Brown, B. (2012, March). *Listening to Shame* [Video]. TED Conferences. https://www. ted.com/talks/brene_brown_listening_to_shame

Brunzell, T., Stokes, H., & Waters, L. (2016). Trauma-informed positive education: Using positive psychology to strengthen vulnerable students *Contemporary School Psychology Vol 20* (1) p. 63-83. doi: 10.1007/s40688-015-0070-x

Brunzell, T., & Norrish, J. (2021). *Creating Trauma-Informed, Strengths-Based Classrooms: Teacher Strategies for Nurturing Students' Healing, Growth, and Learning.* Jessica Kingsley Publishers

Burke Harris, N. (2018). *The Deepest Well: Healing the Long-Term Effects of Childhood Adversity.* Houghton Mifflin Harcourt

Cahill, H. (2021). *Using School-based Social and Emotional Learning Programs to Advance Wellbeing Post Emergency.* [Video] Melbourne Social Equity Institute. https://socialequity.unimelb.edu.au/news/events/school-based-social-and-emotional-learning-programs

Cahill, H., Kern, M. L., Dadvand, B., Cruickshank, E. W., Midford, R., Smith, C., & Oades, L. (2019). An integrative approach to evaluating the implementation of social and emotional learning and gender-based violence prevention education. International *Journal of Emotional Education,* 11(1), 135–152

Carnevale, A., Fasules, M., Quinn, M., & Campbell, K. (2019). *Born to Win, Schooled to Lose: Why Equally Talented Students Don't Get Equal Chances to be All They can Be.* Georgetown University

Carpenter J., & Drabick D. (2011). Co-occurrence of linguistic and behavioural difficulties in early childhood: a developmental psychopathology perspective. *Early Child Development and Care. 2011 Sep;181(8)*:1021–1045. doi: 10.1080/03004430. 2010.509795

Carrol, L., & Gladstone, N. (2022). Sydney's wealthiest suburbs claim the most HSC disability provisions. *The Sydney Morning Herald*, 4 September 2022

Center on the Developing Child at Harvard University. (2011). *Building the Brain's "Air Traffic Control" System: How Early Experiences Shape the Development of Executive Function: Working Paper No. 11.* https://developingchild.harvard.edu/wp-content/uploads/2011/05/How-Early-Experiences-Shape-the-Development-of-Executive-Function.pdf

Center on the Developing Child at Harvard University. (2020). *Resilience.* www.developingchild.harvard.edu/science/key-concepts/resilience/

Center on the Developing Child at Harvard University. (2022). *Activities Guide: Enhancing and Practicing Executive Function Skills with Children from Infancy to Adolescence.* https://developingchild.harvard.edu/resources/activities-guide-enhancing-and-practicing-executive-function-skills-with-children-from-infancy-to-adolescence/

Center on the Developing Child at Harvard University. (2022a). *InBrief: Understanding the Science of Motivation.* https://developingchild.harvard.edu/resources/inbrief-understanding-the-science-of-motivation/

Centers for Disease Control and Prevention. (2022). *What is Epigenetics?.* https://www.cdc.gov/genomics/disease/epigenetics.htm

Centers for Disease Control and Prevention. (2023). *Adverse Childhood Experiences (ACEs).* https://www.cdc.gov/violenceprevention/aces

Cherry, K. (2020). The Different Types of Attachment Styles, *Very Well Mind.* https://www.verywellmind.com/attachment-styles-2795344

Cole, S., O'Brien, J. G., Gadd, M.G., Ristuccia, J., Wallace, D. L., & Gregory, M. (2005). *Trauma and Learning Policy Initiative*, Massachusetts Advocates for Children

Colla, R., Williams, P., Oades, L. G., & Camacho-Morles, J. (2022). "A New Hope" for Positive Psychology: A Dynamic Systems Reconceptualization of Hope Theory. *Frontiers in Psychology Vol. 13*, 2022. doi=10.3389/fpsyg.2022.809053

Commonwealth of Australia. (2022). Australian Early Development Census National Report 2021, Early Childhood Development in Australia

Corey, G. (2021). *Theory and Practice of Counselling and Psychotherapy: Updated Tenth Edition* (10th ed.). Cengage

Cozolino, L. J. (2014). *Attachment-Based Teaching: Creating a Tribal Classroom.* W.W. Norton & Company

Craig, S. E. (2008). *Reaching and Teaching Children Who Hurt: Strategies for Your Classroom.* Brookes Publishing

Craig, S. E. (2016). *Trauma-Sensitive Schools: Learning Communities Transforming Children's Lives, K–5.* Hawker Brownlow Education

Curtis, P., Frey, J., Watson, C., Hampton, L., & Roberts, M. (2018). Language Disorders and Problem Behaviors: A Meta-analysis. *Pediatrics 142 (2)* https://doi.org/10.1542/peds.2017-3551

Cyrus, K. (2017). Multiple Minorities as Multiply Marginalized: Applying the Minority Stress Theory to LGBTQ People of Color. *Journal of Gay & Lesbian Mental Health, 21*(3), 194–202. https://doi.org/10.1080/19359705.2017.1320739

Dana, D. (2018). *The Polyvagal Theory in Therapy: Engaging the Rhythm of Regulation.* W. W. Norton & Company

Dana, D. (2021). *The Body's Safety Circuit: A Polyvagal Guided Approach to Connection* [Conference session]. International Childhood Trauma Conference, Online

D'Andrea, W., Ford, J., Stolbach, B., Spinazzola, J., & van der Kolk, B. (2012). Understanding Interpersonal Trauma in Children: Why We Need a Developmentally Appropriate Trauma Diagnosis. *American Journal of Orthopsychiatry, 82*(2), 187–200. https://doi.org/10.1111/j.1939-0025.2012.01154.x

David, S. (2017). How Writing About Negative Experiences Helps You Move Past Them, *Thrive Global.* 3 April 2017. https://medium.com/thrive-global/how-writing-about-negative-experiences-helps-you-move-past-them

Davidson, P., Saunders, P., Bradbury, B., & Wong, M. (2020a). *Poverty in Australia 2020: Part 1: Overview.* Australian Council of Social Service (ACOSS) and UNSW Sydney. https://povertyandinequality.acoss.org.au/wp-content/uploads/2020/02/Poverty-in-Australia-2020_Part-1_Overview.pdf

Davidson, P., Saunders, P., Bradbury, B., & Wong, M. (2020b). *Poverty in Australia 2020: Part 4: Who is Affected?.* Australian Council of Social Service (ACOSS) and UNSW Sydney. https://povertyandinequality.acoss.org.au/wp-content/uploads/2020/05/Poverty-in-Australia-2020-Part-2-%E2%80%93-Who-is-affected_Final.pdf

Department for Education, South Australia. (2019). *Ready to Learn: Interoception Kit.* Department for Education, South Australia. https://www.education.sa.gov.au/sites/default/files/ready-to-learn-interoception-kit.pdf

Dockrill, P. (2022). 1st detailed study of 'misokinesia' phenomenon shows it might affect 1 in 3 people, *Science Alert,* 20 November 2022. https://www.sciencealert.com/1st-detailed-study-of-misokinesia-phenomenon-shows-it-might-affect-1-in-3-people

Doidge, N. (2010). *The Brain That Changes Itself: Stories of Personal Triumph from the Frontiers of Brain Science.* Scribe Publications

Doidge, N. (2015). *The Brain's Way of Healing: Remarkable Discoveries and Recoveries from the Frontiers of Neuroscience.* Scribe Publications

Domitrovich, C. E., Durlak, J. A., Staley, K. C., & Weissberg, R. P. (2017). Social-Emotional Competence: An Essential Factor for Promoting Positive Adjustment and Reducing Risk in School Children. *Child Development. Mar/Apr 2017, Vol. 88* (2), p. 408–416

Dudgeon, P., Milroy, H., & Walker, R. (Eds.) (2014). *Working Together: Aboriginal and Torres Strait Islander Mental Health and Wellbeing Principles and Practice.* Commonwealth of Australia

Dudgeon, P., Wright, M., Paradies, Y., Garvey, D., & Walker, I. (2014). Aboriginal Social, Cultural and Historical Contexts in *Working Together: Aboriginal and Torres Strait Islander Mental Health and Wellbeing Principles and Practice.* Dudgeon, P., Milroy, H., & Walker, R. (Eds.) Commonwealth of Australia

Durham, R. E., Farkas, G., Scheffner Hammer, C., Tomblin, J. B., & Catts, H. W. (2007). Kindergarten oral language skill: A key variable in the intergenerational transmission of socioeconomic status. *Research in Social Stratification and Mobility. Volume 25* (4), p. 294-305. https://doi.org/10.1016/j.rssm.2007.03.001

Durlak, J. A., Weissberg, R. P., Dymnicki, A. B., Taylor, R. D., & Schellinger, K. B. (2011). The Impact of Enhancing Students' Social and Emotional Learning: A Meta-Analysis of School-Based Universal Interventions. *Child Development, 82*(1), 405–432. https://doi.org/10.1111/j.1467-8624.2010.01564.x

Dweck, C. (2006). *Mindset.* Random House

Dweck, C. (2015). Growth Mindset, Revisited. *Education Week, 35*(5), 24–20

Eanes, R. (2022). Pretending To Be Calm Is Not Helping Our Children, *Generation Mindful.* https://genmindful.com/blogs/mindful-moments/pretending-to-be-calm-is-not-helping-our-children

Early Learning, Everyone Benefits. (2016). *The State of Early Learning in Australia Report 2016*, Early Childhood Australia. http://bjseminars.com.au/docs/ELEB-Report-final.pdf

Eigsti, I.M., & Cicchetti, D. (2004). The impact of child maltreatment on expressive syntax at 60 months. *Dev Sci.* 2004 Feb; 7(1):88–102. doi: 10.1111/j.1467-7687.2004.00325.x. PMID: 15323121

El-Sheikh, M., & Erath, S. A. (2011). Family Conflict, Autonomic Nervous System Functioning, and Child Adaptation: State of the Science and Future Directions. *Development and Psychopathology, 23*(2), 703–721. https://doi.org/10.1017/S0954579411000034

Farrington, C. A., Roderick, M., Allensworth, E., Nagaoka, J., Keyes, T. S., Johnson, D. W., & Beechum, N. O. (2012). *Teaching Adolescents to Become Learners. The Role of Noncognitive Factors in Shaping School Performance: A Critical Literature Review.* University of Chicago Consortium on Chicago School Research

Felitti, V. J., Anda, R. F., Nordenberg, D., Williamson, D. F., Spitz, A. M., Edwards, V., Koss, M. P., & Marks, J. S. (1998). Relationship of childhood abuse and household dysfunction to many of the leading causes of death in adults: The adverse childhood experiences (ACE) study. *American Journal of Preventive Medicine Vol 14* (4) 245–258

Flook, L., Goldberg, S. B., Pinger, L., Bonus, K., & Davidson, R. J. (2013). Mindfulness for teachers: A pilot study to assess effects on stress, burnout and teaching efficacy. *Mind, Brain and Education, 7*(3), 10.1111/mbe.12026. https://doi.org/10.1111/mbe.12026

Fricker, A., & Fricker, B. (2022). 'Decolonising' classrooms could help keep First Nations kids in school and away from police, *The Conversation,* 4 August 2022. https://theconversation.com/decolonising-classrooms-could-help-keep-first-nations-kids-in-school-and-away-from-police-188067

Fuchs, E., & Flügge, G. (2014). Adult neuroplasticity: More than 40 years of research. *Neural Plasticity*, 2014, Article 541870. https://doi.org/10.1155/2014/541870

Gage, F. H. (2004). Structural plasticity of the adult brain. *Dialogues in Clinical Neuroscience, 6*(2), 135–141. https://doi.org/10.31887/DCNS.2004.6.2/fgage

Goodall, E. (2016). *Interoception 101 Activity Guide*, Department for Education, South Australia

Gorski, P. (2019). Avoiding Racial Equity Detours. Educational Leadership. 76 (7), 56-61

Goss, P., & Hunter, J. (2015). *Targeted Teaching: How Better Use of Student Data Can Improve Learning.* Grattan Institute

Government of South Australia, Department for Education. (2020). *HSP426 Wellbeing, Stress and Distress Questionnaire: Questionnaire for Education and Care.* Government of South Australia

Graham, L., Killingly, C., Laurens, K., & Sweller, N. (2021). Suspensions and expulsions could see our most vulnerable kids on a path to school drop-out, drug use, and crime *The Conversation,* 15 September 2021. https://theconversation.com/suspensions-and-expulsions-could-set-our-most-vulnerable-kids-on-a-path-to-school-drop-out-drug-use-and-crime-166827

Green, S., Oades, L., & Robinson, P. (2011). Positve education: creating flourishing students, staff and schools. *InPsych 2011 Vol 33* April, Issue 2. https://psychology.org.au/publications/inpsych/2011/april/green

Greene, K. (2020). What is explicit instruction? *Understood.* https://www.understood.org/en/articles/what-is-explicit-instruction

Greene, R. W. (2014). *Lost at School: Why Our Kids with Behavioral Challenges are Falling Through the Cracks and How We Can Help Them.* Scribner

Grieg, J. (2018). *Linking Unconditional Positive Regard and Teacher Wellbeing.* Berry Street https://www.berrystreet.org.au/news/linking-unconditional-positive-regard-and-teacher-wellbeing

Hampden-Thompson, G., & Galindo, C. (2017). School-family relationships, school satisfaction and the academic achievement of young people. *Educational Review, 69*(2), 248–265. https://doi.org/10.1080/00131911.2016.1207613

Harris, R. (2016). *"I feel happy when I get to be with you". Trauma informed practice in education: Carlton Primary School,* Carlton Primary School

Harris, R. (2019). *ACT Made Simple:* second edition New Harbinger Publications

Haslam, D., Mathews, B., Pacella, R., Scott, J. G., Finkelhor, D., Higgins, D. J., Meinck, F., Erskine, H. E., Thomas, H. J., Lawrence, D., & Malacova, E. (2023). *The prevalence and impact of child maltreatment in Australia: Findings from the Australian Child Maltreatment Study: Brief Report.* Australian Child Maltreatment Study, Queensland University of Technology. http://doi.org/10.5204/rep.eprints.239397

Hayes, S. C., Strosahl, K. D., & Wilson, K. G., (2016). *Acceptance and Commitment Therapy: The Process and Practice of Mindful Change (2nd ed.).* Guildford Publications

Hernandez-Wolfe, P., Killian, K., Engstrom, D., & Gangsei, D. (2014). Vicarious Resilience, Vicarious Trauma and Awareness of Equity in Trauma Work. *Journal of Humanistic Psychology 55*(2): 153–172. https://doi.org/10.1177/0022167814534322

Hernandez-Wolfe, P. (2018). Vicarious Resilience: A Comprehensive Review. *Revista de Estudios Sociales 66*: 9–17. https://doi.org/10.7440/res66.2018.02

Herner, T. (1998). Understanding and intervening in young children's challenging behavior. *Counterpoint, Vol 1*, p. 2. National Association of Directors of Special Education

Hershkowitz, I., Horowitz, D., & Lamb, M. E. (2005). Trends in children's disclosure of abuse in Israel: A national study. *Child Abuse & Neglect, 29*(11), 1203–1214. https://doi.org/10.1016/j.chiabu.2005.04.008

Hesse, E., Main, M., Abrams, K. Y., & Rivkin, A. (2003). Unresolved states regarding loss or abuse can have 'second generation' effects: Disorganization, role inversion, and frightening ideation in the offspring of traumatized, non-maltreating parents. In Solomon, M. F., & Siegel, D. J. (Eds.), *Healing Trauma: Attachment, Mind, Body and Brain* (pp. 57–106). W.W. Norton & Company

Hooton, J. (2019). SHAME: An existential wound. *The Knowing Field June 2019 (34)* 29–44

Innerbody. (n.d.). *Nervous System.* https://www.innerbody.com/image/nervov.html

Jamieson, K. (2018). *ACEs and Minorities*. Center for Child Counseling. https://www.centerforchildcounseling.org/aces-and-minorities/

Jawabri K. H., & Sharma, S. (2021). *Physiology, Cerebral Cortex Functions*. StatPearls Publishing

Jennings, P. (2019). *The Trauma-sensitive Classroom: Building Resilience with Compassionate Teaching*. W.W. Norton & Company

Jones, B. K., Destin, M., & McAdams, D. P. (2018). Telling better stories: Competence-building narrative themes increase adolescent persistence and academic achievement. *Journal of Experimental Social Psychology, Volume 76*, Pages 76–80. https://doi.org/10.1016/j.jesp.2017.12.006

Kain, K. L., & Terrell, S. J. (2018). *Nurturing Resilience: Helping Clients Move Forward from Developmental Trauma: An Integrative Somatic Approach*. North Atlantic Books

Kaskamanidis, Z. (2022). Managing micro transitions in the classroom *Teacher Magazine, 23 June 2022*. https://www.teachermagazine.com/au_en/articles/managing-micro-transitions-in-the-classroom

Kenardy, J., De Young, A., Le Brocque, R., & March, S. (2011). *Childhood Trauma Reactions: A Guide for Teachers From Preschool To Year 12*. Centre of National Research on Disability and Rehabilitation Medicine

Kendrick, A. (2022). 5 ways to create a compassionate workplace culture and help workers recover from burnout. *The Conversation,* 18 November 2022. https://theconversation.com/5-ways-to-create-a-compassionate-workplace-culture-and-help-workers-recover-from-burnout-190489 on November 19 2022

Kezelman, C., & Stavropoulos, P. (2019). *Practice Guidelines for Clinical Treatment of Complex Trauma*. Blue Knot Foundation

Kezelman, C., & Stavropoulos, P. (2020). *Practice Guidelines for Identifying and Treating Complex Trauma-Related Dissociation*. Blue Knot Foundation

Kim, S., Crooks, C. V., Bax, K. & Shokoohi, M. (2021). Impact of Trauma-Informed Training and Mindfulness-Based Social–Emotional Learning Program on Teacher Attitudes and Burnout: A Mixed-Methods Study. *School Mental Health 13*, 55–68 https://doi.org/10.1007/s12310-020-09406-6

Kira, I. A. (2001). Taxonomy of Trauma and Trauma Assessment. *Traumatology, 7*(2), 73–86. https://doi.org/10.1177/153476560100700202

Kline, M. (2020). *Brain-changing Strategies to Trauma-proof our Schools: A heart-centred Movement for Wiring Well-being*. North Atlantic Books

Koenig, A., Rodger, S., & Specht, J. (2018). Educator burnout and compassion fatigue: A pilot study. *Canadian Journal of School Psychology, Vol 33* (4) 259–278

Krupka, Z. (2018). Challenging Snoopervision: How can Person-Centred Practitioners Offer New Alternatives to the Fracturing of the Person in the Supervision Relationship?. In Bazzano, M. (ed.), *Re-Visioning Person-Centred Therapy: Theory and Practice of a Radical Paradigm* (1st ed., pp. 265–276). Routledge

Kuyken W., Ball, S., Crane. C., et al. (2022). Effectiveness and cost-effectiveness of universal school-based mindfulness training compared with normal school provision in reducing risk of mental health problems and promoting well-being in adolescence: the MYRIAD cluster randomised controlled trial. *Evidence-Based Mental Health*. doi: 10.1136/ebmental-2021-300396

Kuypers, L. (2011). *The Zones of Regulation: A Curriculum Designed to Foster Self-Regulation and Emotional Control*. Think Social Publishing

Laakso, M., Fagerlund, Å., Pesonen, A.-K., Figueiredo, R. A. O., & Eriksson, J. G. (2022). The Impact of the Positive Education Program Flourishing Students on Early Adolescents' Daily Positive and Negative Emotions Using the Experience Sampling Method. *The Journal of Early Adolescence,* Volume 43, Issue 4. https://doi.org/10.1177/02724316221105582

La Trobe University. (2022). Supporting teachers' mental health, *La Trobe News 19/6/2022.* https://www.latrobe.edu.au/news/articles/2022/release/supporting-teachers-mental-health

Lanius, R. A., Terpou, B. A., & McKinnon, M. C. (2020). The sense of self in the aftermath of trauma: lessons from the default mode network in posttraumatic stress disorder. *European Journal of Psychotraumatology. 11*(1). doi: 10.1080/20008198.2020.1807703

Lean, C., Leslie, M., Goodall, E., McCauley, M., & Heays, D. (2019). *Interoception 201 Activity Guide,* Department for Education, South Australia

LeDoux, J. E. (2015). The Amygdala Is Not the Brain's Fear Center: Separating Findings from Conclusions. *Psychology Today.* https://www.psychologytoday.com/au/blog/i-got-mind-tell-you/201508/the-amygdala-is-not-the-brains-fear-center

Lemaigre, C., Taylor, E. P., & Gittoes, C. (2017). Barriers and facilitators to disclosing sexual abuse in childhood and adolescence: A systematic review. *Child Abuse & Neglect, 70,* 39–52. https://doi.org/10.1016/j.chiabu.2017.05.009

Lever, N., Mathis, E., & Mayworm, A. (2017). School Mental Health Is Not Just for Students: Why Teacher and School Staff Wellness Matters. *Report on Emotional & Behavioral Disorders in Youth,* 17(1), 6–12

Lewis, K. R. (2015). What if everything you knew about disciplining kids was wrong? *Mother Jones.* http://www.motherjones.com/politics/2015/05/schools-behavior-discipline-collaborative-proactive-solutions-ross-greene

LGBTIQ+ Health Australia. (2021). *Snapshot of Mental Health and Suicide Prevention Statistics for LGBTIQ+ People.* LGBTIQA+ Health Australia. https://assets.nationbuilder.com/lgbtihealth/pages/549/attachments/original/1648014801/24.10.21_Snapshot_of_MHSP_Statistics_for_LGBTIQ__People_-_Revised.pdf?1648014801

Luiselli, J. K., Putnam, R. F., Handler, M. W. & Feinberg, A. B., (2005). *Whole-school Positive Behaviour Support: Effects on Student Discipline Problems and Academic Performance.* Educational Psychology, 25(2-3), pp.183–198

Malchiodi, C. (2021). *Children and Adolescents with Complex Trauma: Restoring the Self Through Expressive Therapies.* International Childhood trauma conference, online symposium, 1–3 June 2021

Malchiodi, C. A. (Ed.) (2015). *Creative Interventions with Traumatized Children.* The Guilford Press

Masten, A., & Barnes, A. (2018). Resilience in Children: Developmental Perspectives. *Children,* 5(7), 98. MDPI AG. http://dx.doi.org/10.3390/children5070098

Masters, G. (2018). What is 'equity' in education. *Teacher Magazine* https://www.teachermagazine.com/au_en/articles/what-is-equity-in-education

McCann, I. L., & Pearlman, L. A. (1990). Vicarious Traumatization: A Framework for Understanding the Psychological Effects of Working with Victims. *Journal of Traumatic Stress, 3*(1), 131–149. https://doi.org/10.1002/jts.2490030110

McCluskey, G., Lloyd, G., Stead, J., Kane, J., Riddell, S., & Weedon, E. (2008). 'I was dead restorative today': From restorative justice to restorative approaches in school. Cambridge journal of education, 38(2), 199–216

McLean, S. (2018). Developmental differences in children who have experienced adversity: Difficulty with executive functioning. CFCA Practice Guide (Developmental Differences: 3 of 4). Child Family Community Australia

Merrick, M. T., Ford, D. C., Ports, K. A., & Guinn, A. S. (2018). Prevalence of Adverse Childhood Experiences From the 2011–2014 Behavioral Risk Factor Surveillance System in 23 States. *JAMA Pediatrics, 172*(11), 1038–1044. https://doi.org/10.1001/jamapediatrics.2018.2537

Mitchell, J., Tucci, J., & Tronick, E. (Eds). (2020). *The Handbook of Therapeutic Care for Children : Evidence-Informed Approaches to Working with Traumatized Children and Adolescents in Foster, Kinship and Adoptive Care,* Jessica Kingsley Publishers

Möller, A., Söndergaard, H. P., & Helström, L. (2017). Tonic Immobility During Sexual Assault – A Common Reaction Predicting Post-Traumatic Stress Disorder and Severe Depression. *Acta Obstetricia et Gynecologica Scandinavia, 96*(8), 932–938. https://doi.org/10.1111/aogs.13174

Moser, E. I., Kropff, E., & Moser, M. B. (2008). Place Cells, Grid Cells, and the Brain's Spatial Representation System. *Annual Review of Neuroscience, 31*, 69–89. https://doi.org/10.1146/annurev.neuro.31.061307.090723

Mueller, C. M., & Dweck, C. S. (1998). Praise for intelligence can undermine children's motivation and performance. *Journal of Personality and Social Psychology, 75*(1), 33–52. https://doi.org/10.1037/0022-3514.75.1.33

National Scientific Council on the Developing Child. (2015). *Supportive Relationships and Active Skill-Building Strengthen the Foundations of Resilience: Working Paper 13.* http://www.developingchild.harvard.edu

National Workforce Centre for Child Mental Health, The. (with Australian National University). (2020). *Adverse Childhood Experiences (ACEs): Summary of Evidence and Impacts.* https://d2p3kdr0nr4o3z.cloudfront.net/content/uploads/2020/02/19102540/ACES-Summary-of-Evidence-and-Impacts-V2.pdf

Neuroscience News. (2022). *Cash Support for Low-income Families Impacts Infant Brain Activity,* https://neurosciencenews.com/babies-brain-financial-intervention-19956/

Noakes, M., & Clifton, P. (2005). *The CSRIO Total Wellbeing Diet,* Penguin Books

Occupational Therapy Helping Children. (2017). *The vestibular system.* https://occupationaltherapy.com.au/the-vestibular-system/

Occupational Therapy Helping Children. (2019). *What is interoception.* https://occupationaltherapy.com.au/interoception/

Occupational Therapy Helping Children. (2019). *What is proprioception and why is it important?* https://occupationaltherapy.com.au/proprioception/

Occupational Therapy Helping Children. (2022). *What is Sensory Processing Disorder?* https://www.occupationaltherapy.com.au/what-is-sensory-processing-disorder/

Ogden, P., Goldstein, B., & Fisher, J. (2012). Brain-to-Brain, Body-to-Body: A Sensorimotor Psychotherapy Perspective on the Treatment of Children and Adolescents. In Longo, R. E., Prescott, D. S., Bergman, J., & Creeden K. (Eds.), *Current Perspectives and Applications in Neurobiology: Working with Young Persons who are Victims and Perpetrators of Sexual Abuse.* NEARI Press

Olson, K., & Cozolino, L. (2014). *The Invisible Classroom: Relationships, Neuroscience & Mindfulness in School.* Norton

Ogden, P., Pain, C., & Fisher, J. (2006). A sensorimotor approach to the treatment of trauma and dissociation. *Psychiatric Clinics*, 29(1), 263–279

Omar, K. (2014). *10 years of HoA playgroup.* Melbourne, City of Melbourne

Paas, F., & van Merriënboer, J. J. G. (2020). Cognitive-Load Theory: Methods to Manage Working Memory Load in the Learning of Complex Tasks. *Current Directions in Psychological Science*, 29(4), 394–398. https://doi.org/10.1177/0963721420922183

Parish-Plass, N. (2020). Animal-Assisted Psychotherapy for Developmental Trauma Through the Lens of Interpersonal Neurobiology of Trauma: Creating Connection With Self and Others. *Journal of Psychotherapy Integration*

Parker, R., & Milroy, H. (2014). Aboriginal and Torres Strait Islander Mental Health: An Overview. In Dudgeon, P., Millroy H., & Walker, R. (Eds.), *Working Together: Aboriginal and Torres Strait Islander Mental Health and Wellbeing Principles and Practice.* Commonwealth of Australia

Patalay, P., O'Neill, E., Deighton, J., & Fink, E. (2020). School characteristics and children's mental health: A linked survey-administrative data study *Preventive Medicine, Volume 141*, December 2020. https://doi.org/10.1016/j.ypmed.2020.106292

Paterson, J. L., Brown, R., & Walters, M. A. (2019). The Short and Longer Term Impacts of Hate Crimes Experienced Directly, Indirectly, and Through the Media. *Personality and Social Psychology Bulletin, 45*(7), 994–1010. https://doi.org/10.1177/0146167218802835

Payne, P., Levine, P. A., & Crane-Godreau, M. A. (2015). Somatic experiencing: using interoception and proprioception as core elements of trauma therapy. *Frontiers in Psychology*, February, 2015. doi: 10.3389/fpsyg.2015.00093

Pennebaker, J. W. (1997). Writing about emotional experiences as a therapeutic process. *Psychological Science*, 8(3), 162–166

Pennebaker, J. W. (2018). Expressive Writing in Psychological Science. *Perspectives on Psychological Science*, 13(2), 226–229. https://doi.org/10.1177/1745691617707315

Perry, B. D. (2008). Applying principles of neurodevelopment to clinical work with maltreated and traumatized children: The neurosequential model of treatment in Webb, N. B. (Ed.) *Working with Traumatized Youth in Child Welfare.* New York. The Guilford Press

Perry, B. D. (2009). Examining child maltreatment through a neurodevelopmental lens: Clinical applications of the neurosequential model of therapeutics. *Journal of Loss and Trauma, 14*(4), 240–255. https://psycnet.apa.org/doi/10.1080/15325020903004350

Perry, B. D., Pollard, R. A., Blakley, T. L., Baker, W. L., & Vigilante, D. (1995). Childhood trauma, the neurobiology of adaptation, and "use-dependent" development of the brain: How "states" become "traits". Infant *Mental Health Journal, 16*(4), 271–291. https://doi.org/10.1002/1097-0355(199524)16:4%3C271::AID-IMHJ2280160404%3E3.0.CO;2-B

Perry, B. D., & Szalavitz, M. (2017). *The Boy Who Was Raised as a Dog: And Other Stories from a Child Psychiatrist's Notebook – What Traumatized Children Can Teach Us About Loss, Love, and Healing* (3rd ed.). Basic Books

Perry, B. D., & Winfrey, O. (2021). *What Happened to You?: Conversations on Trauma, Resilience, and Healing.* Pan Macmillan

Perry, R. E., Blair, C. & Sullivan, R. M. (2017). *Neurobiology of infant attachment: attachment despite adversity and parental programming of emotionality*, Current Opinion in Psychology 2017, 17:1–6

Pfaltz, M. C., Passardi S., Auschra, B., Fares-Otero, N. E., Schnyder, U., & Peyk, P. (2019). Are you angry at me? Negative interpretations of neutral facial expressions are linked to child maltreatment but not to posttraumatic stress disorder. *European Journal of Psychotraumatology*, *10*:1, 1682929, doi:10.1080/20008198.2019.1682929

Platt, M., & Freyd, J. (2015). Betray my trust, shame on me: Shame, dissociation, fear, and betrayal trauma. *Psychological Trauma: Theory, Research, Practice, and Policy, Vol 7*(4), Jul 2015, 398-404 doi: 10.1037/tra0000022

Porges, S. W. (2009). *The Polyvagal Theory: New Insights Into Adaptive Reactions of the Autonomic Nervous System. Cleveland Clinic Journal of Medicine*, 76(SUPPL.2). https://doi.org/10.3949/ccjm.76.s2.17

Porges, S. W. (2010). *The Early Development of the Autonomic Nervous System Provides a Neural Platform for Social Behavior: A Polyvagal Perspective.* Brain Body Centre University of Illinois at Chicago. http://www.terapiacognitiva.eu/cpc/dwl/polivagale/porges.pdf

Porges, S. W. (2017). *The Pocket Guide to Polyvagal Theory: The Transformative Power of Feeling Safe.* Norton Professional Books

Provenzi, L., Mambretti, F., Villa, M., Grumi, S., Citterio, A., Bertazzoli, E., Biasucci, G., Decembrino, L., Falcone, R., Gardella. B., Longo, M. R., Nacinovich, R., Pisoni, C., Prefumo, F., Orcesi, S., Scelsa, B., Giorda, R., & Borgatti, R. (2021). Hidden pandemic: COVID-19-related stress, *SLC6A4* methylation, and infants' temperament at 3 months. *Scientific Reports*, 11, 15658. https://doi.org/10.1038/s41598-021-95053-z

Rao, H., Betancourt, L., Giannetta, J. M., Brodsky, N. L., Korczykowski, M., Avants, B. B., Gee, J. C., Wang, J., Hurt, H., Detre, J. A., & Farah, M. J. (2010). Early Parental Care Is Important for Hippocampal Maturation: Evidence from Brain Morphology in Humans. *NeuroImage, 49*(1), 1144–1150. https://doi.org/10.1016/j.neuroimage.2009.07.003

Reuben, A. (2015). When PTSD is Contagious. *The Atlantic.* https://www.theatlantic.com/health/archive/2015/12/ptsd-secondary-trauma/420282/

Ronken, C., & Johnston, H. (2012). *Child Sexual Assault: Facts and Statistics.* Bravehearts Inc

Rosenfield, P. J., Stratyner, A., Tufekcioglu, S., Karabell, S., McKelvey, J., & Litt, L. (2018). Complex PTSD in ICD-11: A Case Report on a New Diagnosis. *Journal of Psychiatric Practice, 24*(5), 364–370. https://doi.org/10.1097/PRA.0000000000000327

Rudolph, S. (2023). Carceral logics and education, *Critical Studies in Education*, 1–18

Rudolph, S. & Thomas, A. (2023). Education, Racial Justice, and the Limits of Inclusion in Settler Colonial Australia *Comparative Education Review,* 67

Runions, K. C., Pearce, N., & Cross, D. (2021). *How Can Schools Support Whole-school Wellbeing? A Review of the Research.* Report prepared for the Association of Independent Schools of New South Wales. https://www.aisnsw.edu.au/Resources/WAL%204%20%5BOpen%20Access%5D/AISNSW%20Wellbeing%20Literature%20Review.pdf

Russell, D. (2022). Staff Wellbeing: A reflection model for teacher peer support. *Teacher Magazine, 15* August 2022 https://www.teachermagazine.com/au_en/articles/staff-wellbeing-a-reflection-model-for-teacher-peer-support

Salinas, M., & Salinas, J. L. (2021). "We Are from Nowhere": A Qualitative Assessment of the Impact of Collective Trauma from the Perspective of Resettled Bhutanese Refugees. *Health Equity, 5*(1), 762–769. https://doi.org/10.1089/heq.2020.0116

Samani J., & Pan S. C. (2021). Interleaved practice enhances memory and problem-solving ability in undergraduate physics. *NPJ Sci Learn.* Nov 12;6(1):32. doi: 10.1038/s41539-021-00110-x

Sar, V. (2011). Developmental Trauma, Complex PTSD, and the Current Proposal of DSM-5. *European Journal of Psychotraumatology, 2*, Article 5622. https://doi.org/10.3402/ejpt.v2i0.5622

Saracho, O. (2014). Theory of mind: children's understanding of mental states, *Early Child Development and Care*, 184:6, 949-961, doi: 10.1080/03004430.2013.821985

Schmitt, M. T., Branscombe, N. R., Postmes, T., & Garcia, A. (2014). The Consequences of Perceived Discrimination for Psychological Well-Being: A Meta-Analytic Review. *Psychological Bulletin, 140*(4), 921–948. https://doi.org/10.1037/a0035754

Seligman, M. E. P., Steen, T. A., Park, N., & Peterson, C. (2005). Positive psychology progress: Empirical validation of interventions *The American Psychologist, 2005, Vol.60* (5), p.410–421

Seligman, M., Ernst, R., Gillham, K., & Linkins, M. (2009). Positive Education: Positive psychology and classroom interventions. *Oxford Review of Education*, 35(3), 293–311

Siegel, D. J. (2006). An interpersonal neurobiology approach to psychotherapy: Awareness, mirror neurons, and neural plasticity in the development of well-being. Psychiatric Annals, 36(4), 248–256

Siegel, D. J. (2010a). *Mindsight: The New Science of Personal Transformation.* Bantam Books

Siegel, D. J. (2010b). *Creating a Cohesive Life Story: An Excerpt from Dr. Daniel Siegel's New Book Mindsight: The New Science of Personal Transformation.* PsychAlive. https://www.psychalive.org/the-importance-of-making-sense-of-our-pasts-by-daniel-siegel-m-d/

Siegel, D. J. (2018). Foreword. In Jennings, P. A., *The Trauma-Sensitive Classroom: Building Resilience with Compassionate Teaching* (pp. xiii–xvi). Norton Professional Books

Siegel, D. J., & Bryson, T. P. (2011). *The Whole-Brain Child: 12 Revolutionary Strategies to Develop your Child's Nind.* New York, Random House

Siegel, D. J. (2020). *The Developing Mind: How Relationships and the Brain Interact to Shape Who We Are* (3rd ed.). Guilford Press

Siegfried, C. B., Blackshear, K., & National Child Traumatic Stress Network (with National Resource Center on ADHD). (2016). *Is it ADHD or Child Traumatic Stress? A Guide for Clinicians.* National Center for Child Traumatic Stress. https://www.nctsn.org/sites/default/files/resources/is_it_adhd_or_child_traumatic_stress.pdf

Shewfelt, M., (2018). The relationship is the therapy: applying interpersonal neurobiology in psychotherapy *The Neuropsychotherapist, Vol 6*, issue12, pp 63-70

Shonkoff, J. P., & Bales, S. N. (2011). Science Does Not Speak for Itself: Translating Child Development Research for the Public and Its Policymakers. *Child Development*, 2011, Vol. 82 (1), p.17–32

Stavropoulos, K. K. M., Bolourian, Y., & Blacher, J. (2018). Differential Diagnosis of Autism Spectrum Disorder and Post Traumatic Stress Disorder: Two Clinical Cases. *Journal of Clinical Medicine, 7*(4), 71. https://doi.org/10.3390/jcm7040071

Sweller, J., Merriënboer, J., & Paas, F. (2019). Cognitive Architecture and instructional design: 20 years later. *Educational Psychology Review 31* p. 261–292. https://doi.org/10.1007/s10648-019-09465-5

Smith, R., Snow, P., Serry, T., & Hammond, L. (2021). The Role of Background Knowledge in *Reading Comprehension: A Critical Review, Reading Psychology*, 42:3, 214–240, doi: 10.1080/02702711.2021.1888348

Stanley, E. A. (2019). *Widen the Window: Training Your Brain and Body to Thrive During Stress and Recover from Trauma.* Yellow Kite, Hodder & Stoughton

Suarez G. L., Burt S. A., Gard A. M., Burton, J., Clark, D. A., Klump, K. L., & Hyde L. W. (2022). The impact of neighborhood disadvantage on amygdala reactivity: Pathways through neighborhood social processes. *Developmental Cognitive Neuroscience.* 2022 Apr;54:101061. doi: 10.1016/j.dcn.2022.101061

Szoeke, C. (2022). *Secrets of Women's Healthy Ageing.* Melbourne University Press

Teyber, E. & Teyber, F. (2017). *Interpersonal Process in Therapy: An Integrative Model (Seventh Edition).* Cengage

Teicher, M. (2016). *Brain Regions, Pathways and Circuits: Understanding All the Ways Maltreatment Affects the Brain and Their Implications for Treatment.* [Conference session]. International Childhood Trauma Conference, Melbourne, Australia

Teicher, M. H., Anderson, C. M., Ohashi, K., Khan, A., McGreenery, C. E., Bolger, E. A., Rohan, M. L., & Vitaliano, G. D. (2018). Differential Effects of Childhood Neglect and Abuse during Sensitive Exposure Periods on Male and Female Hippocampus. *NeuroImage, 169,* 443–452. https://doi.org/10.1016/j.neuroimage.2017.12.055

Teicher, M. H., & Munkhbaatar, O. (2020). Understanding the needs of vulnerable children: The importance of type and timing of maltreatment on brain development and risks. In Mitchell, J., Tucci, J., & Tronick, E. (Eds.), *The Handbook of Therapeutic Care for Children: Evidence-Informed Approaches to Working with Traumatized Children and Adolescents in Foster, Kinship and Adoptive Care* (pp. 59–79). Jessica Kingsley Publishers

Teicher, M. H., Samson, J. A., Anderson, C. M., & Ohashi, K. (2016). The effects of childhood maltreatment on brain structure, function and connectivity. *Nature Reviews Neuroscience, 17*(10), 652–666. https://doi.org/10.1038/nrn.2016.111

Thomas, J. M. (1995). Traumatic Stress Disorder Presents as Hyperactivity and Disruptive Behavior: Case Presentation, Diagnoses, and Treatment. Infant Mental Health Journal. 1995;16(4):306–317

Tough, P. (2016). *How Kids Learn Resilience.* The Atlantic, June 2016 issue, http://www.theatlantic.com/magazine/archive/2016/06/how-kids-really-succeed/480744/

Tronick, E., & Gold, C. M. (2020). *The Power of Discord: Why the Ups and Downs of Relationships are the Secret to Building Intimacy, Resilience, and Trust.* Scribe Publications

Ullman, J. (2021). *Free2Be... Yet?: The Second National Study of Australian High School Students Who Identify as Gender and Sexuality Diverse.* Western Sydney University. https://doi.org/10.26183/3pxm-2t07

UMassBoston, Still Face Experiment: Dr Edward Tronick. (2009). YouTube, https://www.youtube.com/watch?v=apzXGEbZht0&ab_channel=UMassBoston

Upton, L., Kezelman, C., Hossack, N., Stavropoulos, P., & Burley, P. (2015). *The cost of unresolved childhood trauma and abuse in adults in Australia: A Report for Adults Surviving Child Abuse in Counselling and Psychotherapy,* November 2015, pp. 146–161

Valent, P. (2006). *Transmission of Transgenerational Trauma* [Conference session]. Intergenerational Communication – Working with Holocaust Trauma's Legacy across Three Generations, Limmund Oz, Melbourne, Victoria, Australia. https://www.humiliationstudies.org/documents/ValentTransgenerational TraumaHolocaust_15.pdf

van der Kolk, B. A. (1994). The Body Keeps the Score: Memory and the Evolving Psychobiology of Posttraumatic Stress. *Harvard Review of Psychiatry, 1*(5), 253–265. https://doi.org/10.3109/10673229409017088

van der Kolk, B. A. (2005). Developmental Trauma Disorder: Towards a Rational Diagnosis for Children with Complex Trauma Histories. *Psychiatric Annals, 35*(5), 401–408. https://doi.org/10.3928/00485713-20050501-06

van der Kolk, B. A. (2007). The Developmental Impact of Childhood Trauma. In Kirmayer, L. J., Lemelson, R. & Barad, M. (Eds.), *Understanding Trauma: Integrating Biological Clinical, and Cultural Perspectives* (pp. 224–241). https://doi. org/10.1017/CBO9780511500008.016

van der Kolk, B. A. (2007). In *Traumatic Stress: The Effects of Overwhelming Experience on Mind, Body, and Society.* van der Kolk, B., McFarlane, A. C. & Weisaeth, L. (Eds.). The Guilford Pres

van der Kolk, B. A. (2014). *The Body Keeps the Score: Brain, Mind, and Body in the Healing of Trauma.* Penguin Random House

Venet, A. S. (2021). *Equity-centred Trauma-informed Education.* W. W. Norton & Company

Vernon-Feagans, L., Willoughby, M., Garrett-Peters, P., & Family Life Project Key Investigators. (2016). Predictors of behavioral regulation in kindergarten: Household chaos, parenting, and early executive functions. *Developmental Psychology*, 52(3), 430–441. https://doi.org/10.1037/dev0000087

VIA Institute on Character, (2022). https://www.viacharacter.org/

Victorian Foundation for Survivors of Torture Inc., The. (2015). *Educating Children from Refugee Backgrounds: A Partnership Between Schools and Parents.* Foundation House. www.foundationhouse.org.au/wp-content/uploads/2015/06/educating_ children_refugee_background_a4_online.pdf

Walker, R., Schultz, C., & Sonn, C. (2014). Cultural Competence – Transforming policy, services, programs and practice in *Working Together: Aboriginal and Torres Strait Islander Mental Health and Wellbeing Principles and Practice* By Dudgeon, P., Milroy, H., & Walker, R. (Eds.) Commonwealth of Australia

Walsh, E., & Walsh, D. (2019). How Children Develop Empathy: Empathy is a work-in-progress throughout childhood and adolescence. *Psychology Today* https://www.psychologytoday.com/au/blog/smart-parenting-smarter-kids/ 201905/how-children-develop-empathy

Wang, Z. (2015). Theory of mind and children's understanding of teaching and learning during early childhood, *Cogent Education, 2*:1, doi:10.1080/2331186X.2015.1011973

Waters, L. (2011). A review of school-based positive psychology interventions. *The Australian Educational and Developmental Psychologist Volume 28* (2) pp. 75–90. doi 10.1375/aedp.28.2.75

Weale, S. (2022) .Mindfulness in schools does not improve mental health, study finds: students who engaged with the meditation practice benefited but many were bored with it, say researchers *The Guardian,* 13 July 2022. https://www.theguardian.com/ society/2022/jul/12/mindfulness-schools-does-not-improve-mental-health-study

Williams, K. L. (2010). *The Effects of Narrative Coherence & Mindfulness on Parenting Style & Child Behavior.* The University of Tennessee, Knoxville

Williams, L. M., Gatt, J. M., Schfield, P. R., Olivieri, G., Peduto, A., & Gordon, E. (2009). 'Negativity bias' in risk for depression and anxiety: Brain–body fear circuitry correlates, 5-HTT-LPR and early life stress *NeuroImage Volume 47,* Issue 3, September 2009, Pages 804–814

Winthrop, R. (2022). How to build collaborative relationships between families and schools *Teacher Magazine,* 27 June 2022. https://www.teachermagazine.com/au_en/articles/how-to-build-collaborative-relationships-between-families-and-schools

Wynkoop, B. (2017). *Trauma and the Brain: Understanding Tonic Immobility. Maryland Coalition Against Sexual Assault.* https://mcasa.org/newsletters/article/trauma-and-the-brain-understanding-tonic-immobility

Wolpow, R., Johnson, M. M., Hertel, R., & Kincaid, S. O. (2016). *The Heart of Teaching and Learning: Compassion, Resiliency, and Academic Success* (3rd ed.). Washington State Office of Superintendent of Public Instruction (OSPI) Compassionate Schools

World Health Organisation. (2022). *International Statistical Classification of Diseases and Related Health Problems (ICD-11)* (11th ed.). https://www.who.int/standards/classifications/classification-of-diseases

Yang, Q., & Purtell, K. (2022). Preschoolers' Vocabulary Skills And Inhibitory Control: The Role Of Classroom Engagement, Early Education and Development, doi: 10.1080/10409289.2022.2105625

Yehuda, R., & Bierer, L. M. (2007). Transgenerational Transmission of Cortisol and PTSD risk. *Progress in Brain Research, 167,* 121–135. https://doi.org/10.1016/S0079-6123(07)67009-5

Yehuda, R., & Lehrner, A. (2018). Intergenerational Transmission of Trauma Effects: Putative Role of Epigenetic Mechanisms. *World Psychiatry, 17*(3), 243–257. https://doi.org/10.1002/wps.20568

Zubrick, S. R., Shepherd, C. C. J., Dudgeon, P., Gee, G., Paradies, Y., Scrine, C., & Walker, R. (2014). Social Determinants of Social and Emotional Wellbeing. In Dudgeon, P., Millroy, H., & Walker, R. (Eds.). *Working Together: Aboriginal and Torres Strait Islander Mental Health and Wellbeing Principles and Practice.* Commonwealth of Australia

Zimmer, C. (2018). The Famine Ended 70 Years Ago, but Dutch Genes Still Bear Scars. *The New York Times.* https://www.nytimes.com/2018/01/31/science/dutch-famine-genes.html

ACKNOWLEDGEMENTS

I wrote this book on the unceded lands of the Wurundjeri people of the Kulin Nation, and I would like to acknowledge their elders, past and present. The land I am on has given me so many gifts, for which I am deeply grateful.

I want to thank Claire for relentlessly encouraging me, always bringing an enthusiastic belief in this endeavour, meaning I didn't always have to; and Ella and Noah, who backed me all the way, while also managing to keep it real, as is the role of one's children, and who hardly ever complain when we force them to participate in mandatory family fun. I can't think of a better crew to have been locked down with.

I want to give my enduring thanks to Lucy, Zoe and Rach, who I have known since primary school, high school and university respectively. They all came on this journey with me, there as I took on writing a book, along with study and work, reflecting back to me the various states I ended up in and offering support and friendship, regardless of what state I showed up in.

I want to acknowledge Ellie. We walked the path of student wellbeing, and then counselling, together. We have developed our visions by sharing our work, our passion and all of our feelings.

I offer thanks, too, to Ruth, who has been a wonderful influence on me over many years – a friend and a guide, helping me to find my place in the work that I do; and also to Indra, always my cheerleader.

Thanks to my parents, who instilled in me a passion for social justice and who are role models for serving the community. By sending me to Princes Hill Secondary College, they provided me with the incredible public education that I believe set me on my career trajectory.

Thanks to my siblings: my brother, Rick, with whom I have shared the hardest parts of my job, and my life, and who has always come through for me with support, understanding and solid advice; and my sister, Cassie, who just gets things done, being the endlessly practical one in the family, meaning it is less obvious that I am not at all so inclined.

I have to mention Julie and Lauren. We have worked together for many years, and over those lockdowns we saw more of each other than of anyone but our families. We have been united, along with all our colleagues, in our struggles to make things better for our students and families. I wouldn't want either of your jobs and I know you wouldn't want mine, but I think we make a pretty great team.

Thank you to Olivia Tolich. It is an author's dream to have the kind of conversation that I had with Olivia which, from memory, went something along the lines of her saying, 'Have you ever thought about writing a book?' and went from there. My editor, Jacinta Dietrich, came on board with a firm belief in the project, and that belief and her constant encouragement has been a steadying influence throughout the whole process. Thanks also to my publisher, Amba Press, Alicia Cohen's enthusiasm for the project and ability to make things happen has been so great.

I have met so many wonderful people through my work. So many educators with dedication that builds them up and wears them down; students who bring their whole world with them to school, sometimes joyful and sometimes not, but most often finding care and connection and safety at school; and families who sometimes trust and sometimes don't, but hopefully find unconditional positive regard regardless, and even the same care and connection and safety that their children experience. School is a special place to be and I am grateful to have spent so many of my days there.

ABOUT THE AUTHOR

Rebecca Harris works in student wellbeing and delivers training in trauma-informed practice to schools and community organisations. She also works as a counsellor and facilitator. She has a passion for trauma-informed work, and believes every educator has the potential to make a profound difference to their students' lives.